VAGINA-MITE [NOT]

JOURNALS 2007 - 2008

CHRISTINE FONTANA

VirginiaDiddit

Published by VirginiaDiddit in 2025
Melbourne, Victoria, 3000
www.virginiadiddit.com

National Library of Australia Cataloguing-in-Publication entry available for
this title at www.nla.gov.au

Title: Vagina-Mite [Not], by Christine Fontana
ISBN: 978-1-923221-05-5 (Paperback)
ISBN: 978-1-923221-04-8 (Ebook)

Cover design and typsettting: Christine Fontana

CONTENTS

To my children, again and always xx

Introduction

The Good, The Bad, The Boring, The Interesting

On a good day I'm addicted to re-living the past as I prepare these volumes for publication. On a bad day I find the project more difficult than I anticipated, convinced that the journal entries add up to a lot of *I woz 'ere, and I woz awful.*

The Introduction to *Vagina-Mite* – the first volume in this series – applies to all volumes. It contains a necessary reflection on the nature and impact of personal writing; the delicate handling of people's privacy while satisfying the compulsion to record life with candour; subjectivity as the default setting in the reader/writer relationship when it comes to memoir formats; and the outrunning of the [thievin', violatin'] AI machine. It also explains the performative nature of writing about private life on a public platform, and affectations adopted in the construction of a strong alter-ego (which increase in frequency according to the degree of stress younger-me was experiencing, and which older-me has diligently cleaned up).

Again with the Hashtags

No need to reiterate the social value of Life Writing, which more or less explains itself. Except to say that to publish is to invite domestic voyeurism, and to hope it resonates with readers on some level.

Because we are nothing if not modern (and slightly lazy), the hashtag lens provides a useful shorthand for identifying where this resonance might hit home. So, less eloquently than the first time around...

Hashtag art and motherhood and all of the complications that go with it. Hashtag Australian writer. Hashtag domestic life, the aftermath of a marriage, the raising of an angry teenager. Hashtag the joys of motherhood, hashtag the struggle. Hashtag I am an idiot, hashtag I am not. Hashtag art and economics, hashtag what was I thinking. Hashtag why didn't I just get a normal job. Hashtag I tried, hashtag I failed.

Hashtag I succeeded, hashtag I had no idea what I was doing. Hashtag Tourette's, that simmering, bastard thing. Hashtag love, hashtag sex, hashtag too-much-information. Hashtag queer relationships, hashtag hetero, hashtag unconventional family structures. Hashtag how we mess up our kids. Hashtag school refusal and its poor cousins: cleaning-bedroom refusal and doing-dishes refusal. Hashtag undiagnosed neurodivergence. Hashtag overcoming introversion, hashtag succumbing to introversion. Hashtag – ultimately – *life*.

On That Note

This was it, family life, all of us together in ways that will never happen again. I don't find the elemental concept of relationships with my children difficult the way they do. Their need for independence is pathological. What this means for me as a mother I can't tell you because it belongs to today, when I know more about our strange psychologies. These books contain yesterday, and so that's where I leave it. When I read through them I'm back in that time, for better or for worse. And despite the hardship, it was beautiful.

Vagina-Mite [Not]

Journals 2007 – 2008

January 2007

Happy n' Stuff

That the things I'm doing lately sound very new-year's-resolutionish is just coincidental. In theory I don't do new year's resolutions, because I push myself through resolutions all year round. On January One I give myself the day off.

I feel so content it should be illegal. Winding down until I find myself alone and comfortable inside my own brain. Sprawled across my bed on Xmas night, reading literary articles while it thunders outside, I'm happy inside every single minute.

Literary articles on Xmas night? Come *on*. The first consequence of contentment is that it makes you boring, but I can do with some boring. I'm boring-deprived. And I get boringer. Reformed Hippy Friend rang from Tasmania and after a ten-minute phone call my head was buzzing with book things, because that's what she does to me. The little bit of happy swelled up and didn't leave. I've been preparing mentally ever since – I'm just not sure for what exactly.

Minor detail. Anyways, it means I'm prepped and ready to work hard. I even spent last night alone with the kids, managing to ward off get-together invitations single-handedly. I was far too happy to party.

Not GirlFriend came down before Xmas and we took Son to see *Eragon*, which I thought would be full of every fantasy cliche under the sun – and it is – but it was so damn good I went out the next day to add Christopher Paolini's books to Son's Xmas present. He broke his I-only-read-at-night rule and finished the first one within a couple of days, then left it on my pillow a couple of nights ago (after I'd told him *'Not tonight, I'm too tired'*), with a huge note saying 'YOU KNOW YOU WANT TO READ IT'. Too cute to refute. So I did read it, and have therefore been in Alagaesia for two days and nights. I want for naught.

On the food front, First-Born's so sick of my cooking they've accepted my offer to pay them to be the family cook, and they do a bang up job of it. If they don't get bored with it within a week it'll be a) a miracle and b) a very good year.

It's weird that everything seems good. Where's the catch?

———

On that happy note, I even like the Not GirlFriend arrangement. It's grown on me. I stayed with her a few nights ago and realised I like that my life is different from hers. And I was very mature. For example, she got home from work after midnight, just after I'd fallen asleep reading, and went back upstairs to smoke a joint with her alleged-ex-husband. Technically I was supposed to be upset by this because it's not much fun watching somebody having a party inside their head when you haven't been invited. On the other hand, she was hilarious.

I had to overcome the mother of all ambivalence. As I gazed into her pin-prick pupils, fighting that left-out feeling, she thought *oops* and suggested we break open a bottle of wine. So I went upstairs to get the best quality Passion Pop out of her fridge (I'd brought it with me, to her horror; she had real wine only feet away from the bed), and insisted that we drink it from the bottle. We had another memorable night, sound-tracked by her Neko Case CD. Since we "split up" we've had so many memorable times together I'm scared I'm gonna forget them.

———

Tuesday, 2nd January, 2007.

Piggy in the Middle

I think I'm the piggy. Or my very comfortable bed might be the piggy? Whichever it is, Ex-Husband's gone territorial.

There was a possibility that Not-GirlFriend stay over tonight, and Ex-H just happened to ask if he could stay over, because he's been working on our humongous and much-neglected garden. I said okay, but that she might be staying too. He said *NO* to that [!!!]. He didn't say it in caps lock, that's just me taking a bit o' liberty, because he seems to think he has the right to claim his place in my bed. He said very firmly that he'd be staying as though I didn't have a choice, and that put me in a revolting position where I might have had to say *'You sleep on the couch or you don't sleep here at all'*.

Fortunately she said she couldn't stay because her alleged-ex-husband is back at work, and she needs to be home for her kids. Complication avoided, but I lay awake for a long time last night feeling very uncomfortable. He's my friend – my very good friend – but I don't understand him. I ended our marriage, yes, but he's the one who let it die. Technically he waived his right to this territory years ago. Why does he want to be anywhere near me anyway? He's my EX husband, so as much as I love him I have to say right now that emotionally he's no Einstein.

I feel bad. Bad because I hurt his feelings, and bad because it's not fair of him to put me in an awkward position in my own home. We need to sell this house sooner than I thought, for the sake of boundaries. And I need to find him a new girlfriend (he never goes out so can't find her himself). Someone who doesn't want kids, and doesn't mind him hanging out occasionally with his outrageously sexy ex-wife. I just want him to be happy. Any takers? He's nice, I promise. Anybody? Please?

———

Sunday, 7th January, 2007.

You Must

I've just read Lionel Shriver's *We Need to Talk About Kevin*, and I'm dazed. At first I was put off by the rigid syntax and academic-ish expression, but it gets interesting really quickly. It goes directly onto my favourites shelf, do not pass Go.

———

Not Just An Afterthought

I was saving what I have to say about Friend S for something much deeper, but I'm happy to spend it on boobs, because I think it's beautiful that our friendship had such spectacularly tacky beginnings. She e-mailed me about having omitted her from my almost-Hooters memory. I'd forgotten that when I met her at a literary luncheon she did say she'd go to Hooters with me, but we were partying with the literati and somehow suddenly it was the middle of the night, and she had to go home to her children.

If I was her I'd want full credit for my role in potential depravity, too. On a subliminal level it's no wonder that meeting her was the most important thing [to me] about having won that prize, although the big money that came with it was also handy. And the recognition, that too was nice. I was thinking about this long and hard before Xmas, while I was going through an I'm-really-useless/nobody-loves-me phase (after the demotion to not-girlfriend, which was a big kick in the gut).

My only optimism during those revolting weeks came from knowing I have three particular friends who make me feel more alive than any others, because of who they are and what we share (curiosity about boob establishments included). I cried thinking about it... and now I've lost my train of thought. I think I just wanted to say that she's the best compensation for a wasted Hooter-opportunity I've ever met.

———

Tuesday, 16th January, 2007.

Fuck Beauty

I'd like to thank Zadie Smith for boring me to tears. I avoided reading *On Beauty* forever, because I find the title unappealing. But I picked it up because I love her work – there are passages of *White Teeth* that I can (and do) read over and over again.

I've given it a full 94 pages but *I can't stand it* anymore. Something about the blow-by-blow descriptions of the entry to a dinner party? I like her characterisation, but not what she's doing with it.

Ah, now I feel mean, but I mean that thanks sincerely. Not being hooked on a book = I can do my work, undistracted.

———

Monday, 29th January, 2007.

Big Fat Fibber

On the bright side, I bought conservative clothes for an important up-coming interview, and I look dead sexy in them. On the other bright side (confirming that all bright sides are shallow), my new haircut is stopping people in their tracks.. The more compliments they give me, the more convinced I am that the tools I'm working with here (my looks) are usually inadequate. It's just hair, but having track-interrupting hair comes in handy when you turn up to your little brother's engagement party on the weekend and discover that your childhood friend is in the crowd. A childhood friend who lives in Europe, has a holiday house in Spain (and one at Mt Martha – probably next door to Kylie Minogue), and who hasn't contacted me in about... eighteen years?

Childhood Friend was wearing jeans and a mickey-ish t-shirt that was very *London,* but fortunately for me I had my hair, and two glasses of wine in my gullet. I've never been more grateful for looking "okay", because she hasn't seen me since I was an awkward teenager and was practically falling over herself. Apart from being disgusted by the shallow conversation, I was enjoying it, and I actually like her. I must have talked to her for hours, and seeing her made me happy, which is stupid because I'll probably – and quite happily – never see her again.

I think, actually, it was an important I'm-a-grown-up moment. I realised I can hold my own. Like I've evolved.

On the not-so-bright side, I think Not-GirlFriend lied to me. I'm not sure how much this matters yet. Not a hurtful lie, but it's significant, and was unnecessary. She declares adamantly and frequently that she could never lie to me. Sweet, but if she was to lie, that declaration would mean nothing anyway.

Anyway. I hope I'm wrong. I'm not going to tell her she slipped up, because how embarrassing for her to have gone to the trouble of lying without being smart enough to cover her tracks. I'll just watch quietly and see if this thing is dying or not.

On the other not-so-bright side, I've been thinking a lot about how thinking-a-lot isn't a very good thing. I've been listening to audio books and I know things I don't want to know about the world. I wish I was more like my Mum and Dad. I wish I lived my life simply and traditionally. And not alone. I wish I went to work and came home and watched tv and followed the news, raised my kids, grew old and retired, and that's as complicated as it got. Not an easy life by any standards (theirs), but their complications aren't unnecessary.

I wish shallow things like haircuts actually mattered to me. That's what I wish. (Did she really lie to me? Fuck!)

———

Wednesday, 31st January, 2007.

Blacklist

I've started really caring about haircuts now, because I had the baddest of bad-hair days in the *entire world* yesterday, and discovered that the state of your hair is directly linked to your intellectual performance.

I had my Very Important Job Interview. Dream Job, even if it is on the shit-kicking side. Just admin, but government admin, and part-time, which makes it a Dream Job for both my long-term plans and my single-mother slash art-student "situation".

It's hard enough to get an APS interview, so to stuff it up is sacrilege. And when I say *stuff it up* I mean *really stuff it up*. Starting with the hair, of course, which foofed up even though in the morning I'd stood in front of the mirror with a hair straightener, attempting to get back to my temporarily stunning state.

Hair aside, I looked grown up in my office clothes, and felt great walking around the city with all of the other office-clothes people, like I was in the world properly for the first time in years. Then the interview threw me completely, and I realised I was nervous. I had my personality with me this time, but not my brain. I didn't expect them to ask me the same questions that I'd answered in the written application. *Word for word*. It threw me because I hate repeating myself. I felt like a complete dick (and was about to make an even bigger dick of myself in the work sample test). I tried to give alternative answers in my nervous verbal response, but I think I just achieved giving inappropriate examples.

About that work sample test: ouch. I realised what I'd done wrong five hours later, when it hit me like a right-royal epiphany. I was instructed to write a letter, which should have been easy. I can write letters standing on my head. But do you think I could write *their* letter? They gave me information, a situation and a time limit. I sat there thinking about how if I was in the situation they'd given me there's no way in hell I'd draft a letter containing so little information.

6

I'd use resources and ask questions. I'd take the words they'd given me and change them – see above, *I don't like to repeat things*.

So I wrote the letter, but badly. The epiphany was that they'd *wanted* me to write a vague letter with the little-information they'd given me, repeating it word for word. No improving on their simple language, no finding the secret to better verbal expression, no jumping through hoops to demonstrate your writing skill. It was so simple I'd missed the point, because I was trying so hard to figure out what the trick was. No trick – imagine that! I felt so stupid when I realised.

And the funniest thing? During the interview they'd asked why I wanted this little job when I'm obviously qualified for something more. Qualified-ish. Despite my humble answer, they're now going to read my sample test, raise their eyebrows and say *'qualified my arse'*. They'll slam me onto the APS Employment Blacklist, and use my sample as a PowerPoint demonstration when they hold courses about What Not To Do in administrative job interviews. The audience will laugh, thinking it's the comic relief part of the course. *I am exemplarily bad.*

Next time I'll do better. I'm so glad I think it's funny. Except it's not funny. I'm putting on a brave face.

———

Still Wednesday.

Love Letter

It could be that I'm an emotional sadist, because my lover's suffering is making me very happy. She didn't lie to me. Or if she did, she's un-lied to me since, and that makes it all better.

In fact, even better than better: she's missing me with that little edge of desperation, and it makes me feel very loved. Having gone through an emotional renaissance, she asked me to read the first letter she'd given me aloud to her, and I did, and she said these wonderful words: *I still feel that way about you.*

Now everything's groovy and I take back what I was saying about wanting to live an uncomplicated life like my parents. I'd rather have this chaotic experience any old day.

———

February 2007

Oh Dear, Oh Goodness

On Son's first day at Big School last week (Year 7), I asked him *'Have you had breakfast?'* as we were getting into the car, to which he answered *yes*. I asked what he'd had and he said *'Celery'*. And that carrot stub rolling around on the back dashboard of my car was Son's Friday breakfast.

Don't be alarmed? It gets worse.

I was walking him into school on the first day, reassuring him as we went that all nerdy children get walked in by their lovely mothers, and as soon as we were through the gate he revealed his nervousness by saying *'Oh dear'*. You can imagine the alarms going off inside my head. I tried to steer him towards more palatable exclamations by demonstrating (role-model style) how a kid should behave once he hits Year 7, saying *'Holy crap, this place is crawling with kids'*. I said it emphatically, and then managed to slip the word *crap* into just about every sentence I uttered.

It's not all bad – he's a lovely person, has good friends and a great sense of humour. But really, the oh-dears have got to go. And, it gets even worse. On Friday evening we were down in our yard picking the single nectarine off of the nectarine tree that grew from a stone we'd thrown over the balcony (yey nature!), and somehow ended up in next door's yard picking blackberries. We were chasing a frog, and when it leapt away Son said *'Oh goodness!'*.

I realised then that demonstrating the proper use of exclamations wouldn't be enough. I looked him in the eye and said *'No, no no – you can't say that, Son. You have to say* Holy Shit!,*'* and tried to get him to practise saying *'Holy shit Mum, the frog got away!'*. He just looked at me and shook his head.

8

Tuesday, 6th February, 2007.

Testing Patience

Churchy Friend told me she's sleepy because she hasn't been smoking her dope. I asked her if she's gone cold turkey this time, and she said if that means she's not having any, then yes.

Me: *Good. You should not-smoke the stuff when you go to Your Hippy Friend's place.*

Churchy: *I can have it when I go there.*

Churchy again: *I'm not entering this debate with you.*

Me: *I know; in case you didn't notice I didn't say anything.*

Churchy: *I can hear you thinking it.*

Then I heard her lighter strike up. I'm 99.9% sure she's given up cigarettes. When she told me about the hash cookies she'd made and sent home with her friend last week, there was no doubt left. Within the space of about twenty seconds she'd told me she wasn't taking dope, but also told me – inadvertently – that she had, was, and is.

Saturday, 10th February, 2007.

Scatological

Hours and days and weeks of drawing while everybody else is out at the beach, and I'm feeding my brain with think-food that can't be doing me any good. That in itself sucks and makes me think I'm doing life wrong, but how do you stop?

It's the audio books. Firstly I listened to *The God Delusion* (Richard Dawkins), and it's my new bible. Now when anybody asks me about atheism I can point them towards this book. When they ask me why religion matters so much even to atheists, I can point them specifically to the first chapter, which outlines the gradual rise of xtian fundamentalism in this contemporary world, the nuances of which have been worrying me for a couple of years now.

The bad thing is I followed *The God Delusion* with a lecture series about Zionism and the Palestinian conflict. For years I've listened to news reports without opinion, well aware of my own ignorance.

Now I'm opinionated as all heck, and wish I wasn't. I just wanted to *inform* myself, but when you listen to the nitty gritty you realise how complicated the mess is, and how impossible it is to mend. My biggest new opinion is that human beings are motherfuckers (no offence).

Not happy reading material for summer. You know when your brain shifts into a higher gear? This'll make me sound like I'm a hundred years old, but it happens as you get older; you can pinpoint where you suddenly grew more wise.

I tried to counteract this unwanted understanding of the world by listening to Dan Brown's *Angels and Demons* – all 18 hours of it. It was gripping in some places, but mostly it DRAGGED and by the end I was ready to scream.

Forget the female characters with their almond-smelling hair, sable eyes and firm legs. The point is: nice going, trying to escape the heavy shit of religion by reading a trashy novel that focuses on... religion. The title wasn't enough to warn me off? Sometimes I'm just so blonde on the inside.

I'll finish off by saying that Dan Brown doesn't help the world by promoting the idea that people need religion, and isn't it all nice and fuzzy to let them have their illusion [delusion], no harm done?

Thank goodness this drawing's almost done. It's in my best interests to give up books for a while.

———

Re *The God Delusion*: I think Dawkins woulda been wise to drop the last chapter and end on a stronger note.

Also: limiting the argument to a battle between Science and Religion (so common) is a weakness, when there's so much more to say. And you don't need "evidence" to not-believe in a fabricated deity. He puts the onus in the wrong spot, doing us all a disservice.

———

Sunday, 11th February, 2007.

Guardian Angle

I didn't get the spelling wrong, I just can't bring myself to use the word "angel". While I'm at it, I don't really have a guardian. I was, however, amused to see Not-GirlFriend sent into a spin during the week when Her Sister asked what's going on with me, then gave her an earful about how badly she's treating me, how she should be honouring our relationship, and how I must be suffering. She used a strong word to describe Not-GirlFriend's callousness but for the life of me I can't remember what it was.

I'm almost flattered, but Not-Girlfriend insists that Her Sister wasn't saying it because she cares about me. Apparently she said it because she likes to have the moral upper-hand in the sister-sister relationship. I don't think so, not entirely. I think what Her Sister said to her is what a normal person would think.

Anyways, it made Not-GirlFriend think. She did a lot of thinking, wracking her brain to find ways to treat me proper. She spent Friday with me, went to dinner with her cousin, but came to my house afterwards for the night.

I feel sorry for her, because she's so lost. Today, though, I feel more sorry for myself. Staying the night because she feels she should isn't the same as walking into somebody's life properly.

Also making me sad today is being let-down by Churchy Friend. When she says she's given up the marijuana but is still allowed to smoke it at her Hippy Friend's place, I joke about the probability that she'll go there every weekend and then some.

I just phoned and Her Ex answered. He told me she's sleeping, and that she just got back from yet another night at her Hippy Friend's place. Some days there's no point in trying to find a bit of happy in other people. Having ESP about this isn't actually funny.

———

Friday, 16th February, 2007.

Flogging a Dead Horse

Apologies for the T word, but my thesis was returned today, with three examiner reports. Verdict: passable with revision, which they've given me a whole year to do. Due on my birthday next year, hip hip hooray.

I probably won't do that revision, and probably won't resubmit. Some horses ya just gotta let die naturally, I think.

One of the criticisms could be dealt with by including an exegetical chapter I was forced to remove because of length constraints. That's quite a serious bummer. Some other criticisms are expressed in literary speak, not many of them consistent, and most of them obscure. My supervisor apologised because the thesis was sent to examiners who've never examined this particular form of thesis before (wrong field). I care about this, but it's part of a system that won't change in a hurry. No point in caring too much.

What I do care about is that one of the examiners was literary-theory obsessed, and got personal in one of his/her paragraphs. I read it with raised eyebrows and then with a gobsmacked expression. As in, are they *allowed* to say that? I can handle criticism, I can even handle failure, but I can't understand somebody going out of their way to be mean. And believe me, the comment I'm referring to was *very* mean, totally unprofessional, and most of all, unnecessary.

So thank you, academia. I don't belong there, even though I also do. I just don't care enough about the things that matter to theorists, and I can't impress them. I impressed my supervisors (one of whom is a hard-core literary theory person), and that's good enough for me. My work here is done.

———

Afterthought

I may have said this before, but it's exhilarating to fail (even though I haven't actually failed). It requires that you humble yourself into accepting there are things you're just not good at. Other people have more trouble with my failing than I do, because I seem both capable and competent. It's not tricks with mirrors, I am sometimes those things. There's some other thing missing, though. That thing lets them down.

So it's good that I'm at art school now. I'm in classes with babies and I'm allowed to start my adult life again, only it'll be better this time. Despite being unemployed and non-doctoral after all. And among the most scummy of the scum of the earth.

I guess this is a pep talk. It's liberating to know that nothing I do actually matters, like being on holiday from all expectations. I want to get a job as a cleaner (I'm making a phone call today), so that all of my thinking effort can be put into making art. I want to buy a new computer (RIP old laptop) because I miss writing, and the tools of the trade are important. I want to take this starting-again seriously.

Because what am I now? Nothing, and nothing is the best thing to be. "Blank canvas" makes for a very appropriate pun.

Sunday, 25th February, 2007.

Trolley Rage

This is what you get if you try to brave your way through the big shopping centre carpark on a weekend. The situation was so crazy I was forced [!!] to drive through a No Entry entrance, which by default wasn't an entrance at all. I was there to buy flowers for Ex-Wife, but of course ended up struggling with heavy bags after accidentally stumbling over an amazing fruit shop. Trolley coin thingies aren't user friendly if you're juggling flowers and unanticipated bags of fruit. No more cool, calm exterior for me; I now understand the constant aggression seething inside the skin of Kitchen Nazi Friend.

Ex-Wife deserved a sweet gesture. A couple of weeks ago I spoke to her about our roles Other-Mothers, suggesting she try to *be in the kids' lives properly'*, because First-Born needs to know who their family are and *how 'bout it, lay some love on 'em*. She's been wonderful and loving and my kids are well on the way to feeling comfortable calling her "family".

I also wanted to include a be-ribboned packet of Toffee Pops (Cadbury's, biscuits) in the gesture, because we laughed about how I used to eat her Toffee Pops when we were a couple. Naturally, I planned to remove a few from the packet, for old time's sake.

I read an article about how major supermarkets use product placement and generic copies to run other brands out of business. I won't rant, I'll just lament the fact that when they do this the generic product is usually inferior. No more Toffee Pops. I bought a packet of generic rip-offs and they're revolting. In this game of consumer Armageddon, another one bites the dust.

Monday, 26th February, 2007.

Stuff

I haven't written about how First-Born has been wonderful all holidays, possibly because it was just such a relief.

Today they made me two cheesecakes. Ex-Wife gave them the recipe and took them shopping for the ingredients over the weekend. They're in the fridge and will stay there until my birthday happens. We'll probably have cheesecake for breakfast.

They also bought me three blocks of Lindt chocolate. When I picked them up yesterday, they threw the chocolate down in front of me and snarled *'Happy birthday'*. This after they'd spent the drive home telling me how much I suck, how I'm horrible to live with, and how I've done a pathetic job of raising them.

BUT: they later cornered me in the kitchen and hugged me hard, rocking from side to side in that cute way they do, saying *'We don't hug enough'*, and not letting me go.

I don't know if it was Jekyll or Hyde that left the huge cheesecake-cooking mess for me to find when I got home tonight, but *happy birthday* to me. First-Born thanked me for dinner two hours later, started an argument about my interference in their school work, and then threw rice at me.

Cleaning thrown rice offov the kitchen floor is a bummer. Love/hate, love/hate. Just choose one already and get it over with, please?

Then there's Not-GirlFriend, with her I-miss-you's, I-love-you's, I-wish-I-could-have-more-of-you's, and all of the et-ceteras a girl could want. I even get I-need-you's, and she was avoiding those for a while, so they're significant.

All very nice, until I say I-love-you back. Then I sometimes get *'That's lovely but also a bit scary x x x be careful'*.

It's just love, for fuck's sake. Good feelings are balloons that're blown up and deflated. I float around on them, I plummet. This is called being loved to bits by people who'd rather not. I'm not what either of them want. Another year of not wanting my birthday to happen; I wonder will I ever feel okay about it?

14

Tuesday, 27th February, 2007.

Catch 22

Love is... a heart-shaped chocolate cookie baked especially for you and served up on a plate when you walk through the door after a long day at art skool. Love is also a heart-shaped chocolate wrapped in baking paper that your Jekyll-Hyde child carries downstairs to you. You find they've written *'I love you Mum'* across the top.

They were able to make these affectionate entreaties because they'd refused to go to school today. I've avoided telling the long story about calling a meeting with teachers to discuss attendance issues, and First-Born getting angry at me for said interference. But here's First-Born topping my cheesecakes with cherries and melted chocolate, and spending the school day making chocolate gestures for their chocolate-susceptible mother.

How am I supposed to punish *that*???

Catch 23

Before I got home to my chocolate love hearts from First-Born, I got home to the letterbox and a parcel from Not-GirlFriend that looks suspiciously like a box of chocolates. That's second breakfast taken care of (to follow up on the cheesecake entrée).

She loves me, she loves me not.

I'm right back to that insecure place, expecting to be burnt at any minute, but she's all loving and wondering why the hell I don't sound very happy over the phone. Which shits me because I try very hard to fake it. Why does she do this? I have no idea. But a parcel in the mail: how do I stay upset with *that*?

March 2007

Jackass...?

I prefer to think of myself as intrepid rather than stupid, and seeing as I got away with only one sting on my thigh, I'm doing pretty well.

I propped my tripod up in the overgrown rose garden near the retaining wall – very brave. I was covered up in a zipped hoodie, long cargoes and wasp-resistant moccasins. The wasps didn't mind me one little bit. They flew around all gentle-like. I took lots of photos, but the little beasties were so fast I had to duck inside to get the instruction booklet for the camera. I've never fiddled with shutter speed before.

When I got back I heard loud humming, and saw hundreds of wasps banging against the side of the house. Then I saw the camera. Apparently wasps love (or hate) cameras. The cats went mental, the wasps are still going mental, and I can't get to the camera (which is actually Ex-H's, and is brand-spanking new).

Big Queen Wasp is inside that nest sending messages out to the worker wasps; *What is it? Bring it to me! I must have it!*

My act of courage involved taking the smaller digital out to photograph the wasps swarming around that camera. It looks spectacular. But then one of the little bastards bit me on the back of my thigh and about a hundred other little bastards were banging into my head. That seemed like the right moment to run inside and call for pest control.

So pest control will be here soon. They'll see the camera propped in front of the nest, and they'll know exactly what's going on. It's okay though, I have a plan. I'm going to look them in the eye and say *'Gosh, isn't my [imaginary] husband silly; I tried to tell him not to do it, but you know. Men!'*

16

Bunny Boiling

This story starts with my intuition screaming hysterically at me (reading signs like they're written in large print), and leads to me doing something slightly neurotic, which in turn leads to me discovering that Not-GirlFriend did something far worse, thus justifying my neurotic action. Because the end DOES justify the means.

Strangely, she's been talking about making a real commitment to me for weeks, and did so again on Friday night. She started talking about our future as though it'd be together. She even said *'I'm contemplating spending the rest of my life with you'*.

Very serious – even I wouldn't promise the rest of my life. She sounded genuine, but I knew something was wrong. She's been secretive and distracted, and it was more pronounced that night. Sneaking her mobile phone into the toilet with her, that kinda pronounced.

So I did what any decent neurotic woman would do: I violated her privacy. After the most interesting sex we've had to date – sex that would have led to a whole new-and-improved dynamic between us – she fell asleep and I pried into her mobile phone. I had to, it made me, by beeping with a message at 1 am. A very intimate time of night for a mobile phone to go off.

The opposite of classy, I climbed carefully out of bed, crawled naked along the cold floor to her side, snuck the phone out from under her hand, opened it and found that she'd wiped most things.

That's called covering her tracks, in Sherlock terms. I found some unusual messages and wrote down the numbers. Told her in the morning that I knew she took the phone to the loo, asked her to please fess up to *why*.

She's backed herself out of so many lies this weekend it's not funny. She lied about the text, which was about wet-on-wet painting (hah), and signed off too affectionately to be innocent. Lied enough for me to search further.

Our goodbye was sad and loving that morning, after a very loving night and a very loving wake-up. I knew the end was coming, and asked her during that sweet last embrace if it was our last. She said *no*.

We decided to split up over the phone while I was driving home – nothing to do with the texts. She didn't know what I suspected yet. It was meant to be an amicable break up. We cried and cried. Big babies, both of us. So in love, so not.

But actually it's as standard ugly as any other break up. During our first final-goodbye phone call during her break at work, she confessed to using a women's dating site. I don't know why she told me this, possibly because I was firing questions at her a mile a minute. A huge tactical error on her part. She said that there's nothing going on, but I realised later that if she's using the site she must have a profile. I found her profile, and it's a doozy. I recognised her instantly (sad, because if I'd read that person online I'd have fallen for her instantly).

She tried to make it sound innocent, but she was listed as wanting *'friends, relationships, dates, chats AND casual encounters'*. She said she put it there two weeks ago (about the time she started telling me she wanted to commit properly). She said she didn't put it there with the intention of picking-up chicks, but it coulda been there forever for all I know. It's so detailed there's no way it's not there for chick-picking-up purposes.

There's more, but it doesn't matter. I could dwell on it forever or I could just try to make it through the hell this is and leave her behind.

She wants us to be friends. If I knew how much or little she'd lied, that'd be an easy decision. But I don't. It's safe to assume the worst.

Very rushed entry, this. Getting it over with. My objective for the week: to function. Possibly also not to cry all over everybody I talk to. Possibly also not to throw up (I'm being hit by waves of nausea). Now if you'll excuse me, I have to go off and learn to live within this vacuum she's left behind. I've lost my best friend.

———

Friday, 9th March, 2007.

Epilogue

In my mind Ex-GirlFriend/Not-GirlFriend is two people. I like the she's-innocent-ex much better than the she's-lying-ex, so that's the one I'm trying hard to believe in.

When we met up on Monday she kept saying *'It's just me – I'm just me'*, and I love that "me" of hers. She insists that she didn't cheat on me, that she meant every loving word she said, that she didn't fake all of that emotion, and that the mixed messages she gave me were really a result of her confusion, not lies she told to keep me hanging on. She has an answer for everything, and most of the answers aren't too convincing, but I kissed her and held on and bawled my eyes out, and said I'd think about the whole friendship thing, bully for me.

By night I'm okay being on my own, but mornings are a killer. I get morning sickness every day, on the strength of not being able to believe her. Going to art classes and forcing myself to concentrate is the only way to get relief from the thinking.

She kept in touch for a few days, sending me texts like *'I'm finding it hard not to send u messages about the little things... like I chipped my tooth today x'*, which could have been genuine and I hope they were. But of course, she could be faking those, too, just to let me down gently. I'll never know. My strongest feeling is that she's already replaced me, and so isn't finding this hard at all (except for the guilt).

I'm being big about it, and have gradually begun to eat little bits again. Soon my jeans will stop falling off and I'll be normal. I've decided that I like her enough to be her friend either way (if the things I like about her are real, and that'll become obvious as time passes). I even think it's good to be free of her, so that I can stop being the submissive, weak and quietly "nice" person I'd become in her company.

Okay, over it. Moving right along. I have good friends who've made me feel animated and alive in a way I haven't felt in a long time. They give me intellectual stimulus I've been missing, and bring me back to the real world. Nobody's telling me I'm "not quite good enough" anymore. I think they call this *emancipation*.

———

Thursday, 15th March, 2007.

Advice

I don't know why I even need other friends, when I have a friend like Friend A, who sends me late night texts that say stuff like this:

> *'A thought occurs: maybe you could volunteer at some queer/womens organizations to meet women. Fuck asylum seekers, they won't get you laid.'*

We love Friend A so much we're going to accept the sad fact that people don't use proper punctuation in text-speak, and overlook the missing apostrophe. Even though she's studied Editing, we're not gonna mention it.

———

Still Thursday.

Bouncing Back

Misery is boring. I was so BORED being SAD. I wouldn't let myself do ANYTHING. This is because I knew that whatever I did during the all-important mourning period would be henceforth associated with the emotional faecal matter that is the end of a relationship.

So for a week and a half I avoided reading good books, listening to good music, food (that one wasn't my choice, it just made me gag), and any art that wasn't being shamelessly exploited for its distractive qualities. The only thing that kept me positively distracted was being with people, so when I was alone I had to make like an automaton. I was practically a professional television watcher. As a result, when I snapped out of my miserable phase and plunged headlong into a very healthy I-hate-her phase (I did tell her that if she wanted my friendship she'd have to accept that I think she's revolting, and I meant it), nothing that I love doing had been ruined by bad memories.

I really mean *snapped out of it*; how amazing to go from being so totally sad one minute to so totally happy the next. And then to *stay* happy. It happened Tuesday night, on the train home from Art Skool. I was looking over the man next to me's shoulder, trying to work out a word puzzle for him because he was a bit stuck. I had no idea word puzzles were so much fun. They are, but probably only when you're trying to spoil it for somebody else. So I blurted the answer at him (some kinds of genius cannot be contained), and found myself chatting away as though I'd never been unhappy, and then suddenly I wasn't. Unhappy, I mean.

Now I think I should carry an emergency word puzzle with me wherever I go, just pull it out when I feel like talking to people and can't find a good excuse to interrupt whatever they're doing.

I'm back in the world of the living. I'm reading like crazy and laughing out loud to myself on the train, singing when I walk and talking to complete strangers, focusing beautifully on my work, and even eating. I'm getting so happy it's obscene.

So if I were to tell you I really didn't like Rosalie Ham's *The Dressmaker*, I don't know if I'd be telling the truth, because it was one of the books I tried reading during those long, dark hours of Perpetual Gloom. It was no doubt contaminated with Ex-GirlFriend-Not-GirlFriend's dishonesty. If I try to also tell you that it seemed to have all of the ingredients of a well-crafted novel but none of the soul, don't listen to me. I'm probably wrong. Poor Rosalie Ham. My misery has butchered her book. I should've left it alone.

Saturday 17ᵗʰ March, 2007.

With Eyes Wide Open

Ex-GirlFriend-Not-GirlFriend cried in my arms today. I feel really guilty. Not that I've done anything wrong, but I do have a big fat mouth that I should learn to keep shut. The irony is that by feeling hurt by her, I hurt her feelings. (She cried in my arms!) I wrote her a letter last weekend. It was blunt, angry, confronting, and it belonged to that moment back then.

I warned her of that when I gave it to her (when I was crying into her lap a couple of days after the split). I practically labelled it with Hazchem signposting, just so she'd know the context and keep it where it belonged, in that messed-up we've-just-split-up weekend.

Well, I m-m-made a m-m-mistake. I'd been happy with her and didn't want us to break up, and had therefore assumed that she wouldn't be unhappy about it. I mean, she's the one who ended us. Being unhappy was my job, and I did it with so much gusto I had it covered for both of us. I honestly believed that she felt genuinely bad, but because I didn't hear from her overly much, I thought she must be feeling a bit relieved to be free of me. And there was also that shitful feeling of thinking she'd replaced me.

So when she rang yesterday evening I was surprised. To hear from her, and to hear her say she was missing me, that she loves hearing me laugh, that she's been finding it really hard to cope, and to hear her say she'd read my letter again. I told her she shouldn't have done that, that the moment had passed. Reading it again would lead to feeling bad about things she didn't need to feel bad about anymore. I'd wanted to express them, not accuse her.

Way ta go, Vagina-Mite. (Now can I skip to the bit where she cried in my arms today? That lovely creature.) I'm so mean. And just for the record, I was wr-wr-wrong about her being revolting. She's not revolting. She's not even scum-sucking. I don't even care that she lied. She's only human. While I was out last night with my bitches I kept getting flashes of memory, of her not-revoltingness. And her perfume. I *missed* her. This is all very selfish of me; I've been hogging the sadness to myself without being worried about how she's doing at all.

Anyway, I was even more surprised when she asked me to a movie tonight. So I asked her to join me at the State Library to see the printmaking exhibition first (it's BRILLIANT, by the way). I went to Reformed-Hippy Friend's birthday breakfast (which was at Ceres, which is suspiciously as full of hippies as Byron Bay, so maybe Reformed-Hippy Friend isn't as reformed as I thought) and then made my way to the library feeling a little nervous.

You'd think she was a serial killer, the way some friends were warning me to be careful about seeing her. I tried to explain to them that I didn't need to be careful, because she's never been malicious. The only way to know if the friendship is genuine is to experience being with her. So can you imagine how cool it was to be there in the library gallery, looking at some magnificent prints, with somebody who *loves* art, when that somebody just happens to be somebody I feel so at home with, and to have her spontaneously hold me and moan and kiss my cheek and tell me *she's missed me she's missed me she's missed me*?

It took me a while to get used to her being affectionate. All afternoon it was surreal, and then when we sat in our cinema seats she held onto me and told me how she's not coping and started to cry. This shouldn't make me happy, but it does. I needed to see her emotions. Even though it also makes me sad. I held her and told her I love her, but what can I do? I do love her, but she made a decision that I have no power to change, so I can't even comfort her. Love doesn't scare me the way it scares her. I want to be there to look after her, but I'm not allowed to. What a bizarre situation to be in, to feel her crying all the way through her body. I have to pinch myself to see if today was real.

We kissed cheeks and held bodies, but there was no passionate kissing. I could prattle on about this all night, but I've been running on less than three hours' sleep and need to collapse into bed. I miss her more than ever tonight, only this time I don't miss her selfishly. I'm sad *for* her, not *because* of her, so whatever it is she's done that she keeps saying 'I'm sorry' for, she doesn't need to be sorry. I don't want her to be sorry, I just want her to be happy. Slap me about for it all you like, but I'm still madly – and tragically – in love.

Sunday, 18th March, 2007.

The Movie

We went to see *Notes on a Scandal*, and I think everybody should love what I love so I highly recommend it. I also recommend enhancing the experience by seeing it with a weeping ex-lover in your arms, but if you can't find one of those don't worry, the movie will knock your socks off.

Isn't Cate Blanchett just beautiful.

Isn't Judy Dench just amazing.

And isn't the script just so exceptionally handled.

All that aside, though, the important thing is that Cate Blanchett is ageing. Being in her age bracket I have to assess these things. Forget beauty – I was monitoring the texture of her neck, which looks just as old as mine, oh thank goodness. And her face under the make-up, because she's pale-ish, has the same skin-tiredness (the one that people with outrageous tans don't get – they just look younger for longer and then turn leathery). She's much less haggard than me, but that's okay, as long as she's proving that humans across the board are all the same and my parentally-accelerated ageing process isn't turning me into some kind of freak.

Hollywood's about so much more than entertainment.

———

Still Sunday.

Party Animal

More animal than party, it turns out. Here's a lesbian story that has nothing to do with me, except that I watched it transpire and am trying to work out a tactful way to stick my big interfering nose in.

I went out on the town with my limited number of lezzo-poofter-bastard bitches on Friday night, and nothing went according to plan. Friend A and I met up with Offending Lesbian Friend at The Salty Dog – the only bar I've ever fallen in love with. It was so good there we didn't end up going to the Hotel Formerly Known as The Star, which is just as well because I don't particularly enjoy the Drag kings and wasn't in the mood for scene lesbians. I just wanted to dance with my friends.

I love Offending Lesbian Friend; she's one of my favourite people to hang with, and seeing her so often lately has made me happy. But she's young and stupid and thinks with her penis. It didn't take me long to realise that the focus of the night was on her determination to hit on Late Chick. We all revolved around the vortex of this goal.

At first it didn't matter, because she's fun and The Salty Dog has great food and the Straight Girls were nice, and Friend A's the best person in the world to flop about with in armchairs.

But then we went to The Peel. A night on the town isn't a night on the town unless you've danced with woofters. At the Peel Offending Lesbian started to grow a bit dark. Or maybe it was just the threatening lighting and weird camera angles? She was getting aggressively amorous and wouldn't dance with us, claiming that she won't dance with anybody she wants to sleep with [?].

I later found a text she'd sent me when we were dancing with Late Chick, and it said *'Fucking hell, how do I pick up a non-smoking dancing bitch?'*. Meaning that her usual tactics weren't going to work

24

(the night she tried to hit on Ex-GirlFriend-Not-GirlFriend = they'd bonded over cigarettes).

She made her move, Late-Chick rejected her, so we found and danced with her anyway, thinking we could cheer her up with some wholesome, woofter-boogying fun. But her penis was stiff and she wasn't gonna let a good stiffy go to waste. She spotted some woman who clearly wasn't interested in anybody other than her own friends, managed to manoeuvre our dancing bodies towards them, and then she disappeared.

There comes a moment in any night that's being dominated by your lesbian friend's stiff penis, when you realise that you're not actually having fun. A and I hit that moment then. So we found her again, and took Offending Lesbian home first. That's when she told us her plan to hit on Lovely Straight Chick (who's such a sweet person). Her plan was to get Lovely Straight Chick drunk soon. She was serious about it, as though it's a conquest. That's just plain ugly, especially if you apply the words "date rape" to the scenario. A preconceived, aggressive plot to fuck somebody against their will. Nasty.

She didn't go for Confident Straight Chick – she selected the soft-seeming one. Imagine being Straight Chick, waking up and remembering you'd had a lesbian experience you weren't ready for.

It's scary to see this predatory streak inside a friend you care about. Especially one who doesn't need to resort to these tactics. I'm not looking forward to my next conversation with her. I can't let it go, and she's going to get ashamed and avoid me for ages, like she did after she hit on Ex-G-Not-G. There must be a way I can do this tactfully.

Waitaminute, did I just put the words "I" and "tactful" into the same sentence? This is gonna get messy.

———

Prequel

The night started with First-Born tightening the straps on my bra so much that I couldn't breathe, because apparently 38 year-old boobs aren't allowed to be a little gracefully lower than 20 year-young boobs. So with my boobs in a bra that makes them sticky-outy enough even without the aid of lung-crushing straps, I went to pick Son up from his friend's place, and was asked in to meet his friend's parents. Unfortunately they were lovely. *Really* lovely. I finally get to meet really nice people out in the burbs, and there I am talking to them for an excruciating half hour, thoroughly aware that I must have looked conventionally tarty, only half-dressed and with double-intensity sticky-outy boobosity.

Before going out, I went home and changed into other clothes.

———

Man Stubble

Everything is sex, whether you want it to be or not? I shouldn't be so surprised that we trip over it everywhere we go.

I was following Friend A from the crowded dance floor when I looked up at a hairy chested male. Our eyes met, and we both did double take. It was hilarious, just like in the movies. It wasn't attraction on my part, it was fascination – as in, was he really looking at me like that? It made me curious, so I stopped where I was and let him approach me. He asked me to dance with him, put his hands around my waist and started kissing my neck.

That's bad news, because I'm a sucker for neck kissing, and man stubble feels sexy against your skin. Don't ask me what my body did when he got to my ear. I'm a little surprised by how arousing it was. Obviously, if I'm still remembering it. If it had been anybody else I probably wouldn't have pulled away. (I delayed the pulling-away bit, thinking that prolonging the kissing for one small minute wouldn't kill me. Maybe two minutes. Maybe two and a half.) Fortunately I'm sweet and innocent and had the brains to remember where I was. Because, really, we're talking The Peel here; for all I knew the man was leaving a wriggly trail of sperm across my neck.

Boy germs. Being single is a bio-hazard – I oughta be more careful.

———

Monday, 19th March, 2007.

I Didn't, I Wasn't...

This is my last one. Just while nobody's looking. It's just that I saw her again today, in a this-is-what-it's-going-to-be-like-from-now-on way.

For coffee. Or in my case, hot chocolate. I guess I was surprised when she suggested meeting up again so soon, and was hesitant about it. Maybe I knew it'd be my final lesson in breaking-up. I'm over all the lies and whatevers, and have to get down to the business of simply missing her. Which is much easier on a Saturday night when she's crying all over me and I get to hold her and be in love for one last minute. Not so easy when we're just having a coffee and every time I look at her I want the lovey-dovey emotion back.

This was our first catch-up without intimacy. Some arm touching while we walked, maybe. Little intimacy leftovers. Except that I accidentally kissed her goodbye at the tram stop. Well, she kissed my lips (peck), and I kissed her back more than I should have. Whoops.

I need to train myself to think of her non-emotionally and non-sexually. And non everything-elsely. It's not I-need-to-die sad like it was last week, but really sad all the same. I struggled through a drawing class this afternoon, because somebody played a cd of ambient music. It was instrumental-ish and James Taylor-esque, and I didn't need any help in the sad-feelings department. By the time I was waiting for my train my eyes were watering and I had to hold them back.

This transition to friendship is taking so much more courage than I admit to. I think I'm only pretend-tough. But I can't walk away from her, so when she suggests we meet I'm not going to say no – I'm gonna push myself through this, face it all head-on, get the friendship established and moving along happily, and then eventually it'll be easy. (Won't it?)

———

Still Monday.

Something to Look Forward To

I was walking along the street on my way to meet up with She-Who-I-Promised-Not-To-Mention, in kind of a hurry, and I bumped into the same man about three times because the traffic intersections were so crowded. Eventually he started talking to me, saying something about how we must *'have a connection'*, which was meant to be a joke (I hope). He told me he was looking at me and thinking to himself that

I *'have passion'* in my eyes. Oh puh-leeease. Of course he meant it (pffft), and wouldn't dream of saying something so corny as a cheap pick-up line.

I've never been chatted up at a pedestrian light before. Is this as good as it gets? At least he had the decency to let me go when I said I was in a hurry.

When are women going to start saying crazy things like that to me in the street? And should I be worried that I'm walking around with passion in my eyes, instead of in the parts of my body where it's supposed to be? Do people look at me and see DESPERATION? Like sleazy neck-kissing Peel man, who recognised a complete sucker whose knees would buckle at the slightest touch.

It's difficult to walk away from somebody who's talking to you, even when they're a bit weird. If people like that can spot loneliness from a mile away, I need to lock myself up in a cupboard.

———

Friday, 23rd March, 2007.

Pencil Me In

I've deliberately made no social plans this weekend. Except for finishing off a *Lost* marathon with Ex-H. And except for seeing a movie with my mother. Apart from that, I'm being diligent and planning to work my butt off. (As if I haven't starved enough of it off already. Maybe I should change that to work-my-butt-back-on.)

And just as well, because if I want my personality back I need to fill it up with good, hard slog. My brain just won't unwind unless I've wound it up tightly with a productive glut. So I expect to pat myself on the back by Sunday night. By then I'll have finished off a very important (and yet, not) writing project. Plus I have a shit load of art work to sink into and roll around in, I can't even express how hungry I am for this.

Also, did I mention overcoming a few artistic fears? Writing about it is a way of making myself accountable. Even though the first rule of working really hard is, don't tell anybody about it until the work is done. I hope I haven't jinxed myself.

———

Sunday, 25th March, 2007.

Great Expectations

I touched a penis!! And what a nice penis it was. Technically it's not kissing-and-telling, because we didn't even kiss (the penis and I, nor its owner, who happens to be a good friend and ex-lover). And so ends what is possibly one of my most hilarious sexual experiences to date.

The funny thing is, I feel like a disappointed virgin. I'm serious about the kissing – there was none. I was with this very good friend because it just happened that way. This might have something to do with the fact that I'm giving out slutty vibes, a result of craving mindless, hetero sex. Full-on penetration from every conceivable angle, and no love. Being fucked legless, I think the expression goes – that's my short-term ambition.

You'd think it'd be easy, considering I had the penis in my hand and it was being very cooperative. I wish I was better at being slutty, though. Then I could've gone out with Sex Maniac Friend and found myself a stranger, which might've been more successful. But no. I was with Old Friend, thinking *how weird's it gonna be to kiss him after all this time?*, wondering if I could go through with it without laughing. While I was exploring his body I had to chase away the memory of (and preference for) She-Who-I'm-Not-Mentioning, knowing I had to get her out of my system. So I had that thing in my hand and my body wanted it real bad; I was about to go in for the here-goes-nothing kiss, and I heard him say *'Oh no!'*.

I'm pretty sure that's the first time I've ever been a victim of premature ejaculation. They almost always climax too soon, because once they're inside you they can't seem to hold it for long (and there's nothing worse than being asked to stay preventatively still when you want to let go), but this soon? Before we've even made it to the heavy kissing? My poor, poor body!!

I had to laugh, and I did, but *dammit* – my first man-sex in about a year was a disastrous non-event. I remain, unfortunately, unsullied.

———

On the other side of the coin, I found an older woman clad in rampant lesbian uniform in one of my classes during the week and started a conversation with her. I was talking to her for a long time about dancing at The Peel before her face contracted into an incredulous expression and she asked me if I was "gay". The term threw me. I told her *'Not as such, but...'* and explained, and she kept saying *'You're kidding me? I would never have picked it'*.

I was so disappointed. Am still. What do I have to do to toughen up on the outside? Rugged jewellery? Shave my hair off? Nose rings?

I'm like a blip that only shows up on man-radar. What if I decide I don't like men?

――――

Still Sunday.

Great Plan

If you ever need a sure-fire libido suppressant, take your mother and big sister to see *The Queen* [movie]. Although, I got a kick out of seeing The Queen [person] in her fluffy pink dressing gown. Also, when she walked out of a bedroom holding a dressed-up hot water bottle to her bosom, I thought she might be a woman after my own heart.

When you're back from the movie, go for a long, fast walk, flying over the hillsides because you're so full of energy. Then slow yourself down by listening to Sarah McLachlan (soundtrack of my life at present. Favourite song: *Adia* – so beautiful to listen to over and over again). (Coulda been worse – last week I kept listening to Billy Joel's *Always a Woman*.)

If my libido doesn't start to subside under the stress of this treatment, I don't know what I'm going to do. I think The Queen [person] will have to be the answer; when I climb into bed tonight, I absolutely have to close my eyes and think of England.

――――

Tuesday, 27th March, 2007.

Replica

I was emulated! It was so cute. Last week Young Male Art Student was at the easel next to mine in Drawing, and kept looking at my pitiful work (observational drawing, objects – I can do it ok [as opposed to well] if I love the object, but if I don't love the object I get bored halfway through) and saying he loved the way I do shading, which is rough-as-guts because my objective in these classes is to loosen up. I thought he was just being polite, because other people in our class do some fantastic work.

But this week he was on an easel across the room, and when I went for a looksee at everyone's work I noticed he'd copied my rough-ish shading. He'd done it inside his usual strong lines, a little odd, but how nice is that!?! I hope I'm not giving him bad habits.

Still Tuesday.

Snapping Out of It. Again.

Although my Sarah McLachlan playlist and I have formed such a close relationship over the past few days, my mourning period just ended. Honest to goodness, I feel happy. I even smiled through *The Answer* all the way home. I smiled and couldn't stop smiling, and if you can smile through Sarah Mc after an ugly break up then you're doing okay.

Now I'm embarrassed because I've written about a month's worth of schmaltz into this thing and destroyed my cool, calm facade. The good news is that I don't need feelings anymore, because I have PAINT. Art Skool keeps getting better n' better, and I'm feeling euphoric.

I love that I'm bad at everything at the moment. I'm ready to get back to my political agendas, whatever they are (they've changed since last year), so when I go to sleep tonight I won't be dreaming about her, and I won't be dreaming about deflating premature ejaculations or great sex that could have been. I'll be dreaming about painting. (Waitaminute – is this a good thing?)

Thursday, 29th March, 2007.

School's Out

I'm trying to work out just what school of parenting I'm following at the moment. Is there one called the Watch-What-They-Do-With-Raised-Eyebrows-But-Do-Nothing-Whatsoever-About-It method?

I was about to write a nice little thing about First-Born's outrageously normal recent teenager-ness. They're still a handful, but they're a nice one, who comes into my room when I'm lying across the bed reading and throws themself onto me for a hug. Tonight they passed me on the stairs and announced casually *'I'm going up the road, I won't be back 'til tomorrow'.*

I reminded them that they're only 14 and it's a school night, so *no, you can't go.* But you see, there's nothing I can do to stop them. By "up the road" they mean to their partner's house. (The partner's 18 and has no job; First-Born's 14 and has no motivation = perfect match.)

They assured me they won't be having sex and I had to laugh, because that's not what's worrying me. (According to them, having sex would make them cheap – I think that's hilarious, and don't care if they do have sex, as long as they're sensible about it, which they will be because we've talked about it a lot and teenagers always listen to their mothers' advice.) (No, really!!)

What worries me is that they keep taking days off school, and I don't know what to do about it. I can't just raise my eyebrows and walk away from this one. Can't they be like a normal teenager and bum out because of an ugly drug habit? Can't they get busted for armed robbery and horrendous acts of juvenile delinquency? At least I could find solutions for those. How do you treat a mere pathological avoidance of responsibility? (This question has their teachers stumped as well.)

Maybe I should force them to leave school and work in a McDonald's kitchen for a pitiful wage for a year, then make them repeat Year 9, which they will do because by then they'll have discovered how sad life is without an education.

The most I could do as they walked away tonight was call out that the house rules just changed, and they'll be coming home to something completely different. I delivered this warning in what was probably an ineffectual I-give-up voice, because I know what's coming. My non-arguing holiday just ended; I have to put my reluctant foot down. Doing life tough for a while is the only way. Except, I have a feeling if I send them out into the School of Life, they'll just find a way to wag that, too.

———

Chris Fontana

Friday, 30th March, 2007.

Adios Amigos

Last entry about her, I promise. It's just that I'm now like one of those people who cut their own arm off because it's trapped under a boulder, and then wander around the jungle for days, pulling maggots out of their own fetid flesh wound. Then they escape death and go home n' write a book about it.

No book for me, just this melodramatic little post. Turns out I'm only happy most of the time; the other percentage of time I'm sort of not. When I'm thinking about her. So in one swift and overly-emotional move I severed contact with Ex-G-Not-G. I had to. She's going on a date tonight, and that means our next conversation would have included details I'm not ready to hear. Still too broken by the lies to be able to stomach it just yet.

A few weeks ago she sent me a copy of a reply she received from her internet-dating-site correspondent (she claimed it was her only one, and it's not a "pick-up") (we're generously [?] giving her the benefit of the doubt) and I had mixed feelings reading it. On the one hand, it was nice of her to share it with me, so I beat back the little voice that said she should have shared it as soon as the correspondence started, instead of sneaking around behind my back. *Shut-up, Little Voice*. On the other hand, it was hard to read without feeling hurt because our relationship started with letters, not unlike that one.

Knees together, Huni – you on-the-make isn't something I wanna watch. By reading this letter I could see what Ex-GirlFriend-Not-GirlFriend had written, because the woman was responding to a question about her earliest memory, which is a get-to-know-you-fast question. It made me think about all of the people meeting other people over the internet, and how there must be a list of standard questions that serve this purpose, which makes friendship seem so easy to attain it conversely seems cheap and meaningless. As though you can pick up a friend anywhere. And you'd have a glut of replaceable people you can just use up and spit out.

She told me about her upcoming date like a friend would. I'm really happy for her, but I can't stand this flippant, shallow friendship

33

because it dances around a lot of unresolved issues. Trust ones, mostly. And as much as I like the little squeezes and I-miss-you's she gives me (lost track of how many times she did that when I saw her on Monday), they really mess with my head.

So there ya go, I'm very brave because I just asked a beautiful thing to leave my life. As armless and maggotty as it makes me, I think did the right thing.

———

Friday, 30th March, 2007.

Perspective

Anybody in the mood for some not-starving white class guilty conscience? Just thought I'd remind youse all that we live in a fat, rich country and should be laughing in the face of our not-very adverse little personal adversities. Reformed Hippy Friend forwarded an e-mail from her sister today, describing her experiences as an aide worker in Sudan. And it's true, our mother's weren't tricking us, there really are children starving in Africa.

It's just background noise until somebody you know gives you details. Or if you think about Mlak Mlak and the dollar-fifty Coke machine (*Ronnie Johns** has made it impossible to think about third world poverty and keep a straight face, but is just as successful in conveying the point).

The point is: we've got it so easy. On the bright side, I didn't develop a fistula giving birth to my third stillborn baby before I'd even turned 17. Life, today, should be looking pretty damn peachy.

The Ronnie Johns Half Hour/The Ronnie Johns Good Times Campfire Jamboree Half Hour Show, Now on Television

———

April 2007

Thespian Stuff

I suppose I can manage talking politics on a Sunday night, but only briefly because I've worked hard all weekend. Almost. I decided that my plan to spend the whole weekend alone was stupid, with art or without it. So I worked up until midday today, then drove into Carlton for some literary functioning with Reformed Hippy Friend.

I miss hanging with book people. Even though some of them smell. I won't write about it because I'd have to insult a poet who I quite like, smell notwithstanding.

A couple of rounds of Italian hot chocolate later, we went to La Mama to see *Asylum*. Politics and women in stockings. The politics have me excited because Kit Lazaroo did a really good thing with this play, undoing some of the simplistic (and overly-sentimentalised) approaches to asylum seeking issues that have been bothering me since late last year.

For example, an e-mail was sent out to ASRC volunteers (of which I'm one), complaining about an allegedly damning article that appeared in the Herald Sun newspaper, claiming that it was inciting racism. I clicked on the link, read the article, and it wasn't damning at all. If it was leaning a tiny bit to the right it got away with it, because it was actually a pretty fair account of a racially sensitive situation. I felt angry [at] and disappointed in the ASRC for pushing the antagonism angle too far. Nobody does anybody any good if they deliberately misrepresent an adversarial viewpoint. It's not black and white; nobody should fuck with racial issues just to evoke sympathy.

I can't stand it when people "strategically" fail to properly comprehend a clear piece of writing, it makes me think the whole country's under-educated. Go back to school, people.

Reformed Hippy Friend works in the Immigration Department (does some fascinating stuff), so if you're going to see anything immigration-ish you have to see it with her. Her reaction to *Asylum* was very defensive because she's tired of the way Immigration staff are branded as heartless, when they actually have a tough job to do and most of them work towards reasonable outcomes. But I thought the play conveyed the complexity of bureaucratic decision-making beautifully, and that the presented case was so complex it was impossible to determine the validity of the claim. Which made immigration staff inadvertently look good. The audience aren't given a chance to empathise too much with the asylum seeker and therefore can't really make up their minds about who to trust. I loved that.

Or maybe I've got it all wrong – maybe I'm just so peed off by that email that I can't empathise with asylum seeking characters anymore. Maybe everybody else had empathy seeping from their pores. Maybe I'm emotionally cold and should seek psychological help. But no, that's not true; I still care, I just care differently, and with less patience for blind sentimentalism. I should hunt down some reviews and see what other people thought.

―――

Friday, 6th April, 2007.

Far Too Sunny for Vomit

Yesterday could have been a disaster, but I saved it just in the nick of time. I did this by changing my clothes. You know how you really want the blue knickers but can only buy them in pairs, and the pair they come with is hideously orange (as opposed to good-orange), and you buy them thinking you'll wear the orange ones only when you know nobody's gonna see them anyway, so they technically won't be wasted?

Well yesterday I was wearing the hideously orange knickers and I was so lucky to have gone for a quick pee before I left the house, because the only thing worse than hideously orange knickers on their own is hideously orange knickers worn under otherwise-nice brown cargoes. Clashing colours – if I hadn't realised in time I'd have had to see that colour-clash every time I ducked into the loo during the day.

Crisis averted. As a result, yesterday was a good day. Today, however, is going to take some serious saving, because Churchy Friend is sick. Again. I feel sorry for her because nobody wants to help her when she's sick, due to certain things she does that are hard to stomach. But I don't feel so sorry for her that it makes me want to help her. Even her mother, who's saintly by anybody's standards, will do anything to avoid having to help.

My method of coping with this is to let everybody else deal with her until she's ready to come here, and I look after her when she's in recovery. In the comfort of my own home. On principle I do little more than provide some peace and welcome, and turn a blind eye to the incessant pot smoking, which she still does in front of my kids even though I've asked her not to. It helps get her through this (possibly also causes it, who knows).

But I received a message saying she wants it to be me that comes down to her farm to look after her, because she looks after First-Born for me when First-Born needs to be away from me. Playing the be-fair card. Which is fair. I don't appreciate the edge of nastiness in the request, but still. Fair. Also I have two kids to look after and have to turn life upside down to go to her, but still. Fair.

What I find difficult about the situation is that she can be quite judgemental and actually vicious, and then demanding, but will only accept help selectively. She said something cruel a few days ago, and now I must go to her. If she wasn't so vicious this wouldn't be hard to do. But she is. And if she doesn't let me kick her arse to help her over the drugs (and I do try), then why should I help her with its ugly consequences? Does it make me selfish, if I feel the need to be cruel to be kind? Considering there's no kindness in it whatsoever? I can't get out of this one. I'd better make sure I wear some pretty spunky knickers today; I'm gonna need all the luck I can get.

———

Still Friday.

Oh Fuck

Now I feel really mean. I'm trying to foster a dog-eat-dog attitude, but I keep asking myself, apart from the manipulation and oppressive demandingness and the house full of vomit and dog saliva and cat piss and the long, depressing hours keeping vigil beside her spewy throat-fingering bedside and the possibility that I won't get a wink of sleep on accounta her kennels are full and somebody's gonna have to quieten the barking dogs down in the middle of the night, why is it that I'm so reluctant to help her? Anyone else and I'd drop everything and run to them, but her? All she wants is to feel loved and looked after. Why can't I give that to her? Just because I know she'll try to suck me dry? I feel so guilty. It's just, she gets so *mean*.

(Double fuck – if I go I'll have to feed the dogs bleedy lumps of raw meat!)

Saturday, 7th April, 2007.

Long, Long Weekend

This is my conscience speaking. The guilty one. Churchy Friend didn't try to suck me dry, she was just grateful for the company. She was up and about by the time I arrived, which meant I could happily point out to her that she was able to empty her own bucket. And she's kinda changed – more like a real friend now. A deep comment I don't feel like explaining at the moment.

It was different being there because her ex was away, so the house had a better atmosphere. It was her space, and all I could think as we sat in that soft lighting was that her space is a really nice one. And that I really love her and her company when all of the bullshit is removed.

But then there's the emptiness. Night time is okay because you can't see so far, but then you wake up and a long, empty day is stretched out in front of you. That is, you wake up from dozing after having insomnia from 2 am onwards.

Can't stand emptiness, not right now. Not ever. Makes me worry about how isolated Churchy Friend is. So I filled the morning taking portrait shots of her and her pictorially interesting smoking habit, a little surprised that she let me, and grateful to have a record of the way I know her. Whenever she gets sick First-Born and I start worrying that she's going to die young, because her body seems so weak and un-looked-after. But forget death. It was a nice day, her last weekend at the farm she loves (hence the sickness), so we spent a couple of hours dozing on a blanket in the sun, waiting for me lovely mother to arrive with me lovely children.

I'm embarrassed tonight because I burst into tears as soon as I started my walk after getting home, and cried my way over the hillside. I shouldn't be crying over Ex-G-Not-G anymore, it's been over a month. There should be a rule that when you break up with somebody, you're only allowed one day of mourning for each month you had together. For us it was 11 – we met a year ago on Tuesday. I should have stopped crying about three weeks ago. I need to obey the maths.

———

Sunday, 8th April, 2007.

A Half-Good Read

Finally, I finished reading my first Haruki Murakami book – *Kafka by the Shore*. I feel like I've been reading it forever, even though I only started it on Tuesday. I've been pretty busy with other things, but it felt like it was *never going to end*.

I was nervous opening it, because every time I read a blurb about one of his novels I get put off by the way they're promoted with whimsical or fantastical elements. They all sound like magic realism, and magic realism has had its day. It shits me, in other words, unless it has a powerful purpose behind it, and is written really, really well.

Tough customer, me. I should explain that "magic" is okay, but more often than not it's used to remove agency from human beings, and novels seem pointless [to me] without properly attributed human motivation. But Dad recommended it, saying he enjoyed it even more than he enjoyed *Shantaram*. (I gave everybody in my [VERY BIG] family a copy of *Shantaram* for Xmas, and the consensus is that it's brilliant, but touched with philosophical wankerism you have to laugh off in order to enjoy.)

So I started reading *Kafka by the Shore* regardless of the cat part of the blurb. And now I'm confused because I'm not sure what my opinion actually is. I'd never compare it to *Shantaram*, it's just too different. And I was obsessed with it for days, wishing I had time to run away and read it. I took it everywhere and snatched every spare minute I could find.

I liked it? The writing's beautiful and gentle and it's very Japanese (duh) in every limited sense of the word. The philosophical elements are woven in beautifully right up until the final chapters. Although, just like in *Shantaram,* it's a bit annoying that every person who meets every other person just happens to launch into a heavy philosophical conversation. I think I read it holding my breath, afraid he was about to overdo it and ruin the whole thing.

Which he did, eventually. The final chapters are the ones that wouldn't end. Did they *ever* drag on. I'm frustrated because he did a good thing until he started getting way too far away from reality. It was full-on BORING. I had to wade through stupid descriptions and dialogue that [I think] added NOTHING to the story.

Philosophy, once it stops being skilfully embedded in reality, becomes disembodied from meaning. So I got to the end of the book, and I can't tell you what it was trying to teach us. Makes ya think, yes, but usefully? The meat of the story morphed into utter nonsense. Now I'm wondering if I should read another one of his books, just to see if he does the same thing with it.

Dammit, I really wanted to love this one.

––––––

Monday, 9th April, 2007.

A Fully Good Read

I should've spent this free ten minutes before my lift arrives cooking porridge on the stove top, but we live in a modern world and that means runny porridge because the microwave is nice and fast. Someone should teach my microwave how to cook properly.

Being modern means being efficient means I have time to tell you in twenty words or less that the winner of the Meanjin/Readings novella competition – *China,* by Margaret Innes – is a gorgeous story. In fact, reading it was one of the highlights of this last fortnight, and that's saying something because I had a lotta highlights this last fortnight. (Such as = did about a million galleries and one of my new friends took me to Brunetti's, where I experienced my first ever Italian hot chocolate (LOVE AT FIRST SIP), then Diane Fogwell gave a tour of the printmaking exhibition at the State Library, and the Curvy exhibition launch on Thursday night was more like a disco than an opening, it even had little mosh pits that we had to risk being crushed inside if we wanted to get closer to the artwork, and... oh forget it, I might as well start telling you boring details about what I had for breakfast if I'm gonna list every good thing) (Oh, waitaminute... someone say porridge?) (Good thing I didn't tell you I had it with honey and banana).

China, really good story, made me happy. Competition winners knocking my sox off means the world is getting things right.

Tuesday, 10th April, 2007.

Tough Digits

My toes should hurt. Why don't my toes hurt? Doesn't make sense, because we walked for over three and a half hours along a beach yesterday, and by the end of it my toes were killing me from being pushed up by the sand. Beautiful day; we took the boys and ran up and down sand dunes, and I love listening to Son laugh with his friends. I think he's having one of those idyllic childhoods, despite the fact that he lives in a house with an angry sibling and a lost and lonely mother who feels pretty much like she hasn't provided certain things very well.

On the other hand, I'm not a bad mother, I'm just circumstantially challenged. On the beach I was completely content one minute, and then completely sad the next. But I refuse to go back to feeling dead inside. Dead-inside people are useless. They don't make pretty pictures. They don't even make ugly but-socio-politically-focused pictures. What's the point of living if you're not gonna make ugly but-socio-politically-focused pictures?

So when everybody collapsed in an exhausted heap at the car afterwards I ran down to the beach, stripped down to my knickers and went in for a swim. I'd say it felt liberating and sexy swimming topless if I didn't suspect my boobs had turned blue (so cold!).

So I talked to my kids (again) about moving to somewhere around Brunswick, but they still hate the idea. I can't sacrifice their happiness for my own, even though theirs depends on mine, and I'm older, wiser, and know that life can get much more interesting than it is out here.

I'll just have to work harder. Stop feeling restless. Swim topless more often. Problem solved.

———

Thursday, 12th April, 2007.

Ho Hum

I just moseyed on over to see the *Blasphemy* exhibition at Burrinja gallery, in Upwey. Which was brave, considering that Upwey is the gateway to hippy territory.

I was a bit disappointed, actually. I'd been looking forward to seeing this exhibition because the blurb made it sound like it had the potential for very strong sociological statement (critiquing xtianity). The works themselves are okay, I just didn't leave with any resonating feeling of having experienced anything much. I guess I wanted it to be more sophisticated, and pack a bit of punch. For example, it could have done with fewer crucifixes. Sucks a bit of power out of the imagery if it gets repetitive.

I seem to always be wanting something I can't find. It might actually have been great, and I just interpreted it as *blurgh* because I have a little lack in my lustre at the moment. Or I could just be hard to please. Maybe if I'd waited half an hour, until a more vibrant mood possessed me, I might have liked it more?

———

Saturday, 14th April, 2007.

Ye Olde

There should be a law against wearing lipstick once you turn fifty. In fact, if I had my way nobody'd be allowed to wear it – ever. It's hideous stuff. But it's especially tragic if you wear lipstick once you get old, and I'm traumatised by Older Ethnic Friend and her filthy lipstick habit. So much so that going gallery hopping with her yesterday was a bummer, because whenever she spoke to me I didn't know where to look.

I think the tragedy is amplified by her pride in her European looks. She was attractive when she was young, and likes to talk about how women are jealous of her because she's still a spunk. (She got the "spunk" bit from me, only she gets it wrong and calls me things like "Spunk Freckle"; it's very cute.) Only, after years of looking younger than she is, I noticed yesterday that she suddenly looks her age.

I saw her from the tram, standing at the top of the Flinders Street steps waiting for me, and my heart sank. She used to be stylish and elegant in a natural, flamboyant way, but yesterday she was this bright red blur of old-stereotype. I snuck up behind her, said something to make her laugh, and when she turned to me she executed that laugh with a gaping, bright-red-lipstickied mouth. On her cheeks, the clumsy old-woman uniform smudge of blush. She looked like a Punch and Judy puppet and it was so sad, because she's also walking slowly.

I don't know if I'm sad because I want her to age gracefully, or to just not-age at all. Ageing with lipstick is not graceful. I wish women wouldn't do that to themselves. Mouths don't need dressing up.

So maybe this isn't about ageing. By the time we were sitting down to hot chocolate in Fed Square, I had to look her in the face and I almost couldn't. I can't see my friend under all of that make-up, all I can see is this shiny bright muck. I should probably dig out some tact and tell her, but this is a woman who insists that putting yoghurt on your face does wonders for your skin, and who rubs so much olive oil onto her neck and cleavage that she looks like she's been polished.

Ever notice how older men don't look hideous? There's a lesson in that for everyone.

Still Saturday.

Words, Thoughts, Please – No

There needs to be a new category of books, where we can stick well-written works of thought-provoking pointlessness. I just finished reading *The Accidental* by Ali Smith. I saw a woman on the train reading it weeks ago, and thinking I should be more like other people (and less like myself) I decided to give it a go.

43

This is the second book in a row that I've read that's started beautifully and ended... badly. I love the way Ali Smith writes – LOVE it. I got sucked in by the narrative voices in the first two chapters, but then the next two were dead boring, the plot started to reveal itself, and I experienced that big let-down feeling. The plot goes something like *family go on holiday and each of them think many [entertaining] thoughts, then wild girl wanders in out of nowhere* (so clichéd, so unlikely) *and asserts herself into their family holiday lives; mysterious wild girl does wild and stupid things but wins the hearts of all of said family, and makes them think more [less entertaining] thoughts; wild girl is forced to leave their [thoughtful] lives, they go home and not much happens but they continue to think [less and less entertaining] thoughts.*

Fun but pointless. I think I read to the end only out of loyalty to the beginning. Yey Astrid and Magnus, but the rest of the characters can go fuck 'emselves for draining the fun out of my Saturday afternoon. Now I have to find an effective way to shake the pointlessness out of my head. Stupid reading-on-train lady – next time I have to pay more attention to people's expressions as they read, and if there's any trace of book-induced emptiness I need to keep the hell away.

(Or just try Ali Smith's other books, because she has a great mind. The titles *Other Stories and Other Stories* and *The Whole Story and Other Stories* crack me up. Could be she's really good in small doses.)

———

Sunday, 15th April, 2007.

Inky Dreaming

Fucking nature. Nothing but NOTHING comes between me and my sleep, especially not motherfucking possums and their motherfucking frolicking over my motherfucking balcony in the middle of the motherfucking night. First-Born and I took shifts at trying to scare the shit out of them, but they kept getting away, so I had to go back to bed and comfort myself by singing a *Curse-of-Millhaven* mantra (Nick Cave song verse, about the little creatures who all gotsta die) over n' over in my head. For the extra motherfucking hour and a half that I was awake because of them.

For about the fifth night/morning in a row, when I finally did sleep I dreamt about printmaking. These dreams are elaborate and theatrical and my brain is racing with them. If only I was working as hard as I'm thinking about working.

The problem with printmaking is that it's so slow to learn, and my teacher told me not to *'jump the gun'* when I asked her if I could try some new things out of class hours. I want to jump the gun, there's so much to learn it'll take forever if I don't. In my dreams she lets me. There's a technique I desperately wanna get my hands on, so I might have to spend my next class begging. Again.

And in the meantime work out what I care about – I'm still in an unusual stalemate when it comes to deciding upon images. Come on reality, catch up.

(For the record, they don't really gotsta die. On a good day I love possums. When they're properly contextualised, away from my balcony during nocturnal hours.)

———

Wednesday, 18th April, 2007.

Busy Busy Busy

Gutsy is my middle name today. Fear? What's fear? I wagged skool so I could spend a whole day doing something (an art thing) that I've been too scared to try. Also to avoid Picasso – bit sick of Picasso. I worked hard. And I did this thing, of which I was afeared.

Now I'm practically invincible. Still having those printmaking dreams. I've been waiting for a long time for this feeling to kick in, where I become obsessed with what I'm doing, and it feels this good.

I have to find a way to sneak extra time in the printmaking studio, because I don't have enough experience to take advantage of free access times. It'd be bliss to be in that room without Evil Monday Student (don't ask). Even Very Nice Teacher has trouble keeping herself calm around Evil Monday Student. She must have nerves of steel. I watch, but have only caught her laughing twice.

What I really want is three weeks of uninterrupted studio time in that room. Then the possums can fornicate on my balcony all they like, because I won't need sleep. If the universe would see fit to deliver this to me, I'd be very grateful.

Also my gaydar seems to be working. By accident. And that's how it should be, by accident. You see somebody around and think in the back of your mind that she looks nice, like somebody you could like, but you don't actually expect her to be somebody you'd like because looks don't mean anything. Then you see her where you didn't expect to see her and you say *hi* and start a conversation, because you're brave like that. You don't think too much about it but then it's Monday and you see her again, just five seconds after you've thought *'Imagine if she was here right now'*, and she looks happy to see you, so you ask her her name (which you forgot to do the first time because you were too busy pretending you weren't thinking "that way", convinced that if you start to like her you'll find out she's straight or married or a bogan or has bad personal hygiene or hates reading or tells big lies to her girlfriend[s]).

Next time I'll move the conversation on to horrorscope exchanges and favourite colours.

Anyway, it doesn't matter if she's any of the above. It's just nice to know there are nice people out there, and when I find them I can ask their names and that's perfectly okay. If they all turn out to be smelly bogans, who cares? I have printmaking to think about. And painting, and drawing. I couldn't possibly fit a woman into my dreams, there simply isn't enough room for her.

———

Saturday, 21st April, 2007.

Up-Sucky

I stooped so low. As somebody who hates celebrity arse-kissing, I'm disgusted that I accidentally did some of that. I didn't mean to – I wanted to approach said "celebrity" as one human being to another, but that's just naive of me. I don't think it's possible in certain contexts, because when a person's standing in their own limelight they're IT-and-a-BIT and you're just the Adoring Public.

Anyway it's not my fault. There were a few things I liked, but there was only one work in the whole of Art Melbourne at the exhibition centre that I loved. One!! (There was also one exhibit that I hated, some artist clearly ripping off the work of Rosalie Gascoigne. The factory of stolen things. Nothing will be special anymore if they don't stop.)

This thing I was curious about (not mentioning any titles), because it was different and multi-layered, and monitored by the artist-in-question (not mentioning any names), and it excited my brain. Getting excited makes me talk. And I did, right at/to/with the artist.

Now I wish I hadn't, because this artist probably needed to not have their arse kissed. That's not what I was trying to do; I was touching on common ground, because we'd both had work published in the same journal. But even before we finished talking I could see their media spin happening, and by the time I'd said goodbye and wandered off I was starting to feel sickened by it all. I took myself off to some small galleries for the afternoon, needing to feel cleansed by something more quiet and less commercially vulgar.

I've since then learned how far the media side of the event has been taken, and I'm appalled but also fascinated. By a certain person's ego, and the cloying neediness behind their fame. I'm so glad I'm not a celebrity-type person. Being invisible and unimportant rocks.

———

Friday, 27th April, 2007.

They Smell

It's rough taking the train home at night. Last night I had to sit next to a hippy, because I can't ride backwards on a train without feeling sick. I had to take the only forward-facing seat.

It spoke to me. There I was, nauseated by the fug of stale incense and bourbon & coke (which it was drinking surreptitiously from a can), not to mention the weird stink of the steaming hyper-organic vegetable ricey-legumic take-away fodder it was eating, and it interrupted my staunch attempts at withholding my repulsion by speaking. How do you ignore it and hope it goes away if it *speaks* to you?

It said something disparaging about the rail police people who'd just asked me to take my feet off the seat (sorry – I was tired and needed to elevate them before they fell off), and I looked at the seat opposite the hippy and saw enormous mud smudges that matched the colour of the mud caked onto her stinky hippy docs, and thought about what a stupid selfish fuck it [she] was. Is.

I should've just ridden the train backwards, because her grubby hippy garb, with its layers of hempy natural fibres and her filthy dreadies and the foul texture of her bong-stained skin and her bloodshot eyes, mixed with the gross miasma of her being-at-one with the filth of the universe, was making me wanna puke up my Mars bar.

It told me to have a nice night as I got up to leave, it's way of spreading goodwill to all creatures throughout the universe. Isn't it ironic, that if I sit next to a Normal Person I can exchange words and wish them a good night with complete sincerity, but the stinky good will of the stinky world-loving hippy made me wish she'd fall over in dogshit.

If you're planning on loving the world and all its creatures? Have a shower first. Use soap. Wash your clothes regularly. And go easy on the incense. Please.

———

Still Friday.

Big Bother

When I was wallowing in the cheated-on person's Pit of Despair and lounging around in front of the television, searching desperately for distraction, I saw the ad for *Big Brother* and thought '*Hallelujah!!*'. I knew then that if I couldn't find a reason to exist in a hurry, I could substitute *Big-Brother*-watching for the Meaning of Life and have a reason to get out of bed every day. My horizon, in other words, didn't look so empty.

So just as well I got happy in time to avoid needing the stupid thing, because it's actually boring. In an interesting way. I mean, I *have* been watching it. But only a bit, and only because it's so much fun picking on the Mormon. First-Born and I bond over sport like that.

Anyway, about the Real World. Being extremely innocent, I realised that I hadn't looked properly at Nice Woman's body. What kind of pervert am I going to be if I don't actually do any perving? I only knew the silhouette-ish shape of her. I'd been drawn mostly to her rather lovely face and head and the potential personality conveyed by the way she carries herself. So when I saw her this week I made a concerted effort to *check her out*, and I'm pleased to be able to tell you that yes, she's *very nice*.

But that's where the fairytale ends, because I don't see her enough to get her alone or find out much about her. There's *mysterious*, and then there's *mysterious*, and unfortunately she's the latter. Although, we've now had two whole [brief] conversations – two and half, if you count fly-by hallway comments – and she knows my name, and uses it with great gusto when she says goodbye. Can you base all hopes on somebody knowing your name? Perhaps I should keep my hopes and dreams bound up in *Big Brother* after all.

———

May 2007

What Year is it Again?

Sitting down here with the computer is like sitting down to talk to an old friend. I don't have time for my real old friends. I neglect most of them, and then bump into them in weird places. and have to say stupid things like *'I was just thinking about you'*. This happened today, twice, and I was telling the truth, I really was thinking of them, both, only it sounds so lame. I made a date to have drinks with them one night soon, forgetting that it'd be Son's Birthday, and had to ring them to cancel, entering a whole new dimension of friend-neglect.

So as much as I'd love to dump a few thoughts here, I might just have to neglect this old friend also. Been to Sydney, I can dump that, there's a weight off. I love aeroplanes. And I love Sydney. Melbourne's the marriage and Sydney's the affair. (Brave of me to use an infidelity metaphor so soon after having my heart ripped out through my nostril.)

Anyway, I'm still processing the experience because it was huge. I must have done a million galleries in a very short time and my brain's swollen with the happy glut. I don't know how people's brains don't spontaneously burst all over the streets in that city, there's so much stimulus. When I'm up in Prodigal Niece's apartment I rush to the window every five minutes just to gape at how much life there is everywhere you look. And there's something thrilling and strangely comforting about falling asleep to the sounds of sirens tearing through the streets down in the Cross, and stirring during the night to the distant drug-fucked sounds of *pleeeease, somebody help meeeee* floating up from the gutters. Makes me smile to myself as I roll over and let some other good Samaritan call the police for them.

Home now. Tired and busy. That's a good thing. You know life's going well if *Spiderman* doesn't even make it to the top ten of your list of things to do. He'll have to be postponed 'til next week.

Saturday, 12th May, 2007.

Lez-be Friends

Okay, not lez-be, but try telling my body that. Plain old let's-be-friends is what she said. Just so you know.

I woke up thinking about art again, as I do every day. Art makes a good mistress. This proves that I'm still in a good headspace. I don't wanna be in love with anybody at the moment.

Ex G-Not-G contacted me a couple of weeks ago. I contemplated inviting her to Sydney with me, but then thought heinously bitter thoughts about her not giving us time together when we were in a relationship = she doesn't deserve time together now, so the invitation didn't happen. I thought *'fuck you'* instead.

But then, you know. Texts morphed into e-mails and it turns out that every time I say the littlest thing I accidentally hurt her feelings. It's like I walk around with my foot in my mouth. I don't mean to do it, I just say what I'm thinking (it's not my fault the words "you lied" sneak their way into otherwise positive comments – I'd prefer it if they weren't even in my vocabulary). Despite this, she tells me she misses me and she's not over me and it still hurts her and she thinks about me a lot, and I'm amused that I could matter so much to somebody.

I had no intention of seeing her, until she texted yesterday morning and suggested meeting for coffee.

Way ta go with the strong resolve. I finished my printmaking and walked over to meet her. Didn't feel anything in particular until I saw her leaning against a tree outside the State Library, chewing on her thumbnail. I recognised her by her silhouette because of that nail chewing. It's nice knowing a body and its habits so well. *That* made me smile.

So anyway, the hugging: nice. The smell of her: nice. Her touch: nice. That she gave me a print she'd just whipped up in the studio, so hot off the press that the paper was still damp: very, very nice.

Apparently we *can* be friends. I don't feel traumatised from having seen her. We had our Brunetti's Italian hot chocolates and I walked her back to skool. We hugged goodbye. My left hand did a reflexive move to her right breast and I got embarrassed because it was another *oops*. We kept hugging, so damn close that my mouth had this natural urge to kiss her and I had to hold it back. I told her that if we're going to be friends, I'll have to tie my hands behind my back and suture my lips shut.

I'm too focused to go backwards. I have no idea why I mean the least little thing to her, but I don't need to know. I don't need to know anything, really. I'd rather have her as a small, nice thing in the present than a huge, bad memory in the past.

———

Saturday, 19th May, 2007.

Mild Overload

Arthur, Martha, I'll answer to anything right now, I'm that busy. As long as Arthur likes wearing black stockings to work. This because I've discovered that *wearing* black stockings is as sexy as *dating* somebody who wears black stockings. I had no idea.

I rediscover this fact every week at work (waitressing), because I wear a skirt with a split in both front and back, and I can feel this really nice breeze against my black-stockinged legs as I walk to and from the kitchens. Don't ever let anybody tell you that carrying heavy trays of food and plates through a function centre isn't a sensual experience.

Driving home, the splits in my skirt come in handy because I can't resist running my hands up and down my own legs, because they look like somebody else's when they're dressed up in stockings. If I die in a car crash in the small hours of a Saturday morning, you'll know why.

I don't even have time to be sitting here writing this. I have a house full of smelly boys, here for the weekend for Son's party. I'm breaking out the incense when I get back from my walk. And then, when I've fed them, I'm getting back to my painting, which I had to interrupt to go to work yesterday. What happened to my good intention to return to the easel by 8 this morning? Do I really need sleep so much that I slept through my alarms – all three of them?

I wish I didn't have quite so many things running through my head right now. Or that I at least had time to offload them. Or had a nice woman to distract me from them, black stockings optional. Or could just work uninterrupted on my "stuff". Or that I couldn't hear lots of thumping coming from upstairs right now. Those smelly boys are destroying my finally house-worked house.

Good on them. May their minds be under-burdened and their bellies full of Cheezels. It's the better way to be.

Monday, 21st May, 2007.

Rapture

I must have tickets on myself, because Ex-H takes me out to a concert and I think of it as *me* doing *him* a favour. But only because I don't like interrupting my work when I get so little time to spend on it as it is. This woe-is-me single mother attitude suits me quite nicely.

I said yes to this outing because he's moving to Mackay soon (really soon), and because *Carmina Burana* is his favourite, and because it's my favourite, too (I think, but possibly only *O Fortuna*). Also because I learnt a long time ago that I shouldn't avoid doing good things just so that I can work, no matter how much I want to, because I always (always!) end up looking up from what I'm doing and thinking '*Gee, I could be there right now instead of lonely old here, aren't I a dick*'.

Now I'm excited because I've never heard it live before and the Melbourne Chorale et al were wonderful. In fact, just being in the Arts Centre was wonderful – I haven't been there for years.

Orff = fun, but the Bartok pieces – no. I felt like a misbehaved child because I couldn't love Bartok's music and just wanted to play. Except, the performers were fun to watch. The pianist reminded me of Bugs Bunny, belting away at the keys with a tempestuous (but restrained) force channelled all the way through his body.

Best of all was the percussiony thingy, which sounded like a marimba but had pipes so might have been a glock or a xylophone and damned if I can remember which is which. I LOVE marimba, and I MISS it, because First-Born (before blossoming into the unmotivated teenager we know and love) was once upon a time a gifted percussionist. I use the word "gifted" in all its poxyness, but truly, they were amazing – I have a recording of them playing *South Wind* with flawless timing.

(I say that as though I know what flawless timing sounds like; it was her teacher that was astounded – I was just impressed.)

It's a part of First-Born I miss a lot. They were part of an ensemble and therefore a provider of much live music in our home. When they brought the instruments home for weekends you could hear them play all the way up the street and back. If I had a spare $4000 to play with I'd buy a whopping big marimba and leave it lying around on the off chance that they'd pick up the beaters and start playing again.

Problematically, the percussionists only got bit-parts (Bartok's fault?), and most of those bit-parts were girly high pitched fluff designed to highlight the pianist's angst. It must have been frustrating for the musicians, surely? To have to stand there all that time and only hit the odd little key? There are some things about the way music is thrown together that I'll never understand.

Anyway it doesn't matter; *Carmina Burana* was brilliant. Almost as good as the beer commercial using the *O Fortuna* score. I love that beer commercial! We could have saved ourselves time and effort if we'd just stayed home and watched that over and over instead.

——

While We're on the Subject

If we told her to, Sinead O'Connor could write a fantastic modern opera. I've been listening to *Troy* on my iPod, and think she'd translate to opera in a big way. If I had some "my people", I'd get "my people" on to "her people" and get this thing started.

——

Saturday, 26th May, 2007.

Refuge

Sitting down was a dumb idea. The thought of getting up again to set up beds for a handful of hungover emo's isn't very appealing at this time of night.

I love my bedroom. I'd like to hide in here forever. I'm suffering major violations of personal space, not just because of the crowd of emo teenagers here for First-Born's party.

Have you ever noticed how emo's try so hard to look different that they all end up looking the same?

Back to the point: I can't get a minute alone. I need to paint, and I need it badly. I was going to paint all day and then paint all night, but there are people everywhere. Although, the party's been good and isn't actually the problem. One of the teenagers sang along to Abba with me. And some of them kept saying 'Your Mum's cool as' whenever First-Born tried to insult me. And some of them were raving about my art (teenagers – they don't know much). And I did get to throw a bucket of water over Boy From Up the Road's head when I caught him pissing over my balcony (my idea of fun?).

The problem is that Ex-Husband's staying here for a short while before moving to Mackay. I feel guilty for being annoyed, but I can't help it. I thought it'd be okay, and he's a lovely man, really. But there's so much man-ness in the house I can't stand it. And all of those habits of his. (Hair in my sink!) He takes up personal space like you wouldn't believe. I try to overlook it but everywhere I turn is *him*.

It'd hurt his feelings if he knew I was getting annoyed, so I'm biting back my impatience. Really, he's lovely. I just wish he'd go and be lovely somewhere else.

I was just thinking about how good it is that this party will finish eventually, and I'll have the day to myself tomorrow because my kids will flake at about 5 am and not get up until a hundred o-clock, and that means I can paint (if I can overcome the distractions). Then I remembered that Ex-H is staying here and will be back tomorrow. He's gone to his mum's tonight because he didn't want to be here for the party, being a bit of a wet blanket. He spent the day making the most annoying anti-party jokes. He is, above all things, anti-fun. I can't stand his presence taking up every spare piece of brain-space, in such a negative way. And that means I'll get no peace and no privacy, and that means no painting.

I don't want this. I feel mean, but the things I've had to deal with this week, you don't wanna know. And it's not that I don't love him. It's that separated people are by default toxic to each other and if one of them has so many negative opinions of the family he was once part of, they shouldn't be in the same domestic space.

I'm knackered and cold and dreading the next few minutes of un-sitting myself down and getting those kids to co-operate, so that I can sneak some sleep.

———

Sunday, 27th May, 2007.

Day of Rest?

Maybe refuge was too strong a word. Did I mention that Ex-H doesn't handle stress very well? And that First-Born is so cute and friendly to me when they're drunk that I'm considering slipping vodka into our water supply?

I had a really nice day. Not much art, but lots of planning and project-thinking in the morning, and then lots of vacuuming and mopping, resulting in an immaculate house full of sunshine and fresh air. And, blissfully empty of excess teenagers.

Now Ex-H is asleep on the reclined front seat of his car at the bottom of the driveway. Because it's quiet out there. Possibly even peaceful. Which is what my house was like before he got home tonight and rested his grumpy body on top of the other side of my bed. I walked into my lovely me-bedroom and discovered it had been transformed into miserable old him again. He doesn't respond to my friendliness, and I'm starting to get really, really territorial. I'm thinking of barking if anybody goes anywhere near my room.

I wanted to enjoy his visit. I even thought it'd be fun having him here for a while. It's turning out to be one bit of stress after another. And then another. And another. And so on.

Sleeping in the car like that is Ex-H's way of making a grand statement about the shattering noise of family life, and all of its impositions on more sensitive folk such as himself. It's his way of making his rejection of a life that includes parties and post-party clean up days LOUD and CLEAR.

Anyway. The plan is not to get insomnia tonight, though I don't know how I'm going to manage that when I know he's going to wait until we're all in bed before slipping into the house again, waking me up in the process. I'm going to be so aware of his performative misery that I'll feel about as rotten as I feel right now.

Here's a message to all depressed/depressing people: no offence, but you're so fucking contagious you should banish yourselves to some wet and miserable island and leave the rest of us the fuck alone.

Between First-Born and Ex-H, I don't stand a chance. This week's a write-off. Luckily he was out in the car tonight when First-Born started yelling about the computer. What'll happen when I'm not here to make sure there's a protective barrier between them? How will I be able to stay at art skool all day when I know that I should be at home guarding my space and their space and his... his whatever it is that needs guarding?

How do you make an insistently miserable person happy?

I'm going to have to stand Reformed Hippy up tomorrow night, even though I've been looking forward to seeing her all week, because I can't leave First-Born and Ex-H alone together without risking some serious conflict.

I wish Other Son hadn't gone home tonight – I miss him. And the pillow fights at bedtime. And how happy he makes Son. How *normal* he makes us, because we can walk away from the screaming and there's this happy face there to cheer us up.

This week, like last week, my life doesn't belong to me. I hate that. Some depressed people take up all the oxygen. The rest of us hold our breath and *wait it out.*

———

Tuesday, 29th May, 2007.

Joy and Exclusion

It's funny how when you're in the thick of it you give such a damn about things, but as soon as you're at Skool with your wonderful Skool People you just stop caring about what may or may not be happening at home. Especially when you step foot inside the print studio and this feeling of utter calm and purpose kicks in.

Bugger everybody.

I gave Ex-H a stern talking-to before leaving yesterday morning, telling him he had to cheer the hell up before the rest of us got home.

So after a really good day, I took my blistered, hard-working hands off to meet up with Reformed Hippy after all. (Half responsible-adult,

I rang to check that everybody was okay before promptly leaving them to fend for themselves.) She said at one stage, *'You're the only friend I can go out with who doesn't think it's weird when I just want to have chocolate for dinner'*. It was then that I realised we'd had chocolate for dinner.

We saw *The Science of Sleep*, and if that movie can't make you happy then nothing can. Except when Stephane's behaviour gets obsessive/aggressive towards the end, making me wonder why people around him didn't read it as schizoid and dangerous, because we could see life from his perspective but they couldn't. So wasn't the girl taking him in just another woman forgiving a crappy man for violent behaviour?

And I think of this as feel-good stuff, why? I guess my recommendation comes with a clause in the fine print; if you can overlook that unpleasant element, you'll piss yerself laughing. Until you get home and watch the late news and discover that The Peel has fought for the right to exclude women and heterosexuals.

Devastating!! We were talking about going there just yesterday, because it's been a while and I'm hanging out to dance, and now there's nowhere for me to go. I don't *like it* anywhere else.

I can understand why they want the exclusion, but doesn't letting hetero people into the Peel encourage tolerance in the general community? Doesn't it give poofterism a great name, because everybody has so much fun there?

This could be the end of fun as we know it. Although they do have a female bouncer on the door, so maybe they're just making sure the rampant gawking patronage is under control. Stupid gawking patronage have ruined it for everybody.

———

June 2007

Sunday, 3rd June, 2007.

In the Love of the Common People

I could turn into a snob if I wanted to. Although I'm wondering if somebody who uses cheap eighties' song references would even be allowed into the snob club as a guest, let alone as an exclusive member? It's just that those towel-flicking, football-obsessed meat heads in the staffroom at work numb my brain. As do the Mothers of Small Children, who think it's exciting that they're going to do an infant gym instructor's course (part time, while their own kids are at kinder) so they can make a career out of spending even more time with even more small children, because their maternal cups so fucking overfloweth. Also, the women who think the best thing about waitressing is that it makes you burn calories.

Gimme a break.

No, don't gimme a break – make me work so I don't have to sit down and listen to their boring conversations. It's excruciating. When did I become such a bitch? They're actually nice people. When they don't speak. Someone to smile at when you pass by in the hallway. Someone to laugh with while you're scraping leftovers off the plates during clear up (because have you noticed that debutantes don't actually eat their food?), giving you a good excuse to muck around with the only woman in the whole place who you're sure is a rampant lezzo poofter bastard, because she's funny and relaxed and fairly unattractive in a way that's different to the other funny and unattractive women who you know for a fact are not lezzo poofter bastards but mere Bogans with a capital B.

No offence to all funny, unattractive lesbians who fit *that* particular stereotype. Just so you know, I find that strangely appealing, so I'm dreading finding out that she, too, is a Bogan mother of boys in the local Bogan footy club, where all of the strapping young towel-flicking,

59

meat-headed men seem to play. Except I never will find out, because she's a kitchen hand and has different break times. Probably with more interesting people.

You can see how desperate I am to amuse myself. But I love my job, where everybody's really friendly, and I don't have to think. I love being active and busy. Except that every week I feel like I'm doing something wrong, because in every other field of my life I know if what I've done is good enough only when somebody else has looked at it and approved. Everything takes a lot of research, visual and otherwise, and (when it comes to teaching) a lot of prep work. Not so, in waitressing. Isn't that bizarre. Makes you realise how much you push yourself in your real life, when you're more uncomfortable doing a manual thing that has no right or wrong attached – it just is, you just do it, and then it's done.

Good job, soldier. Last night, every time I picked up a tray of plates I told myself *'Tonight's the night you're gonna drop it'*, because I was sure that nothing's meant to be this easy.

This is what it's like to wear somebody else's skin.

But even in this other-world in which I find myself, some things are the same. I wrote this whole entry because I wanted to tell you about the boobs I saw last night.

Debutantes and their guests are mostly UNsexy, by the way, with their overly young boobage and flitty personas. No offence to all debutantes. And their guests. But on Friday night there was this woman (a guest) who was at least a double D cup, and she was wearing at most a C cup sized dress, because she was quite slim. The other waitresses were raising eyebrows and laughing (which was mean – maybe I'm not the bitchy one, after all), but I thought she was fantastic. Her boobs were squished into this voluptuous three-pronged shape and were straining against the fabric, totally asymmetrical and utterly awkward and so worth drawing I wished I had a pencil on me at the time.

But last night's boobs – wow. I should share my thoughts during break time, to make the staff room a little more interesting. The universal appeal of perving might transcend the barrier created by my colleagues' obsessive interest in football? Because there was one woman who was otherwise boring, whose dress was of seriously deep plunging cleavage variety. I think I stared. *Very* nice. That's all I wanted to say. End of story.

———

Friday, 8th June, 2007.

Blah blah. Blah.

All of the time I should have spent painting this week I spent working on copper plates, and I've been obscenely happy because of it. Today I knicked into the studio to proof my etching – my first grown up, nobody-told-me-what-to-do etching. It's not finished because I don't have time to aquatint yet, but it's finished enough to see that my lines have worked.

I love being single, because I can work as much as I want and never feel bad about it. (Except when I neglect my kids.) So it's a pity she felt so nice to hold today, because it reminded me that I should feel lonely. I wonder if I do. Do I? Not really. But still.

———

Tuesday, 12th June, 2007.

Domestic Goddess

Because I don't think these things should pass by unnoticed, I'm telling everybody that I cooked. For a man!! Ex-Husband left for Queensland on Sunday so I took the morning off to make him some pancakes. They were *good*. I should have photographed them and printed them up as Xmas cards. Also, when you slow down enough to cook pancakes you end up potting around the kitchen, and before you know it you've not only done the dishes, but you've ENJOYED doing the dishes. I think if I wasn't such a preoccupied person (i.e. dish-hating lazy slag) I'd make a fantastic housewife. For about a day, before getting bored out of my brain.

Anyway, his leaving was a sad thing. Since I gave Ex-H a stern talking-to about how he's so holier-than-thou that he separates himself from all decent humans (i.e. me) and is going to grow old and die alone if he doesn't cheer up and be nice, he's been lovely. We settled back into our old companionable friendship, and it was even nice to have him around. It's going to be strange with him gone – he's like a cross between close family and old furniture. I'll miss him.

During the few minutes before he left I felt like a cruddy person, because I've been so busy during his last few weeks I didn't even a) go with him to the movies, b) take him out for a goodbye dinner, c) watch the rest of *Lost* and *Desperate Housewives* with him, or d) have goodbye sex. Actually probably just as well re the sex – it'd be weird, because we haven't had sex with each other since before Ex-G-Not-G. But it would've been nice to give him some warmth before he went off into the world alone.

I think the alone bit is what's making me sad. I don't want him to be lonely. He sapped my mental space, is a complete fuddy duddy and occasional pain in the arse, but he's my friend and I love him, and I'd like to make sure he's okay.

I'm a bad, people-neglecting person. After my folio's in and assessment over with (should have been today, but First-Born's not well so it's been delayed) I'm going to cook for my children. I'm going to cook a lot. Somebody's gonna have to cross my name out of the definition for Neglectful in the dictionary, and put me in BOLD CAPS under the definition for Good Woman. Sounds like a decent enough short-term ambition – I can work my way up to Perfect from there.

———

Friday, 15th June, 2007.

Perfect Score

I spent yesterday cringing at the thought of my folio being looked at by teachers. You don't want anybody to see your learning-curve work until you feel like you've actually got something to show for what you've learnt. So after I picked my folio up, I didn't even look at my essays until I got on the train. Then I swore out loud because I got 100% for one of them.

This will sound dorky, but writing those essays changed my life. For the past two weeks '*Did you get your essay in?*' was the start of every conversation, and because I get carried away by whatever excites me, every time somebody asked me I'd start blurting out everything I was thinking. Then I'd feel like an idiot and remember Ex-G-Not-G's *'Sometimes you're over-enthusiastic'* comment. But I'd look around me and see that the one-person I was talking to had grown to a small gathering of people, all fully engaged, and just like that our interest in art expanded to include a shared interest in the broader world.

It's not enough to love what you're doing, you have a responsibility to get it right every time you speak or write or draw a picture. Those grades mean I'm on the right track. And I'm allowed to be doing this. And I'm in the right place, with the right people. Now I can put my head down and work away quietly, and nobody's going to mind.

———

Friday Night/Saturday Morning (12:46 am).

Good News and Strange News

The strange news first: Ex-H started his new job yesterday, and when I spoke to him last night he didn't sound overly pleased with it, but I didn't expect him to ring at 7:30 this morning to tell me that he's going to quit. After one day. Part of me thinks it's hilarious. Good on him for knowing what he wants and for doing what he needs to do. And for having such a spectacular mid-life crisis.

I advised him to give it a month, then reduced my advice to give it a fortnight, and then to give it a week, and then to give it until after the weekend. Then when I realised he *really* hated it and couldn't stand the idea of being in that office for even one more day, I just said *what the hey, good luck, lemme know how you go*. I haven't heard from him since. I've called and called all day, and I'm worried about him.

He probably hasn't charged his phone, or he might be driving back to Melbourne and out of range. He has the luxury of living off his long service leave money for quite a while, but it won't have occurred to the poor boy to take a holiday. He'll probably arrive on my doorstep some time tomorrow afternoon and collapse in an exhausted heap.

Wouldn't it be nice if he were to let me know he's not dead in a ditch somewhere.

The good news is that I've been short-listed for an art prize and that means being exhibited soon. I've been bouncing off the walls and talking to a hundred million lovely friends, no wonder I'm so tired, but who wants to sleep? I doubt I'll be lucky enough to actually win but that just doesn't matter. I entered this particular prize because I care so much about the theme (Reconciliation) and it's so rewarding to have been selected for the exhibition. Especially at this point in time.

So I'm pretty happy right this minute, AWOL ex-husbands aside. I have so many celebratory glasses of wine teed up with my friends that I'll be able to sustain the happiness for quite a while. I'm glad I didn't have to work tonight – what a lovely way to end the week.

———

Tuesday, 19th June, 2007.

Who Says Ethics Isn't Sexy?

Bit sick of myself, but I'm sitting here for a chat anyway. To express my surprise that Peter Singer's book about the ethics of globalisation is actually NOT porn. I wish somebody had told me that *before* I got on the train this morning, so that I didn't read it with a porn slant.

No, I don't know what I'm talking about either. Something about almost having sex with Ex-H the other night, because he's here and I'm here, and opportunity has made my body, how you say, begging for it. (I kissed him. Passionately. But then I stopped myself, very sensible). Also something about Ex-G-Not-G telling me last night that she's fantasised about me, and being very surprised. Combine begging-for-it with Ex-G telling you something provocative, then read Peter Singer on the train and tell me ethics doesn't make you squirm on your seat.

Other things that suddenly seem sexy include cold weather, red bricks, standing up, sitting down and, of course, breathing.

So even though today was a happy day, I'm feeling flat tonight. It's so much easier being alone when you have nobody to think about.

———

Saturday, 23rd June, 2007.

Things that Shit me #1

Why doesn't anybody speak proper no more? It's bothered me for a while now that television presenters are getting lazy with their language. Is this a new thing, or have they been doing it all along? It's making me feel anal as I sit there correcting them. Out loud. I'm ready to be one of those grumpy old women who perch themselves in front of the nursing home tele and bitch about how the world used to be.

The things that shit me most = when people say "there is" for a plural. For example, *'There's a lot of people in here'* instead of *'There're a lot of people in here'*.

I thought it was just the Big Brother people at first, and was willing to overlook it because they're morons, but now it's happening everywhere, even in the news reading. Everywhere I go people are getting it wrong. Because they watch the news and are easily influenced? Nobody cares – why don't they care? If we can't get people to care about their 'is's and 'are's, how are we going to manage World Peace?

Last night at work some people were saying "much" where they should have been saying "many", and it was doing my head in. How does a body get over these things?

––––

Things That Shit me #2

I asked Ex-H to find a covering for the manhole because the smell of the annual rodent population currently decomposing inside the floor/ceiling between upstairs and downstairs was getting overpowering, and he said *'It'll fade quickly'*.

Let me tell you something about decomposing rodents: the smell DOES NOT fade quickly.

You could argue that I should have covered the manhole myself, but I'm a *girl*, and as a *girl* I want the job done, I want it done *now*, and I want not to have to do it myself. What's the point of having a Y chromosome in the house if he's not at my beck and call? This is why men shit me. They make you dependent on them by hankering to your own laziness by doing everything for you, then when you really need something done they don't do it.

In the end I summoned my reluctant independence, found a piece of cardboard and pinned it to the ceiling to cover the hole. Ad hoc, which is pretty much my style, but it worked instantly, so I feel like a domestic genius. No more stench of death.

Now if somebody could tell me how to get the stench of there's-a-man-in-the-house out, I'd be very much obliged.

———

About Those Dishes

My house is lived-in, but it's also very clean. Unless I'm finishing off a piece of writing, or a drawing, or a painting, then I let it go a bit. In fact, if I've got work in the finishing stage, I'm a complete scrag with the housework. It's fantastic. And let's face it – if you have an older ethnic friend who visits and always says upon inspection *'Gee, your place is so clean'*, then you must be a top of the range scrubber, because her standards are so high.

Clean? I'll give you clean. Motherfucker.

So if I'm willing to put up with a less than perfect kitchen every now and then because I'm insisting that my kids do their fair share of cleaning, that's my prerogative.

Who cares anyway? Dishes schmishes – Ex-H is really clutching at straws to find a way to assert the Necessity of Himself.

———

Monday, 25th June, 2007.

Pest Control

I'm sitting here with a glass of Kahlua and milk and I'm calling it breakfast. That's my daily intake of dairy, right there. Do you see how he's driving me to drink? Forget oats – oats are for people whose ex-husbands aren't hanging around for longer than they should.

At least I have the decency to feel bad about it. Not the Kahlua, but about wanting him to leave. In fact I feel downright guilty, and am willing to acknowledge that I'm being a princess with this attitude, but I can't help it. Technically he's the dream house guest (guest?). He's quiet, he goes about his business, he fixes things and does the dishes. In fact, my kitchen hasn't been this clean this regularly since... since ever? (Or it seems that way, see *I'm-going-on-strike,* above.)

BUT, *we're separated*, and this is my home space, where I live with my family, of which he's no longer an immediate part. If he doesn't like the arrangement, then we need to sell the house. I don't know why he avoids this selling-of-the-house.

I asked him to go to his Mum's this week, as per our mutually agreed upon arrangement; he's supposed to be here a few days, there a few days, as a way of mitigating the extremes of his general intolerance of "us". But he got offended. He has no right to be offended, because we're not *married* anymore. I just want to be alone with my kids.

Plus this week is the last opportunity to have the house to myself before school holidays start, so I'm desperate to be alone with my work. I guard work time like a pit-bull — nobody but nobody fucks with my work time (except for my kids, because I love them), and he knows it.

If we were in a poor country I'd have to be grateful for this whopping big roof over my head and for even having my own bedroom and indoor plumbing. But we're not. Gawd bless the selfish big western world, where I'm allowed to be a spoilt brat.

When I asked him to leave (actually, I was going hysterical by this stage, because of his negative attitude), he listed the things he's done around the house and said '*You don't cope on your own!*' [!!!!!!!!].

I cope fine on my own (don't I?). I have plenty of *blah* to say about it, but will skip to the bit where I'm confused by my own bitchiness. I don't want to hurt him, but the longer he's here, the more I start to hate him. While I was going hysterical, I screeched something about not wanting to live like we're married, *we're not married, we shouldn't be in each other's space like married people, surely there are things about me that annoy you just like they did back then.* To this he repeated his theory that '*We only separated because of First-Born*'.

No. I mean Yes we separated because of First-Born, but it's not that simple. I spent a year begging him to understand them, putting up with his sulking moods and his judgement and the way he shut himself off from us until there was no marriage left, and I was disgusted by him by the time I kicked him out. I hated him for doing that to a child. From my perspective, "because of First-Born" means "I fell out of love with him because of how he treated First-Born".

Now I'm recoiling from his presence, even though he's my friend, because he doesn't belong here like this. He does his old-mannish things and I have to bite my tongue, and the more I bite my tongue the more likely I am to explode inappropriately. OhmiGAWD it makes me want to SCREAM. (Am I selfish? That poor, nice man...)

————

Still Monday, 25th June, 2007.

Bitchin' n' Moanin'

If I don't vent this here, it's going to be barked out with much decorative language to his face. Because I suspect he's doing this on purpose. As soon as I started work this morning, he walked right back in. I told him to stay away during school hours so that I can work 100% undisturbed. Now it's 1:30 and he's still here. He's going to his Mum's, but isn't leaving for another hour. The bulk of today's work time is down the toilet. I'm furious. As any self-respecting princess would be.

The reason I think he's doing it on purpose is that I had to sit in here to condense an artist's statement and write a biography for the exhibition, and while I was doing so he came in, sat at his computer, and started watching a television broadcast. I asked him to please go and watch the real tv upstairs, because (duh) it was distracting me from a difficult task (I hate writing my own biography). He got shitty at me as though I was being unreasonable for wanting to concentrate.

Is he a *child*? Is he trying to make a point about his own righteousness by hanging around like this? Who plays the television when somebody's trying to write? At least now I'm *allowed* to be angry. Feeling guilty was the absolute pits.

————

Still Monday.

Going, Going...Gone

I'm the meanest mean person that ever meaned. Meant. Whatever. Here's this man who has nobody and nowhere else to go, and I can't even be generous enough to put up with his quiet, helpful company. But thank fuck he's gone.

Maybe it all comes down to how much responsibility you should or shouldn't have to take for somebody after you've separated. I can't keep feeling bad for his loneliness, because it's not my fault, and I can't fix it for him. I'd like to, but I can't. Then again, he helps me with things all the time. But double-then again, there are boundaries that should be observed, and if I didn't make it hard, he might try to stay here forever.

So I shouldn't feel mean for asserting reasonable boundaries?

Maybe I'm just slapping too much red paint onto that canvas and it's doing its subliminal colour thing to make me feel aggressive. I apologised for booting him out before he left. Maybe if I get the red painting over with before he gets back, everything will be okay.

Same Monday, Different Subject.

Intervention-ing

Last night's news report about military and police measures being taken to deal with the sexual abuse of indigenous children was alarming. Also that those news reports neglected to offer an indigenous viewpoint. But today's *Age* carries that viewpoint, and as expected it raises so many questions about the integrity of our Government.

Such as, isn't the blanket approach an act of racial demonisation? Doesn't this situation call for sensitivity? Don't they need to earn the trust of the children before examining something as personal as their bits? And what about infrastructure and the bigger picture?

Biggest question of all: have politicians learnt nothing from history? Because in this particular situation, self-determination for indigenous people (with government support) is a necessity.

One final question: are Australians willing to see what's happening in this country now, or are they going to keep pretending that they don't see the significance of this kind of violation?

I'd like to see the government try to pull this off in a non-indigenous community and get away with it.

Wednesday, 27th June, 2007.

Political Machismo

I watched *Lateline* last night, and Noel Pearson made some really good points. I could almost eat my words. But I think he's wrong about naysayers *'wishing for failure'*. Granted, the accusation of a land grab is ridiculous, but the fact is that most of us don't trust our government to do this properly. You let them take a little bit of power, and the next thing you know they've taken too much. You let them neglect a crisis for decades and then bring the military in with a theatrical election stunt, rather than pulling their thumbs out and getting the necessary resources organised, you might just be asking for trouble.

What people are angry about = that if the resources had been made available before now, along with all of those funky billions of dollars or "whatever it takes" Johnny's suddenly offering, this righteous coup would have had a much more reasonable, and less frightening, nature.

So I'm not eating my words yet – I'll sprinkle them with salt and put them in the fridge for later.

―――

Friday, 29th June, 2007.

Smelling the Flowers

Thought I'd take a moment to say something non-angsty, because I've gone back to being happy. This is the state I was trying so hard to retrieve last year. 2006 was an existential toilet, but all's well because it's over now.

There, I managed to write this before Ex-H gets back and I go back to being uncomfortably selfish. I just hope I get Current Project finished before he walks through that door.

―――

Saturday, 30th June, 2007.

H-Ex

I got the strangest e-mail last night. It was from Evil Ex-Friend, telling me that she's going to send me a thank-you letter, because she remembers my niceness and "generosity" and et cetera. It's such a nice thing to be told that I feel guilty writing about it here, because it's probably a highly personal thing for her to have sent. But I'm bowled over. I'm wondering if she's signed up for some Evil-Person's Anonymous group, and this thank-you is part of her twelve step program? It's so out of the blue. Maybe I'll wait until I get the letter before thinking any more about it, other than that it's a brave and sweet thing for her to do.

Now that Ex-H is back I can't find any of that [alleged] generosity lying around. I've realised that I'm actually censoring what I say to him, walking on eggshells to avoid upsetting him. Last night, while I was making friendly conversation as part of my Salvage-the-Friendship project, he started with the judgements again.

Sometimes Ex-H is the spokesperson for Doom and Gloom. This time it was an accusation that I don't police what the kids are watching (tv, movies) enough, because First-Born was asking to see *American Psycho*. Notice I haven't given it to her; I haven't seen it myself therefore have my reservations. The man is not only wrong, but he has a pole up his arse when it comes to kids and their culture. If it didn't worry me so much I'd find it amusing that somebody who forfeited his parental rights because of his sheer resistance to youth still feels the need to impose so much control over the household.

Needless to say I don't feel guilty for wanting him gone – small doses as a friend, fine, but he really doesn't belong here.

———

I know it's a shame, but I have to sacrifice the cleaning of my oven [again] this weekend just to get by. This juggling act of modern womanhood is overrated, and I feel scatter-brained. There are too many things to focus on. I spent a couple of dawn-to-dusk days writing solidly, and by last night I was so spent I accidentally watched *Clueless*. I watched it from a chair all the way over at the kitchen table, just gazing off into the distance, because I couldn't be bothered moving. It was horrifying when I realised what I was doing, but by then it was too late.

Today I think I should do nothing but read. Take a deep breath, and plan ahead for a very full-on week.

———

Never a Day Without Incident
It's not that I'm going to keep a log of Ex-H's annoyingnesses, but I'll mention two more so that I have a record I can use to prevent feeling guilty for wanting him gone.

Last night, while we were watching *Lost*, he made those judgemental comments again, this time about First-Born's music being on. Actually, they kept the volume quite low, and they're a *teenager,* so a bit of music is to be expected. In short, First-Born was doing nothing wrong.

Then this morning, I was about to have a shower but had to go upstairs first to get my conditioner from First-Born's bathroom. I could see him about to sneak into my bathroom so I said *'No, I'm about to use that, go and use the other toilet'.* He snuck in there anyway, so I had to wait (someone oughtsta tell him that selfish princesses do NOT like to wait). When he got out I very firmly said *'That was bad manners, why didn't you use the other one?'* His reply was, *'Well I would use the other toilet if those signs weren't all over the walls'.*

My blood is boiling. The signs he's referring to are, yes, a bit dumb. Not the one I wrote, which hangs above the loo and says *'If you're reading this then you're probably missing the hole'.* (I was tired of cleaning up after Son's friends. Come on guys – how hard can it be to get it into the hole?) But First-Born went a bit far about a year ago by putting a framed sign on the door that says *The Shitter*, and a poster describing some crass Shitter rules that amused them and their friends at the time. I protested, but in the end I thought about it being part of their exploration of toilet humour and creative self-expression, and I let it go.

Let's just say his intolerance of children and family life makes my whole body go tense, and I'm now faking the friendliness because of it. Frankly, I don't want to smell man pee when I'm about to step into the shower. (Princess, I warned you.) Have you noticed how when somebody is making you consistently angry and defensive of your children, their physicality starts to become intolerable? I know I'm being repetitive, but he just needs to *leave.*

———

July 2007

Tear-Jerker

If I look radiant at the moment it's because of my warm maternal glow. This happens when you re-introduce Chinese Checkers and Uno to the household. Son loves games, and when I asked First-Born the other night '*You wanna play?*', they surprised me by saying '*Yes*'.

They surprised me again on Friday night when Son got the Uno cards out (that's the problem with games – you play one or two and then suddenly every time you sit down Son ambushes you with it, and you have to play a hundred), and First-Born leapt up and said '*Deal me in*'. For this, they left their boyfriend and friend-from-school behind on the couch. I said they should maybe invite them to play with us, and they did, so now we're One Big Happy Family with One Big Happy Family Friends.

My evil together-time plan is working. First-Born is so, so funny (I love watching them with their friends), and they and Son are getting along really well again. Everything is *peachy*.

So last night I took Son to the movies. He chose *Bridge to Terabithia*, knowing (because I told him) it's the only one I could even remotely stand the idea of sitting through. He chose to see this WITH ME (as opposed to seeing one of the other movies with his friends) [!!].

That glow I've got going is practically radioactive.

The truth is I didn't expect to like *Bridge to Terabithia*. I expected the magical bits to be so ridiculous they'd make me cringe. So you can imagine my surprise when it got to the sad bit (nobody warned me about any sad bits) and I cried. In fact, I bawled my eyes out. Slipped down in my seat and hoped nobody could see the cinematic glisten of tears streaming down my face. I'm so *embarrassed*; it wasn't even *ET*!!

Still Sunday. Night.

This is becoming suspiciously like live tv, with me reporting from the middle of what now seems to be a war zone.

I don't know why such a nice man has to be such a prick. He was sitting behind me in the computer room down in the dungeon, and when he got up to leave I could tell he was shitty. Blatant rule-breaking. He's not allowed to be shitty at me for being shitty at him for something shitty he's done. So I let him have it, begging him to stop judging the kids and to just be tolerant, et cetera.

He raised his voice, made comments implying that I'm a bad mother because I don't teach the kids consideration (First-Born's music) and that they're out of my control (signs on the toilet door sending message to her friends that she runs the roost) and that I supposedly let them run wild (adult rated films, as though they're not supervised and guided and lectured-at from all possible angles – I'm a semi-academic, remember; there's socio-cultural analysis going on all over this house on a daily basis).

A reminder here: my kids are wonderful, funny, happy, intelligent human beings who have a nurtured life. One of them's hard work, but that's okay. Pick on my cooking all you like, but never pick on my motherhood, because there's nothing wrong with it [most of the time].

I'd very much like to swear right now. A lot. Instead I'm going to go calmly upstairs and be with my kids, and I'm going to find a way to fix this without damaging the Ex-Husband/Ex-Wife friendship. Outside of his family, he only has me in this world. I told him I don't want to hate him, but he's so stubborn with his opinions I don't know where it's all going to go.

On the Goodness of Kids

First-Born has a few woolly-woofter friends, and even one bi friend (male). It's good to see teenagers accepting homosexuality as commonplace. These kids are open and comfortable and happy. In some ways the world is getting better... or has it been like that for a long time and I just haven't noticed? Whatever. It's just nice.

———

Monday, 2nd July, 2007.

Love and Dish-Pan Hands

Some people make me so happy. That's why I'm getting no work done, not because I'm lying awake for hours at night worrying about certain other people who don't.

I love everybody right now. This because my kitchen bench is shinier than it's ever been in its life. And that because I received a text from Friend W-L (ex-sister-in-law, mother of two nieces) just after midnight on Saturday, telling me that Niece One (First-Born's age) said something funny, and '*she laughed and omg, she did a face exactly like u and it was so cute and it made me feel all warm and fuzzy. Luv ya!*'. (Niece One's face must be very pretty!)

Sounds like drunken ramblings, but she put her love where her mouth is by turning up at our house yesterday and doing the dishes that First-Born had left from the night before. She kept telling me she loved me, and doing those dishes is an act of true friend-love if ever I've seen one. Next time somebody tells me they love me, I'm going to point to my kitchen and say, '*Oh you do? Well there are the dishes, so why don't you prove it?*'.

 The best thing is that she insisted I take the credit for her bang-up cleaning job. She's hysterically funny, Friend W-L, so by the time my mother had come for a visit and then gone, and Kitchen Nazi had dropped her son off to stay, and Ex-H had returned from his stinky-mood day of working down in the garden, I'd taken full and multiple credit for that shiny, dish-free bench, and my side was splitting. I have to count my blessings, because I feel so looked-after.

Later, when I picked First-Born up from a party in the middle of the night, one of their woolly-woofter friends came up to me and asked if I'm First-Born's Mum. I said *yes* and he threw himself at me for a huge hug, exclaiming '*First-Born is awesome, they make me laugh so much*'. Then other kids hugged me for the same reason, and I'm feeling like such a proud Mum.

Sad thing, though; just before I left to get them, Ex-H had made some harsh and disapproving comment about the skeleton incense burner he'd given me for my birthday being used in First-Born's bedroom that day. (That's right – he gave me a present, and four months later is trying to control what I do with it, because how *dare* I share it with my child.)

Hence my lying awake for hours thinking about his doom and gloom and worrying about how much damage he's doing to First-Born – AGAIN.

But then, this morning I walked into the kitchen and said to Son *'I hope you didn't feed Kitchen Nazi's Son cabbage for breakfast'*. I looked at the bench and saw his breakfast cabbage trimmings all over it and had to laugh, because kids are the funniest creatures to have around. (It's okay – he had cabbage himself, but gave his friend cereal.)

So even if Ex-H insists on spreading misery, it's impossible to be unhappy. There's so much love 'round here it'll make you wanna puke.

———

Wednesday, 4th July, 2007.

Oh Feck

I just realised (as I was typing the date onto this file) that I didn't call my Dad for his birthday. You know how you remember something so much you forget that you haven't remembered it? That's a piece of unforgivability I'm going to hate myself for for a long while.

Well anyway, it's 2:15 am and I'm really tired but I'm too scared to go to bed. I hate insomnia and know by the state of my mind that I won't be able to sleep. That state qualifying as "nut-job", actually. I was about to get into bed and thought I CAN'T STAND IT (*it* being *him*) and I've snuck into the dungeon to get some alone time, figuring that if I empty my head it'll get better. I mean I *literally* snuck in here – lights off, tip-toeing, scared to breathe and regretting not writing this on my laptop because this other keyboard is so loud.

Suddenly I notice how much this chair creaks when you sit on it in the middle of the night.

Everything's bad because I'm selfish. I asked Ex-H to leave yesterday. I said some blunt things [justifiable], he said some revolting things [not justifiable, and not acceptable], and then we made the decision to sell the house [finally!]. But in the meantime, he's still here. Long story, sick of own voice, can't be bothered.

Something I learn every now and then: he's very nice when he's in our lives, but if I contradict him, or do something like, say, try to kick him out on his arse, he gets very ugly. Is he only a fair-weather good-ex-husband?

End result = that I made an effort to bring us back to friendliness and I succeeded. Genuinely – I value him and fully intend to keep the friendship intact, no matter how ugly it gets. But do you see what I've done? I've felt guilty because of my selfishness, because I can't stand hurting his feelings, and that guilt has made me completely forget what he said to me yesterday. By forgetting, I'm able to spend the day accepting that he's here (easy because I myself was out with friends), and keep it friendly with the thought that I can handle it for a short while.

Until... it's bed time. Before I go to bed I unwind and start to think of tomorrow and what I'll be working on. I can't do that when he's here. His presence gets into my head and won't leave. I try to override it and think of something else, but I can't. This is where I go completely nut-job – it's all mental, not very rational, but I can't help it.

It doesn't help that he's lurking in the background when First-Born disobeys my request that they not burn incense in their bedroom at night. Not a big deal, except that my relationship with them is none of his business (my objection here = related to the ugly comments he made yesterday). I realised tonight that one reason I hate him being here so much is that I don't want him witnessing us. His criticisms are foul. How he expects to be welcome here after saying those things is beyond me.

So why am I the one who feels guilty?

———

Sex and Somnolence

Earlier tonight I finished watching the second series of *The L Word* with First-Born. It's good, if you can get over that crappy intro music. And you *can* get over it, with a fast forward button. Thank goodness for that.

The sex scenes in this series are much better. I therefore spent much time rolling my eyes and whistling towards the ceiling – I really have to stop watching that kind of thing with First-Born in the room. Uncomfortable is an understatement. I soften the embarrassment by [as usual] criticising the amount of prominent bone visible under the women's transparent skin. First-Born's theory is that the show is targeting men. I don't think they're right, and yet they might as well be. Very few non-skeletal women. I know I've asked this before, but don't American lesbians eat?

Less awkwardly, I watched *First Tuesday Book Club* (LOVE!) and Margaret Fulton was very wise. She was talking about a house that was built on a swamp, a significant feature of a major childhood idyll within her memory, and how she can never get back to that place or back to that memory via the place because the house sunk into the bog and is just plain gone. Poignant, that's all. On that soft note, perhaps now I can sleep.

———

Friday, 6th July, 2007.

More Blah

I can feel my facial muscles not working the way a dead person's facial muscles don't work. You know how you can hardly recognise the dead when you view their body, because their whole face has stopped smiling? What a depressing thing to write – I'm clearly under the influence of a life-killing force.

I've been awake all night. Sort of. I was working on a copper plate in the garage last night when a migraine kicked in, so I went to bed at 9:30. Migraine and unhappiness are perfect cures for insomnia, because they both make you need to crash. I used ear plugs so I had silence, and was relieved to feel myself falling asleep.

You can imagine how awful it was to wake up, look at the clock and see that it was only 10:40 pm. One piddly hour!

I heard an ABC radio segment on insomnia once, and it advised not to fight it, because if you relax your body you still get valuable rest. Insomnia is your *friend*. So I stayed relaxed and could feel that I was breathing as though I was asleep. Bit bizarre, really, to be wide awake and asleep at the same time, but it worked until 2:30 am. After 2:30 my eyes were wide open and I was breathing like a stupid old awake person and I wanted to get up.

This is not good. I'm supposed to spend today at the print studio, but don't know how I can do that if my face isn't smiling. I've been trying to work out why I can't just be gutsy about this horrible situation and keep on trucking. That life-killing force feels very real, is sapping the happiness out of my bones.

I have this girly bad feeling that something's even wronger than it seems. Maybe it's just because I've shocked him with the extremity of his unwelcome. Am I afraid of him? Or is that just me responding to the control he's managed to wield without my realising it? Ex-H does so many nice things for me, and I've always thought he was being just that – nice. I don't ask for many favours, and the ones I ask for are things he does for himself anyway (computer things, audiobooks, references etc). Beyond that he does things I don't ask for. It's making me feel really ungrateful, but I'm not ungrateful. Gratitude is part of my whole saintly make-up.

Then I remember his perception that I "don't cope" without him.

This is not what's keeping me awake – what's keeping me awake is the general ugliness and my lost time. But I feel like he's in a position to pull everything out from under us, and I'm wondering if he will.

———

Between a Rock and a Hard Place

Niceness aside, there are things about Ex-H that I can't overlook. Such as, he wanted to be the one who lives in this house when we separated. I stayed because he's one little person and I'm three big ones (i.e. kids). He didn't want us to sell. So every time he asked me to move out so that he could live here, I felt hurt on behalf of my kids. Son still calls him "Dad", but that "Dad" would boot him out of his home, knowing that rent for us would be much more expensive than it'd be for him. The idea of one socially inept man living in this big house alone while his supposed children live in a much smaller place just seems wrong. I mentioned this to him the other day, and he said *'Well Son can stay here with me'.*

You do *not* say that to a mother. No wonder I feel so dark. These are the things that are stuck in my mind.

Another thing: when we separated, he took his precious dvd collection. He even took the ones he'd given me as gifts (eg. *Fight Club*). I don't care about that – he likes to be encyclopaedic, so it's unpleasant but not necessarily malicious. But what I can't get over is that he took the kids' movies. He took *Monsters Inc* and *Spy Kids* and *Toy Story* – things Son loved watching. If we wanted to watch them we had to put in a request and wait for him to bring them over. I find this memory really, really depressing, because he's supposed to love my kid. Also, he's open about hating kids generally, and so will never actually watch these movies that he clings to so much.

The worst thing is that Son doesn't want me to send Ex-H away because he likes having a man around. He's fallen for the illusion of stability, because Ex-H has waltzed in and asserted himself at the head of the household. I told him I didn't want Son getting too attached to him being here, but maybe it's too late? Another thing to feel bad about. First I get accused of not coping on my own, then I get called a bad mother, then he makes the casual suggestion that Son could live with him as if that's okay, and then the situation arises that Son is going to lose his sense of stability and it'll be all my fault because I'm ordering his step-father to leave.

Because of his current presence here, when he leaves I'll have lost something important in every area of my life. Most significantly, Son is going to suffer. I hate that Ex-H is nice to me, as though he didn't say or think those revolting things he said the other day. Because of his pronounced sense of righteousness, I don't think he ever questions his right to make this kind of impact. Some strange combination of nice-meets-inadvertent-malice.

I don't think my trusty women's intuition is playing tricks on me – whether he means it in a malicious way or not, I think Ex-H is prepared to cause a helluva lot of damage in the name of this sense of righteousness. He truly believes that I'm inferior, and that he's therefore entitled. Even being here when he's not supposed to be – technically he's right, he owns half the house. And yet, we're separated. He doesn't understand that inserting your-uninvited-self into the home of a family you're no longer compatible with, and then refusing to leave because you think you have the right to be there despite the law saying you do not, results in real psychological damage.

I prefer trying to understand his perspective than to hate him for it, but the consequences of being inferiorised are so dire. Yes he's nice, but you don't just leave a bad marriage; you escape it.

———

Friday, 6th July, 2007 [fully day].

Light of Day

Forget lesbian sex – I slept!!! For a whole 3 hours!!! And I would have kept sleeping if I didn't get woken at 10 am to drive kids around. It feels good to be alive again. Obviously long-winded whinging helps clear the mind. But I have to stop that – Ex-H is just a human being trying to survive like the rest of us. I can't handle that I'm being so mean. I'm not going to get into heaven if I keep this up. Mind over matter, that's all I need. None of this I'm-hard-done-by diatribe.

I hate that I can't just be nice to him and let him stay. Nobody deserves full-on rejection like that. It's not his fault he's so negative about life he makes me feel dead.

———

Sunday, 8th July, 2007.

Rhymes with Spoke

I've really put the scrag back into my scumbag single-motherhood now. There are no words for it. Except for these ones, and I have to get them right or I won't be able to pass myself off as cool. Last night I got baked. Or trashed. Or wasted. Or stoned, if you wanna be old fashioned about it. But it wasn't like being stoned, exactly – I've been there, done that. This was different, it wiped me out.

I was at Churchy Friend's little place in the country with a few of her friends. It was her birthday, and we were being merry n' such when she lit up a joint. She offered me some, and I accepted but only because I had no goon with me. I thought it was a good opportunity to do one of my random experiments, to see what all of the drug fuss is about. I've done this before – gotten stoned and found the experience so inferior to alcohol that it reinforces my view that dope-heads are dumb. Plus, birthday; I figured if I wanted to bond with my dope-addicted friend, this was the way to do it. I was dripping with magnanimity.

But a mutual friend brought her a batch of "special" cookies. I've wanted to try his cookies for a long time (curiosity), so I had one. Three bites into a four-bite cookie, he saw me and said *'Whoa, don't eat the whole thing'*, because they're potent. *Now* you tell me. For a whole half-hour I didn't believe him, but then it kicked in and by that I mean it *really kicked in.* My body thought it was sick and I was panicking because I had kids with me. Not only my kids, but Son's friend, who I'd have to drive home later.

But then I sat down and realised that the humming feeling in every inch of my body wasn't sickness, it was pleasure. And so began the most internalised buzz I've ever felt in my life. I couldn't move, for hours and hours. First-Born thought it was hilarious and kept asking me to pass them things because they knew I couldn't identify simple objects. (*'That's right, Mother, the Coke can, pass me the Coke can, Mother, it's the red thing on the table..'*)

Not the best way to meet your friend's new friends; there's a little local farming community out there thinking I'm the mute [comatose] relative. But the worst thing is that I don't know how I'm going to warn my kids against using drugs, when it felt so *good.* Why wouldn't you throw your life away for the stuff? Go ahead – it's worth it! And all this time I've spent trying to get Chruchy Friend over her addiction, I should have been telling her *'Don't be stupid, just stay stoned'*!!

I've put in an order for some cookies to keep on hand for when an opportunity arises, with friends and without kids. When the next blue moon comes around. But now I'm gonna to spend the next few years worrying that my kids will try drugs and like them. I just hope First-Born's willing to take my hypocritical don't-do-it advice. Oh *bugger.*

―――

Homophobe Alert

I was overly optimistic in thinking that the world was changing when it comes to teenagers and homosexuality. We were driving home (much later than expected) last night when Son's [BEST] Friend mentioned "gays". I don't even know how the conversation started but the kid's a bigot. He even called gay people "abominations" [!!!!!!].

I stayed silent, but Son and First-Born tried (and failed) to talk him round to a more healthy level of tolerance. I was shocked by the vehemence in this little kid's voice. I knew his brother was like that, but his brother has Asperger's so his intractability is more understandable. Although, he has to have gotten this intractability from somewhere. Apparently his whole family think that way – even his mother.

Did I mention I've stayed at the tail-end of the suburbs for this many years so that my children could keep their good friends? Did I also mention it might be time to move the hell out of here? And First-Born wonders why I want to move us all to Northcote.

I always liked that kid, but I find myself feeling repulsed. Next time he comes to visit I'm gonna burn his food and give him the smallest piece of chocolate. I fully expect to one day wake up and find a brutal red X painted across my front door, because eventually he's going to find out about our checkered history, which come to think of it isn't exactly historical. I hope he doesn't hurt Son's feelings.

Dammit – why can't the world just be nice?

———

Monday, 9th July, 2007.

New Leaf

The only artistic thing about me lately is my temperament. I have to get over this [melo]dramatic tantrummy phase. Because I could continue to lament the loss of the last four weeks' worth of work time and the wonderful schedule that could have and would have been if I'd been left alone, or I can kiss them goodbye and let life start again tomorrow.

No pressure. No more kicking of self. No more hating of Ex-Husbands who are really very nice people, just because he KILLS MY VALUABLE ROUTINE. Still, it's amazing how settled I feel when he's not here. And how not-working on something can drive me nuts.

A few days ago I was painting stop-out onto a printing plate, and I felt so at peace it was overwhelming. Ex-H wandered up from the garden where he'd been slaving his guts out, and I think he was bowled over because I started chatting to him as though I hadn't been a complete fruitcake up until that moment.

A working me is a nice me. Let that be a lesson to anybody who tries to fuck up my work schedule – put a paintbrush in my hand and I'm a saint, but get in my way and I'll bite your balls off.

So, I'm ready to be a machine. But not 'til I'm back from interstate. It's hard to dive into work when you know you have to stop again, so I might as well enjoy myself. Due to a happy coincidence, while I'm away I get to catch up with a friend I haven't seen for seven years. And I know it's bad manners to remember sex when somebody's married to somebody else, but one of my favourite sexual memories belongs to Capital Friend. And while we're on the subject, he has the softest penis skin you've *ever* felt. You probably didn't need to know that, but I've been out to dinner and I've had wine so I'm quite in the mood to tell you anyway. Something else interesting about Capital Friend: he's one of the most beautiful, sensual kissers I've ever kissed. So is his wife.

But it's not going to be that kind of visit and I'm honest to goodness not that kinda girl. Still, having nice memories of intimacy makes you feel close to somebody in a sweet way, even after seven years, so I'm looking forward to seeing them. And making new memories that have nothing to do with sensual kissing or soft penis skin.

In fact, this trip is very much about art. I realised today that I'll be meeting other artists and they'll all probably be nice people. If they're not, it'll be fun anyway. I can't really complain that life's been nothing but parties and dinners and lunches and more lunches and more dinners (which is like being given the reward without having done enough work to earn it), because it means I have good people, and by the end of the week I'll be partied out and ready to settle back into that longed-for work/family routine. Work/friends, friends/work – I don't know which thing to look forward to the most.

———

Friday, 13th July, 2007.

Feeling Lucky

I had the nicest holiday. Friend K said I should call it a junket because it was all paid for and professional, but that makes it sound like the spewy pink dessert Mum used to mix up from a sachet. Isn't it wonderful that in the world of art, all business is fundamentally enjoyable? No matter how hard you work, life's a holiday; nothin' wrong with my terminology.

I know just how Harry Potter felt when he arrived at Hogwarts for his first welcome feast, because the Great Hall in the National Museum was decked out and feast-ish. Our art had been transported over from the exhibition venue for the night, and was displayed on big easels in front of black velvet curtainy walls under perfectly subtle lighting.

I feel lucky, because life is rich when you get to experience this kind of celebration. Someone somewhere had an idea for a spectacular event and it was organised beautifully. Spectacular is an understatement – the aesthetics of the whole thing made it unforgettable.

I'd write more about it (aeroplanes!) (all of those nice artists!) but I'm tired and should save it for the thank-you letter anyway. (HAPPY!)

———

Misidentitifcation

This comment left under an entry:

> *I was browsing the net for reviews on crystal showgirls, and found your blog. I don't really know about the place but you sound like a great person to get wasted with.*

How amusing; someone has mistaken me for "cool".

———

Still Friday.

No Offence, But...

Mere-Male Art Friend told me that if he hadn't gotten to know me before reading my blog he would have been scared of meeting me because I'm such a man hater. Am I? *Nah*. But as soon as he described this ball-shrinking response to my harmless little words, I decided to stop criticising those motherfucking penis-possessing sorry-excuses-for-human-beings we call men. Wouldn't wanna hurt their motherfucking little feelings.

Before I stop, I need to criticise them one more time, because while I was away I sent First-Born to stay with my parents, and left Son here with a representative of that gender, embedded in our house.

Son and I were fooling around happily over a game of Uno tonight when he asked *'By the way, what was I supposed to have eaten while you were away?'*. I asked *'What do you mean, didn't Ex-H feed you?'*. He said no, and told me he'd cooked eggs for himself at 9:30 last night.

Honest to goodness, *men*. If you're charged with the responsibility of looking after a child, shouldn't it occur to you to feed him? Feeding the children is part of the job, clearly detailed in the position description. Ex-H can actually cook, so this surprised [and horrified] me. I guarantee you, that man will not have forgotten to feed the cats.

I later asked Ex-H in a friendly voice *'Why didn't you feed Son?'*, and at first he answered in a critical way with *'You didn't leave anything for him'*. Well duh; I thought the man my son calls Dad could handle the provision of food without being directed by the absent woman of the house. When I expressed concern at the lack of initiative [and care] this revealed, he changed his unfriendly "reason" to a less-critical "excuse", by saying that he didn't cook for himself (he doesn't eat every day, more ascetic than a monk) so he didn't think of it.

Dear Men-in-General: please stop being such dickheads so that I can think something nice about you. Sincerely, Me.

———

Saturday, 14th July, 2007.

Getting Lucky

Such a stupid expression. Not sure I should have done that. I did, after all, promise not to have sex with my past again. But you know how it is; mind says no, body says you shouldn't say no to food when your stomach is grumbling.

I did, however, learn a few things. I learnt [again] that I'm not a casual sex person. My halo may be dodgily stuck together with clag and sticky tape, but it's still on my head. And by having sex with a man I learnt that I probably shouldn't be having sex with men at the moment. I couldn't worship him – I didn't even kiss his neck. I hardly kissed full stop. No necks, minimal kissing? Until this week I wouldn't have imagined that possible. I don't know why he seemed so happy – I was the most selfish, inattentive lover on the planet.

If only penetration didn't feel so damn nice.

So here's the deal: if you're a man and you want sex, keep away from me. I won't kiss you, head jobs are absolutely out of the question, and you'll be lucky if I even touch the stupid thing. (Okay that's a lie – kinda hard to avoid.) I'll want one thing from you and one thing only [with its many variations], so I'll use you up and spit you out.

Don't bother asking me to respect you in the morning. I won't even stick around for breakfast. And if I have wake-up sex with you, it's my body begging for it, not my mind. That's why I'm facing the other way. When my morning orgasm happens to be surprisingly intense, it doesn't mean I'm not hating having sex with you at that particular moment. In fact, my thoughts will be so far inward that in reality it'll be like I'm having sex with myself, which means that you'll be reduced to nothing but a glorified piece of equipment.

The good thing about having sex with an old friend is the laughter and genuine comfort. We laughed all night. That was nice. The bad thing is that I lay awake while he slept, thinking about how I miss innocence and how life could be a lot less complicated without sex. I like that my focus in life is on work and family and friends, and I honestly don't need anything else. Sex is just part of being in your body, so forget other people, you can handle that yourself quite nicely.

In the middle of the night I swore I'd never have sex again. And I was quite happy with that decision. The problem is that when I least expect it, my body starts letting me know that that's a crazy idea. It remembers the sex without my prompting.

I'm just going to have to thwart its plans until it forgets what it's missing. I'll start by concentrating on getting sleep. I've snuck into the computer room on tip-toe after bedtime again. After a literally sleepless Wednesday night in the hotel, I had the best sleep in ages at Capital Friend's house last night, so buggered if I'm going to let insomnia creep back in by going to bed before my mind is empty.

This time I remembered to bring my lap-top with me – soft, silent keys, still a dream keyboard. From now on I'll just make love to that.

Sunday, 15ᵗʰ July, 2007.

Exodus

It's a good thing I'm alone and unloved, because that's what I deserve. I sort of cracked it at Ex-H again tonight, so I feel like shit. It occurs to me that I might be more than a bit mean. If somebody tries to take my time away, I'm not very nice anymore. I start to fucking hate them, and they probably don't deserve to be hated.

Am I really so obsessed with my work time and my pissy little projects that I'd hurt another person to protect them? [Yes!]

Anyway, I cracked it because he's meant to be away during the week and he keeps not being away, and after a long and uncomfortable argument he said he's leaving tonight. So I got my selfish way, and then I thought about how mean I am, because here's this person that just needed somewhere to be, and who's quiet and is really no trouble. (Again, when I feel guilty I forget all about our history, the revolting comments he makes, the ugly et ceteras.) So I told him don't go, I told him he's right and I'm wrong, that he doesn't have to leave. I told him I shouldn't be so mean. I should, really, just get over myself.

NEWS FLASH: I ATE HUMBLE PIE. But he's leaving anyway.

NEWS FLASH: PSYCHO BITCH SCARES AWAY KIND MAN.

Now I feel truly, seriously guilty; no matter how many nicenesses I commit in my lifetime, I'll always know that when it came to the crunch, I wasn't willing to help another person when he needed me, all because I want to be alone to work. (And, yes, because of the aforementioned history, but don't interrupt me when I'm contemplating my own selfishness.) I am, in short, a fundamentally cruddy person.

So. Trying to proactively get the hell away from my past, I stopped doing homework and started house hunting again tonight. Now I'm wondering what kind of adult I am. A stupid one, I think, who can't even *afford* to be a proper grown up. I feel very insecure, like I should have done everything differently. No drawing, no writing; I should've gone out and gotten a career, gotten married, bought a house, waited until we owned two cars and a turdy big dog before bringing healthy happy babies into a Very Stable Family. (Obviously, Ex-H gave me the you-should-be-working-full-time speech tonight.*)

I've been looking forward to Art Skool, but I don't want to go to tomorrow morning's class. I haven't finished my homework, and it's a class that requires strength of character. The kind you don't bring your emotions to. (*Dear Scarily Professional Teacher, I didn't complete my homework because I was feeling sad.*) I took my girly emotions to that class just after I'd split up with Ex-G and I cried and cried and it was a) embarrassing, b) unproductive, and c) really, really embarrassing.

I'm so tired. Ex-h, who seems to be taking a long time to go through with this leaving business, is packing up. For good? Looks like he's not coming back. That's not what I asked him to do. I just wanted him to stick to our deal – here on weekends, away during week.

I know how stubborn he is; why can't he just communicate without the power games? I explain everything I say to him, there should be no games. And now it's gotten ugly. Fuck. I think I just lost a friend.

(**I avoid telling people that motor tic + full-time work = impossible. For some reason I think it's unacceptable to admit to this impediment out loud, even though it's visible to everybody who knows me. I fear Ex-H calling it an excuse or dismissing it as evidence of being pathetic. Am I pathetic? Yes I am?*)

––––

Thursday, 19th July, 2007.

Strange

Today's been a strange day. It's been such a strange day the word *strange* doesn't quite cover it. To top off the preceding strangenesses, I received my strange letter from Evil Ex-Friend tonight.

It's actually a very nice letter. Full of apologies, full of thank-you's for my utter wonderfulness, and full of memories. Most strangely, it contains a humble request that I call her for a '*careful, gentle conversation*'. That's nice, but I don't think she remembers me properly, because I don't do gentle. I do loud and excited. Okay, that's not true, I'm very gentle – but we have a history of me asking for this particular kind of conversation, and her delaying it until she's "ready".

I waited a very long time for the most basic communication, and then she was gone. Waited forever, just like I waited for Ex-G for ever. So much waiting, and I'm frankly all out of patience. People who make

89

you wait for them to be decent to you are generally full of shit. Who says I don't learn from my mistakes? It just takes me a while.

But I will call her. She's my favourite Babba date – our dancing chemistry is pure gold. I have no idea when, or what I'm going to say to her. Can you revive dead friendships? Ones that were murdered in cold blood? She hurt me quite a lot, but I do understand that it's because she's damaged. And she won't hurt me again, because if I fall back into friend-love (obviously I will) it'll be as a stronger, less gullible person.

Whatever. I should proceed with caution, is all. Like I'm any good at *that*.

———

Monday, 23rd July, 2007.

Location Location Location

It's out of character for me to wag skool, but I wagged skool. I was running late anyway, and was hoping to be able to justify the day off with the shit-load of work I was going to get done. But then I found myself curled up on the papasan chair in front of the window, basking in the sun until I was well and truly cooked, and it occurred to me that I'm feeling very down. I'm also feeling stupid because I didn't recognise that I was feeling down. As in, why is my smile the wrong way up?

So now I wish I hadn't spent the day alone. I'm not very good company and the work I ended up doing was rubbish. I'd say *what's the point,* but there are people who'd slap me for it, so I'm just going to think it out loud.

There are a few things bothering me, but I'll show mercy and only write about the most worrying thing today. I noticed a few days ago that the rose bushes have been pruned, which means Ex-H has been coming here when I'm away during the day. To double check this theory, I turned his computer on this morning and checked his e-mail dates, and sure enough, he's been here checking his e-mails.

I don't know if I'm bad for thinking his presence here during my absence is creepy, but while I had his computer on I did a send and receive, and he received two e-mails from Content Barrier, tracking my internet use. Every site I've visited over the past week was there in front of me. Let me spell it out for you – HE'S SPYING ON ME.

90

Well, good luck to him, because frankly, I'm not that interesting. They're almost all arts sites. Although, I did kinda leave my account open when Son had a friend here on Saturday, and after I saw those e-mails I did have to ask him *'What were you doing looking at sex sites on my account, Son?'*. His facial expression was priceless.

If Ex-H is spying on me in this way, what else is he up to? I've noticed a few of my passwords aren't appearing where they should be appearing on this computer. Has he really been delving? Maybe I'm just hurt because he's being so unfriendly, but I've had this sense of menace from him for a while now and I can't define it. Like something's really wrong. Maybe it's not wrong; maybe it's just unpleasant. I thought I was being paranoid, but perhaps I wasn't?

I spent the morning house hunting again, so I can get us the hell out of here. There's not much use though. Where do I go? I'm a bad mother who can't provide for her children. Don't nobody love me. My art sucks. We're fucked.

If the universe were kind, she'd balance it all out by giving me something to look forward to, but the universe is being a skinflint.

———

Nice thing: the view's really pretty from my piece of hillside today – yonder mountains are a rich, clear blue. You only get this clarity at certain times during the year.

I just let myself drift off to sleep, until I overheated and had to move. Yes – overheated! In the middle of winter!! That's so cool. I was in the papasan chair because all I wanted was to be alone. I haven't been alone in the house for so long, and First-Born stole my alone day on Friday by staying home from skool again (gee, where do they get that habit from?).

Mission accomplished, calm restored.

———

Tuesday, 24th July, 2007.

Just in Case

Maybe I'm wrong. Maybe he's not spying; maybe he's just a nice person whose e-mail address just happened to get tagged to my internet account. He'll probably have a good explanation and I'll feel bad for thinking otherwise, when he gives it to me. If he ever answers my calls. Maybe I should stop being a typical female and speculating about the worst before I know the facts.

All's Well That Ends Well

I might be pre-empting the end a little too soon, but all's definitely well. Firstly because painting cures everything. I shouldn't ever let a day pass without picking up a paintbrush. But also because Ex-H asked me to help him retrieve his car tonight, and I did, and as soon as I picked him up he was friendly.

Let this be a lesson to anybody who chooses to take on misery as their life-long hobby; when he's friendly he seems happy, and when he's happy he's lovely to have around. I got a glimpse of my old friend, and worked out that he's relaxed when he's not around me for too long. Something about being hen-pecked that doesn't work for him?

He's probably not spying on me and he doesn't seem creepy anymore because he's not sneaking around in a foul mood, pretending to be my enemy. I can't believe how relieved I feel knowing he's out there not-being-mean. I even miss him. Now we can go back to being friends? I'm so glad I live in la-la land half the time – it's the best place.

Saturday, 28th July, 2007.

Readin'

Even though I don't have time, I really need something good to read. Doing Etgar Keret isn't doing it for me. Although, I did have a nice moment on the train one morning, reading his *Bus Driver/God* story; the last paragraph is beautiful. I was smiling to myself because it was so beautiful, and I looked up and saw the lady sitting across from me smiling as she read her own book. When she looked up and out of the window, still smiling, and her smile turned into this cheesy daydreamy face, I thought *gosh, what's she reading? It must be really good.* So I manoeuvred myself to see the title, and she was reading *Seven Steps to Wealth.*

Sigh. I can't blame Etgar for that. But I can blame him for the rest of his stories being about gawd and devils and angels (with wings – fuck *off*). Religion written into fiction in the form of embodied concepts is what you do before you mature as a writer. You go there, and you come back. Then you look back on your religion stories and get very embarrassed, ultimately feeling relieved that you found your way back to realism before somebody published you and you got a name for yourself, so that this isn't what readers are gonna find when they go looking for you.

I don't hate his stories, I just can't love them. Although to his credit, he comes out with the occasional really good thing, like the dwarf with a load of heroin crammed up his arse. And descriptive use of a polar bear's rear end – I liked that, too. Is it possible I only like stories that involve arses? Something to analyse.

I tested Etgar on Son in the doctor's waiting room on Friday. Figured I'd see how he did with grown-up literature that isn't Robin Hobb (his latest addiction). He said something like *'Meh'*, but he didn't stop reading, so I ended up stuck in a waiting room without a book or a sketch book.

I need to find something I can't put down, so I can complain about having no time to read it. Am I allowed to end an entry like that? As in, you know how some people say not to finish a sentence with "it"? Or is that "is"? Waitaminute, did I just end a sentence with "is"? (Fuck *off*!)

———

Sunday, 29th July, 2007.

Maternity

I'm embarrassed to say that I miss having young children around me. I've had this revolting impulse to cuddle other people's infants when they pass me in the supermarket. Just pick 'em up, squeeze 'em and say *'Oh it's so cute, can I keep it?'*.

I know this is happening because parenthood sucks. If you're planning on having kids, DON'T DO IT. I adore my kids, and I adore other people's kids, I don't regret having kids, and I'd do it all over again, but I can't help looking at people who breed and thinking they're monumentally stupid.

Young kids, though. What's so nice about being around young kids is that they just want to be a) loved and b) happy. Me too! Well, I can do love, and I can do happy, but I can't do be-yelled-at-every-day. I'm plum worn out.

Ex-Wife looked at me across the table last night and said '*You look really content*'. I'd just spent my first two hours of being alone in the house for what seems like months, drawing in the peace and quiet. More significantly, I was spending my first whole day without First-Born for probably the same amount of time.

I don't want to play this game anymore. First-Born says they love me but actually I think they don't. They certainly don't like me.

I just want our home life to be happy. Yes, I know, a good little woman has to put up and shut up. It's bad manners to say that parenthood is anything less than joy.

––––

Don't Go Changing

I'm experiencing some kind of existential anxiety and think I must really suck. It's not just ordinary sucking – I think there's no way for me to not-suck. I'm stuck in a cycle of you-suckness that I can never get out of.

I was trying to work out who I'd have to be for First-Born to think I'm a good mother, or what I'd have to do, and I was stumped. Who am I supposed to be? They want me to undo the past, but [obviously] that's impossible. Then I remembered how Other Son let something slip after Ex-Wife left last night. He said that on the way over, Ex-Wife was saying that I'm "hopeless", and that she bet the screen door was still broken, because I'm so hopeless I don't fix anything [etc.]. (True – I don't. If something breaks I just step over it and wait for somebody else to care enough to fix it.) (Well, who has time for fixing?)

They had a laugh when they arrived and discovered the screen door had been fixed, which is why he was accidentally telling me about it. With his foot in his mouth. And it got me thinking about how I'm pretty lucky. I have a lot of friends who give me an outrageously huge amount of affection. They really lay on the love, so whenever I feel lonely I just flick through my phone messages and my e-mails and there it is, in writing, no less. Or somebody will call at exactly the right moment. Love absolutely makes my world go round.

BUT.

Ex-Wife also loves me – she says so all the time. And if she loves me but says I'm hopeless, what if everybody else thinks I'm hopeless, too? What if what they actually feel for me is Pity that they misidentify as Love, and that's why they give me so much affection? Because it's true, I AM hopeless. The more I get into my work, the less willing I am to do the things I'm supposed to do. Cooking? I hate it. Gardening – too time consuming. Housework? Sometimes I love housework, but when it's really getting in the way of other things, it makes me grumpy. Son actually went and hid while I house-worked on Friday afternoon. And then there are things like mowing the lawn and checking the car oil and water, and I hate all of it.

The only way to justify being this hopeless is to produce lots of work. I used to think being independent was so important, but now I just want to be looked after, so that I can be a work-producing machine. Does that make me hopeless, per se, or hope*ful*?

———

August 2007

Tiny Corpses

A fly swatter is a girl's best friend. The annual dead rodent population in our walls stopped smelling a while ago, but has recently started to emit dirty big black flies, and they're somehow getting into the house. This has never happened before. At first I didn't want to hurt them, and I do say *sorry fly* with each swat, but when there are so many of them you realise they have to go and you therefore need to override your interspecial sympathies, to accommodate the heartless demands of wholesale slaughter. (Same as with mice – at first you watch and can't imagine harming them, but when they multiply into a plague suddenly a flick switches and you're calling the Pied Piper Hotline, knowing full well that he leads those critters to the local sausage factory.)

I've cultivated the required heartlessness and now, honestly, I'm enjoying playing tennis with them. Because it's winter they're a bit slow and dopey, so you can lure them into the computer room with the light and then whack them mid-flight. (Death is immediate, no torture involved.)

I've grown very fond of these flies. They're almost beautiful because they're big and silent and just kinda float or hover around the ceiling. In fact, if they weren't fat from feeding off the decomposing innards of rodents, and weren't likely to breed in our foodstuff, I'd keep them as pets. Also if they promised not to leave fly-specks on my art work. (Can't clean fly specks off anything, gawd knows I've tried.)

This probably isn't painting a pleasant picture of my homely surroundings, but it's like a mausoleum in here. Beady little corpses are sitting in the corners of this room. When the living flies stop arriving I'll vacuum up the lot, counting them as I go. Then I can tell you how many flies you get out of a dead rat. In case you needed to know.

Saturday, 4th August, 2007.

Novelty

As in, worn off. I am so over flies. 114 at last count. Ick.

Wednesday, 8th August, 2007.

TMI

This will sound selfish, but I'm not sure I like it when Churchy Friend is happy. Theoretically it's good, but if she's happy it usually means she has a man, and if she has a man it means she's having sex, and if she's having sex she's talking about it. [A *lot*.]

If it was anybody else that'd be fine, talk away, I'm all ears, but not Churchy. Some friends are so close they're supposed to be like barbie dolls and have no genitals.

Let me tell you what Churchy Friend's genitals have been up to. Her new boyfriend lives interstate, and during his three-day visit over the weekend he's given her fifteen [alleged] orgasms. Not only that, but one of those orgasms went for [allegedly] three minutes.

Three minute orgasm! Well, firstly, this is Churchy Friend we're talking about, so *ewwww;* secondly, who has time for three minute orgasms? It's just not efficient. And it couldn't have been that good if she had the presence of mind to time the stupid thing.

I think I'll keep my orgasms to a 15 second maximum, thanksomuch. But bugger it, now I'm wondering how long an orgasm actually lasts, so next time I'm going to have to count, and that's definitely going to ruin the moment.

Sunday, 12th August, 2007.

Just Checking In

Dammit bugger shit bum fuck. You ever been really busy working on a self-inflicted project and not seemed to be getting anywhere with it? The wag-school, call-in-sick-to-work, neglect-your-children, alienate-your-friends and lock-the-cats-out-of-the-house variety of busy?

97

What *the fuck* am I doing? Meeting a deadline a couple of weeks ago just about killed my [poor old] body, which was not designed to bend over a huge table drawing until 4 every morning, and then getting up early to draw some more. My next deadline's as good as missed, but I don't want to stop.

This isn't my usual, uptight style of drawing. It's like some cool person has invaded my body and is doing fun stuff that the real me is too timid to try. If I stop, Cool Body-Invading Person might exit and I'll be stuck in my boring little life with monotonous old 6B graphite pencils. (No offence to 6B graphite pencils.)

I'm behind in just about every subject at art skool, and given this stupid obsession am about to get even more behind. I'll catch up [??], but in the meantime I'm becoming well-advanced in Getting Nowhere. Working my way up to Failure. (It's good to have an ambition?)

Note to self: the minutes spent writing this would have been better spent with a pencil.

———

Numerical Data:

Dead fly count: well over 230. I had to stop counting when I eventually sprayed, and they were dying in secret corners without witnesses. I now wish I hadn't vacuumed some of them up, because they could be usefully collected and put into a jar. (Pretty!)

Orgasm count: I can't be much of a woman, because my rough estimate is about 9 seconds, maybe twelve, maybe seven. Certainly not 180. It's a good thing some of us have better things to do.

———

Wednesday, 15th August, 2007.

What the Feck?

[Some] Americans have the stupidest sense of humour. They're practically begging to be the object of racial hatred. I had the late news on in the background while I was drawing and was too busy to turn it off, so I was accidentally subjected to David Letterman. Seriously, if that's what American people find funny then they shouldn't be allowed to breed. And their hands should be tied behind their backs to stop them from clapping, because they're way over zealous.

If I meet Americans on the street I'm gonna slap them [gently] and say 'That's *for laughing at Letterman's crappy jokes'*. Actually, soon I'll be able to slap Australians, because our conversion to Americanism is getting pretty near complete; I just heard Australia's removing the maximum cap on tertiary student fees. The wild speculation is that they'll remove HECS altogether, eventually. Motherfuckers.

I'd very much like to rant, but I'm too tired. Easier just to swear.

———

Friday, 17th August, 2007.

Sincerely, Saint Shane

If the news reporter was telling the truth when claiming that the generous sending of a cricket bat to a disadvantaged yet-outrageously-cute young indigenous boy by SHANE WARNE wasn't a cheap publicity stunt (because why would somebody as famous as SHANE WARNE need to do such PR stunt-ing), then why were there camera crews crawling all over the situation and turning it into a feel good circus story designed to enhance the cruddily turgent dick-sticking reputation of SHANE WARNE?

News Headline: *Famous Person* (SHANE WARNE!!) *Does Something Nice*. National heroes (shudder) are so much deeper and sensitiver than their arsehole machismo behaviours would lead us to believe. And see? Nothing wrong with our race relations, because us whitefellas are so fucken grouse. *Maaaaate*. Makes me feel so proud to be an Australian.

p.s. SHANE WARNE!

———

Thursday, 23rd August, 2007.

Perfume

Or spring. Something's making the world smell nice, in that erogenous ohmigawd-nature-is-telling-me-to-mate way. It's like women haven't worn perfume all winter and now suddenly they are and it's driving me crazy. Although Issey Miyake needs to be outlawed, because it's Ex-G-Not-G's perfume. Somebody was wearing it outside a gallery tonight, and frankly being able to smell her does me no good at all. My gut reaction is both to run away from it and follow it all at once, and I spin around on my heel to get closer to whoever. My stupid body almost can't believe it's not her standing behind me. It smells like her, therefore I must kiss it. I *loved* that woman.

Love schmove, I have other plans. Or not, I haven't made up my mind yet. I got asked out on a date, sort of. I wasn't sure if I was being hit-on, actually, but it was confirmed when another friend who'd (unbeknownst to me) been watching us talk came up to me afterwards and said '*Your friend is cute*', with raised eyebrows. I had to turn around and ask '*It's not like that....is it?*'. I'm so dumb. I usually don't know I'm being hit on until somebody's shoving their tongue down my throat, but I guess this time I have advance warning.

She's not unattractive, but she's not somebody I could fall in love with. And yet, I don't particularly want a lover, but I also do, and wouldn't mind if it was her. And I should because I can, because what if nobody ever wants to date me again, and I get to the end of my long and ugly life and regret not taking the very last opportunity to extract some affection from the world?

And yet, I'm too happy being busy n' don't want the complications. And yet-yet, other people do this all the time and it's no big deal.

We'll see. If she wore perfume I'd be a goner, but fortunately she doesn't. Saying no will be easy. I'll just lock myself away in the studio, never sit beside her in the dark, never be alone with her, and not look into her [rather pretty] eyes when we talk. I'll die a lonely old spinster, but will have produced an enormous body of work, the impressive sum total of all the casual sex I didn't have throughout my life. My priorities are completely fucked.

Friday, 24th August, 2007.

Hippy for a Day

I'd hate to impose my viewpoint upon anybody, but you need to all think what I'm thinking for a moment and do something good for the world. GetUp (lobby group) are finally doing something about Gunns (bad-arse forestry corporation) in Tasmania, so we have a window of about hardly-any-days to make public comment on their proposed whopping-big paper mill and the subsequently vast desecration of life as we know it. We need to tell them to please shove their paper mill, because this CANNOT GO AHEAD.

If you don't know anything about Gunns and the proposed mill, you a) are an ignorant git, and b) need to educate yourself very quickly. There was a brilliant article in *The Monthly* a couple of months ago (April? May? The one with the revolting green cover) which described the control Gunns has over Tasmania and, for that matter, the rest of the country.

If I had my way I'd make everyone I know read that article, so they can see just what corporations are capable of getting away with. I please please *please* want everybody to get involved, because it's not just about the trees. And you needn't be afraid of doing something like this – I promise you that unless you're a twat, if you write a protest letter you won't get a mad impulse to suddenly wear tie-dye clothes and eat lentils. So *do as yer told*. (PLEASE!)

Sunday, 27th August, 2007.

Just Unwinding

I'm far too happy to go to sleep. I've been sitting under a lamp at my table with a bottle of ink and a brush and could sit there all night. It feels like time has stood still. Everything's perfect. I'm still behind in my skool work because I wagged a lot of skool to work on a couple of drawings (also to soften parental stress, which was getting out of hand), but I'm catching up. And frankly it's uplifting to walk into my room and see these drawings, which are like nothing I've ever done before. I almost can't believe they came out of my head. Nothing beats giving yourself a couple of weeks of obsessive work on a single project, so I don't care if they're good or bad, I'm just happy that they "are".

Now that I've done my own work for a while (as opposed to skool work) I feel pumped up and am steam-rolling ahead. Except when I'm lounging around doing nothing. I had the house to myself yesterday afternoon, and it's been sunny, so instead of working I as-usual stripped down to knickers and lay in the sun by the window to read *On the Road* (Jack Kerouac), which is just the kind of book you should read half naked in the sun. The whole world smells of perfume and warm skin and doing nothing.

About that book: as the quintessential choice of reading material for my younger adult male peers, I've been meaning to read it out of curiosity for half a decade. After the first couple of chapters I started to worry that it was completely shallow, just some drug-fucked dudes hitching around the country calling out '*Whoopee*' and '*Yahoo*' every five seconds, because life's such a hoot and freedom is so euphoric. So and so gets on the back of a truck, another so and so gets off, blah blah blah. But then just in time, Jack K lets some meaning slip in, and suddenly it's slapping you in the face. I love it. I sometimes don't believe the he-wrote-it-in-three-weeks legend, but at other times it's so scatty I believe he did. The whole experience is one big joy ride.

Maybe I'm a cliché and it's just Spring making me so happy. I love the heat. Tonight = wattle smell in the air + driving home with Thai takeaway in the dark, in a tank top and bare feet + happy kids + Abba on the radio (*Whoopee! Yahoo!*) + having dinner with candles + no one being mean to anybody else. I'm sure this is how normal families do it. Normal's good. I *like* it.

Tuesday, 29th August, 2007.

Synchronicity

Disclaimer: if you're a hippy and you're reading this, no, I am not your soul mate, I don't believe in orchestrated coincidences, and you should probably go and have a bath.

And yet, apparently Mother Earth has nothing better to do than fiddle with my circumstances. Today I for-no-apparent-reason decided I should wag school and paint Reformed Hippy Friend's portrait, so I did. And because this morning I was thinking of a story I'd submitted to a literary journal about forever ago, I had that literary journal's initials written in blue ink on the back of my hand, so that I'd remember to e-mail them to chase it up.

Well I finished my underpainting and was feeling happy because it's sunny and warm and peaceful, and then I went to the computer to write that e-mail but there, without my prompting, was an e-mail from the editor telling me they want my story. That's when I remembered that the story is the one I wrote for and about Reformed Hippy Friend (who I just painted), and damned if that aint a happy coincidence.

Dear Universe, you are *so* cool.

Thursday, 30ᵗʰ August, 2007.

Phew!

Imagine, just imagine if you were really stupid, so stupid in fact that you went out onto your balcony to spray some fixative onto your life drawings, and when you came back in you bumped the backing board of your easel and turned around just in time to see the portrait you painted of your lovely friend FALL TO THE GROUND, and then you tried to catch it, knowing as you did so that you'd be leaving stupid big fingerprints on the fresher surfaces, and then you picked it up and saw that the blue-black you'd painted on yesterday was smeared across your lovely friend's face, and you were tempted to CRY LIKE A BABY until you remembered your painting teacher quoting Other Ace Teacher who had just the other day said *'Oil painting is great because it's so forgiving'*, because you can wipe it off when it doesn't work, so you went running down the stairs three at a time (still not crying, because you can keep your head in an emergency) to grab your paints, then you wiped off that blue-black smear and restored the fingerprinted background, thinking as you did so *'Gee, isn't painting up here in this danger zone nice'*, knowing that you're more than likely to make the same mistake again.

No, I can't imagine being that stupid. Really.

September 2007

TaskMaster

Remind me never to become a personal trainer – I think I almost killed my poor old mother. It was such a nice day yesterday we decided to meet for a walk at the reservoir, an easy walk if you stick to the dam wall (dam as in dam, not dam as in fucken), but somewhat boring on the way back, seeing as by then you've exhausted all of your *'Wow, look how low it is'* conversation. So this time I suggested we *'walk the bush track at the other side of the park after we've done the wall'*.

Mum said *okay*, but little old [?] women shouldn't be so obliging. Whereas I'm accustomed to long and hilly walks on sunny days, it's a long way for unaccustomed little legs. We were having such a nice time, though. I kept asking if it was too much and she kept saying she was fine. There goes my mother's sainthood – she's obviously a liar. An hour and a half later she finally accepted my offer to run off and get my car, pick her up, and drive her back to her car. I was so worried she'd die while I was gone I broke about a hundred park road rules, calling out a giggling apology to park rangers as they gaped at my blatant wrong-direction driving.

My Mum's way too sweet to be bumped off by my stupidity. And anyway, when did she get so fragile? Fragility is for other mothers, not mine. So you can imagine how bad I feel today, having just spoken to my father and been told *'Oh your mother's just gone off to the doctor – she woke with a bit of a fever'*. This is the stuff of nightmares and my guilt is working overtime.

Forget Father's Day; when I visit today, I'm taking flowers for Mum and she's getting all of my attention. I'll explain to Dad that until he pushes himself to the brink of death for the sake of enjoying my company, he's just not as good as her.

p.s. The water levels really are amazingly low. It's kinda pretty, the water so blue, the dry banks like beaches. Also there's an island in the middle that wasn't there before. And if Melbourne's water supplies run dry, it's close enough to my house for me to get there in time to survive, by frolicking in the dregs while the rest of you die from dehydration.

Monday, 3rd September, 2007.

Life, Universe, Everything

First-Born will never be young again. This is a profound realisation. I noticed the change a couple of weeks ago, when they were sick (really sick, not just faking it in their chronic school-wagging way) and I wasn't allowed to look after them. They were angry because I have a no-school/no-internet rule. They swore at me and then went to stay with their partner instead.

You see how it is: a kick-arse mother will never back down on her rules, but a kick-arse mother will as a result lose her child.

According to the Underground Parental Handbook, we're allowed to secretly love it when our kids are unwell because they're floppy and cute and warm, and you get to cuddle them a lot. (Unless it's cancer or something horrible; I mean little-sick, not big-sick.) Especially angsty teenagers who are usually so yelly-screamy and don't let you near them for weeks on end; when they're sick it's like a holiday from the awfulness of life.

So here I am being outrageously happy with life generally (last week I was bouncing-off-the-walls happy because First-Born was on camp, and it's not that I don't love them, but gosh it was peaceful), but with an undertone of sadness because they won't be sick properly. They need to need their mother more. Who wouldn't need me? I'm pretty good. Someone needs to tell them that.

I want my baby back. Now they're telling me they want to leave school and do all sorts of other things, including write a book – a little me-clone running around the planet, that's just what we need. I can guide them to do it properly but I can't really stop them. Should I stop them? They've got an enormous personality and are [is] stronger than

I ever was, so maybe I should just let them go, accept that they're going to grow up before they're ready. (They're not ready.)

The problem is that I remember wanting to leave school when I was young because I knew that if I didn't I'd have to spend the rest of my life thinking, and that's exactly what they're saying they don't want to do. The sheer effort ahead of them, all of that trying and pushing and rat-racey expectation.

Let me see – there's easy not-thinking life [yey], and there's difficult thinking life [boo]. Sometimes I wish I'd ignored my elders and chosen the not-thinking life. Can you imagine not taking your work with you everywhere you go? It'd be so nice to be free. But then I remember that not-thinking Australians vote for John Howard and I think *Phew, that was close*.

I don't know. Maybe I lost them years ago. Gosh knows I'm stupid enough to have taken this long to notice. Spending three years bending over backwards trying to save something that's just gone. They seemed to need me quite a bit, until they didn't. Parenthood's such a bitch.

p.s. Their partner's not really stupid. But they should give First-Born back to me. They're mine, I had them first.

———

Tuesday 4th September, 2007.

Back Track

It got better. First-Born came home to tell me that an intolerant teacher wants them to put tape across their new piercing, so First-Born's going to write 'PIERCING' across the tape. I'm supposed to give them a lecture about respect for rules and authority, but I think it's outrageously *funny*. Gosh I love 'em. Sometimes parenthood isn't a bitch at all, sometimes it's just plain fun.

———

Wednesday, 5th September, 2007.

Day One

As far as time-wasting goes, this entry is momentous. Today was a Big Day, in which I resolved not to waste any more time.

Off to a flying start, then. The un-wasting of time would be achievable if there weren't so many distractions. For example, if Rampant Lesbian Woman hadn't said something erotically charged to me over the phone yesterday; if I hadn't downloaded that groovy Timberland song and been listening to it all day; if I wasn't desperate to go dancing to expend the excessive sexual energy incited by said erotically-charged comment. (Close eyes. Think of England.)

Also if I wasn't lost. I've rediscovered the quiet space I work in at night, and out of sheer discipline have been doing visual research for a project. Except, I can't get over the fact that I really don't like the teacher. The project's interesting, but I don't want to give this teacher anything interesting, in case she ruins it.

I'm not exactly into teacher-hating, but she craps all over our happiness. Apart from crushing our confidence and demonstrating overt disinterest in our ideas, she looks at us with *that look*, and she won't smile. I'm not imagining this; everybody leaves that usually-ace studio after the deathly silent Monday morning classes wanting to slash their wrists. It's as bizarre as it is awful, and she's not even as mean to us as she is to her Friday class.

I hate unfriendliness, especially from a teacher. I don't give a rats arse that she's respected in her field (she is), and I like her work, but if she can't be friendly then she shouldn't be teaching. She should at least fake it.

Anyway, enough. I'll block her out of my thoughts with Timberland-on-repeat, and get back to work. Although it is kinda late; maybe the First Day of my New Life should start tomorrow?

Friday, 7th September, 2007.

Setting the Record Straight

Or not-straight, whatever. In order to protect the privacy of Woman Who Asked Me Out on a Date, and maybe also to avoid being watched while I make up my mind (mind is made up, answer is no, she's being too pushy), I haven't told my Conniving Art Friends who she is. This has backfired on me, because they've ironically assumed it's somebody else and they're watching me anyway. Just because I walk around with an erect penis, you don't have to look.

I stupidly made friends with Foreign Student, before I knew she was a rampant lesbian (which, in retrospect, should've been obvious – my gaydar still sucks). Now when we talk I see them sniggering away at the other side of the room and have to shake my head.

Just because she sometimes blushes when she talks to me. And gets too close sometimes. And occasionally says something provocative. There's nothing to it, she doesn't mean it that way. I was just extending the arm of friendship (meaning the ARM, not the PULSATING VAGINA) and given that there's a dearth of lesbians in my life, finding another dancing friend is a good thing.

Plus I like her, she's nice.

My solution yesterday was to dress like a nun in loose clothes that went all the way up to my neck. I was uncomfortable all day because I can't wear too much (i.e. anything) around my neck without my motor tic kicking in. Then I snubbed her. I could tell from her text messages that she was confused, so now I feel guilty.

It's hard work taking on a new friend, but I like the idea of being a tourist in my own country and showing her around. Falling in love's out of the question because she believes in reincarnation and ghosts, and practises Feng Shui. I couldn't possibly.

On the other hand, I don't have time for a new friend. I'm full up. When I'm at school I just want to be with my [conniving] peeps and do my work. I feel torn, because I want to make sure she's happy and not lonely, but I don't want to be away from these friends. Different languages = slow conversations = pleasant, but also = pain in the arse.

Can I ease myself out of this without hurting her feelings?

Priorities

Mine are tied up in knots. I wag a bit of school here and there so that I can get to work on time when they give me extra shifts, because single art-student mothers can't say no to extra money. And now I'm wagging work so that I can do some school work. Let's not mention all of the other wagging or the other art work or the parenting. Let's just wonder why I don't actually do what I'm supposed to be doing *when* I'm supposed to be doing it.

Why is my Brand New Not-Time-Wasting Life just as complicated as my old one?

———

Saturday, 9th September, 2007.

We All Live in a

Bush Brother turned fifty (AKA HALF A HUNDRED) so we almost-all drove to his little piece of forest outside of Bairnsdale, a place that makes me want to hug piles of dirt. I took photos of the stupidest things, just so that I could bring them home with me. And now I feel lonely because I couldn't share it with anybody. There's my family, but it was one of those visits that leaves you feeling happy but disconnected.

I watch Mum (reigning champion of a game he invented, who can knock over white goods with a single throw) and wonder if she sometimes looks around at us and thinks '*Wow, I made these people*'.

Brother's Friend, in addition to making art and building houses and raising children alone after his wife ran off to Melbourne with a scary looking bull-dyke, plays the guitar. He, his new wife and some friend formed a trio, and they performed for us around the camp-fire. Good folksy songs, mostly, but as a token gesture they sang *Yellow Submarine*, so we could sing along. We were all variable degrees of drunken and one hundred percent merry.

My family never sing together, so I have one criticism. Musicians performing around a campfire – if they were truly generous, having seen how happy we were to sing together – would have chosen a repertoire of singable songs to encourage more of that. After *Yellow Submarine* I kept waiting for songs that'd allow us to be more than passive. After a while the one-sided performance seemed self-indulgent and tiresome. I contemplated putting in requests but decided it'd be bad manners, and later went to bed hungry [for this].

Regardless, you just can't fit this much happiness into one weekend, it's too much of a bizarre contrast to everyday reality. Maybe that's why I'm feeling the plummet at the end of a natural high I've been riding along on for weeks. Or maybe I just desperately need sleep.

Friday, 14th September, 2007.

Blemish

Forget life-threatening illnesses and natural disasters: this week I'm a pimple survivor.

Last night at work I dealt with this by concentrating on people who have worse things on their faces. For instance, Tough Blonde Chick – what *is* that on her face, anyway? Whatever it is it made me miss an important dildo conversation. I was sitting with everyone during break, thinking something along the lines of *'I have a pimple on my face; I have a pimple on my face; I have a pimple on my face...'* when I noticed her hideous thing sticking out from outrageously inadequate concealer. No sooner had I thought *'Well if she can have a weird thing, then I'm allowed to have a pimple',* than I heard the word "dildo". Then they launched into a discussion about the flappiness of women's vaginas after they've had fifteen babies.

I'm dumbfounded, actually. When did they make the leap from football and their "little ones" to flapping vaginas? Last week the discussion was about religion, and I found out that they ALL go to church. (Needless to say I don't tell them too much about myself at work.) And now dildos?

Dear Effing X-tians, you cannot have sex with each other before you marry, but you may shove a rubber-coated piece of industrial-strength plastic up your clacker any old time, just be careful not to damage that hymen. Sincerely, Gawd.

Anyway, back to The Mother of All Pimples, who now has a daughter. I feel ripped off. I thought Mum had made a trade-off with Nature, agreeing to subject me to general ugliness in exchange for clear skin. It's just not *fair* to have both. Damn you, Nature. Damn you to hell.

Sunday, 16th September, 2007.

Victim of Crime

When you're supervising a debutante rehearsal, you're pretty much being paid to sit and read. Or draw. I come prepared for whatever whim might take me, and therefore had a sketchbook and pencils on the table. So what a pity today's little debutantes were thieving cnuts.

Quick, too. We left our table for less than three minutes to pack up the stage, and by the time we got back they'd raided my pencil case so that they could fill out forms. Say goodbye to my lovely, soft new charcoal pencils. (CNUTS!)

Unfortunately I can't be angry at them, because they were from my old school, and when I was a student there I stole like crazy. This was my comeuppance. And if I think about it, karma's actually being very gentle with me. Merciful goddess of cosmic justice – thank you.

After all that I didn't draw anyway. Today was the first time in forever that I got to sit down with the Saturday newspaper and read the arts pages from one end to the other. Now I have tranquility coming out of my ears, and am peacefully reacquainted with my book half, which has this year been starving. What – just coz I got paid to supervise debutantes, doesn't mean I actually had to *watch* them.

––––

Monday, 17th September, 2007.

Sulk

Someone was mean to me. I know I should grow some backbone, and I kinda deserve it, because it involves a teacher I said mean things about a few posts ago. It was true, I didn't like her at the time. But actually, I don't dislike her, I'm just scared of her.

I told her that today, because I didn't think it was right to have so big a problem with somebody and not say something. I'm a student rep and also didn't think it was right to bring it up in the rep meetings without first showing her a little respect, by sorting it out off the record. Plus I want to enjoy her classes like I used to, and to find out why things had changed. Plus I have a big mouth.

So I told her I'm scared of her, that other people are scared of her, gave her anonymous examples of how extreme the problem is, and my voice didn't crack once. I was, in short, very brave.

And that's when I found out somebody had been mean. It was devastating, but suddenly things made sense. All semester I've been trying to work out why this particular teacher had gone cold on me,

111

and when everybody else said it was happening to them too, I thought it must be a general thing. But now I know it was actually personal. She told me the second-year students had overheard me tell my friends I deliberately hide my work from her, during studio access time. She said something like '*I'm well aware of your opinionated discussions...*'.

But they got it wrong. I did say those words, but it was about not showing her my extra-curricular work, because she'd actively discouraged me from doing any. That particular "opinionated discussion" was in reality a serious expression of surprise that a teacher would discourage any student from doing extra work, and the worst thing I'd said was that I felt unwelcome in the studio.

(In contrast, the course co-ordinator was very welcoming and said I could use the studio whenever it was open. The unwelcome feeling was confusing, but it wasn't imagined.)

There's more to it, but in the end it comes down to the fact that a frankly honest and earnest conversation was repeated out of context, and that conversation has coloured the way she sees me. An icky, vomit colour, I think. Absolutely clashes with my hair.

The up side is that the teacher was much friendlier during today's class, the atmosphere better. Judging by some of the things she said when I spoke to her, I don't think she's going to change her opinion of me, but at least she'll relax with the others now. I'll just have to accept that, and fortify my thin skin.

Wednesday, 19th September, 2007.

Th-th-th-th-th-esis

After all the effort I make to dumb myself down, I now have to put my grown-up's hat on and go back to being smart for a while. It's time to revise my thesis.

I'm ambivalent about it, naturally. Part of me's excited about flexing cerebral muscles, like those show-offy body builders that slick themselves with oil and crack walnuts against their biceps. I've been reading the reports, though, and am repelled by the things they want me to do. Such as tackling reader theory, which takes common sense and complicates it with the most ridiculous amount of polysyllables.

If you're smart you can knock it over with a few neat sentences (such as: you cannot pre-empt a reader's response to your story because readers bring their own experience to the work etc, therefore a writer's intentions are irrelevant etc, and anyway all books are filtered through societal systems etc, such as publisher selections etc, which are influenced by marketing demands etc, and critics etc, and academics etc, all of which determine a society's cultural content etc, therefore ideological examination is impossible etc, because writers are trapped within their own sociological milieu etc, making an objective critique impossible etc, therefore none of us are really capable of thinking etc, so we might as well all be vegetables etc etc etc), but they won't like you for it. I dismissed it so cleverly and succinctly in my footnotes, but they want about a hundred pages on this ~~shit~~ material.

I don't know. Should I even be doing this? Just because I can? I suppose *hell yes*? I flounder if I'm not working. If I have a project, though, I concentrate and work my guts out. I'm floundering now because I have too many projects to choose from, so this'll make me sort out the mess. And now that I'm committed to it, I'll probably start neglecting it. Imagine how much art work I'll get done while I'm neglecting my thesis! The next few months could end up being fun?

Friday, 21st September, 2007.

Moral Flux

I bought a book from Borders. I didn't *mean* to, it was an accident. I only buy books from Readings or Dymocks (and Amazon, but only if I can't get it in Australia), because they're not giant corporate bastards.

I thought I was just browsing, but when I picked up a couple of titles and started reading, it felt so good I wanted to keep going and found myself at the counter. When I realised what I was doing it was TOO LATE! That's how people get pregnant. They get pregnant and all the profit goes to a megalomaniac book pedlar and then Readings has to close because people like me don't stop to think.

What am I doing buying a book anyway? Aren't I too poor to be buying books? I can justify it by saying that I like authors to get their royalties (of course I do – if I was rich I'd be buying books all the time), but really, this is too much moral flux for one person to handle. I should just go back to buying chocolate, which raises no moral dilemma whatsoever *and*, as Foreign Student Friend points out, is a very good substitute for sex.

Well, *that* explains a few things.

———

Speaking of...

The Kids' Biological Father was visiting on the weekend, and while I was typing away down here he sat behind me to give me a very good massage, of the non-sexual variety (I forgot how nice it is to be touched!). Although, with him it's always hard to tell because his hands get so intimate in their wanderings. In fact, his strategy works because he really knows how to touch a woman. He can turn any part of your body into an erogenous zone, and when you're enjoying his massage-y embraces you kind of forgive the wandering, and don't want him to stop. You wait until he gets right to the unambiguous point before you say '*Stop right there, buddy*'. I'm pretty sure that's how he manages to seduce so many women.

I'm lucky because I'm unseduce-able by this man, so I can have my massage and not regret it later, but he tells me about some of the women who are far less fortunate in this regard. I was treated to the story of his latest trip to America, where he met an older, celebrity-connected and ex-Playboy-Bunny woman, and it was interesting to witness his confusion about growing attached to her. It's even sweet, because he's liberated her from the trap of habitual existence, and now she wants to leave her husband and come to Australia to be with him, because her marriage made her feel dead inside. Plus he gave her over a hundred orgasms. In ONE night.

What is it with the orgasms and counting thing? Whatever it is, this upping-of-the-ante makes Churchy Friend's three-minute orgasm seem minuscule. It's so ridiculous I know he's not making it up; if you were gonna invent something like that, you'd cap it at about thirty, maybe? Plus I know him well sexually, and if anybody can do it, it's him.

I have to laugh. I wriggled my way out of the massage when he told me that. Because who even *wants* a hundred orgasms? Who wants to care about sex *that* much? Your pelvic muscles would hurt for a week. Your left ventricle might explode. Gosh, people are interesting. I must be humble, because one good one does me just fine. One orgasm and a snot-load of chocolate; what more could anybody possibly need?

Thursday, 27th September, 2007.

Holiday's Over

I know it's mean, but I secretly love it when Churchy Friend cracks the shits with me and doesn't call for ages. I wish she could last the distance; I was enjoying the break, because she's been getting nasty. Fucking x-tians have no stamina. She only lasted a week and half.

Of course she did. Who'd want to not-talk to me for a week and a half? That's just crazy. If I was my friend I'd wanna call me every day (like she usually does). I'd want to have a picture of us together as my mobile phone wall paper (like she does). (Or did – I got replaced recently by three-minute-orgasm-man.)

This time she's shitty for no good reason, pretty much the same as last time. Something about me being late to my mother's birthday lunch, even though it was impromptu, so I only had an hour's warning. If Mum was the type of person who rolled her eyes skywards in exasperation, she'd be rolling her eyes skywards at [very punctual] Churchy-Friend. But Mum simply says gently '*She doesn't seem to understand that you have kids*'. Mum's the champion of my disorganisation. Damn right I've got kids. Damn right Churchy doesn't.

So she punishes me by not talking to me over lunch (that's when I knew I'd hit the jackpot), then she not-calls me, then she one-day sends me funnies via email, then the next day texts to ask a not-personal question and replies with a xx-ed thank you (testing the water), then today she calls as though nothing ever happened.

But now I'm not interested in anything she has to say. Normally this'd make me feel guilty, but frankly I've had enough of her tantrums. If I piss her off so much, why does she even like me? No point talking to somebody who dicks me around so much, so all I'll be doing for a while is listening. I'm certainly not giving her any emotion. There comes a time when people take it that one step too far, and you're totally allowed to think *fuck off*.

———

Latent

Damn, now I feel guilty. Sorry Churchy Friend. Sorry sorry. But let the record state that I was tough for about 24 hours there – my best effort yet. Next time I'll take my 24 hours of kick-arse attitude and build it up to a lifetime, and will no longer be tortured by the idea of her suffering. There'll be no more forgiveness. Forgiveness is *so* new-testament.

That'll learn 'er to turn on me without warning. People are such bad animals.

———

Friday, 28th September, 2007.

Flagellant

I think I'll sit here and hate myself out loud for a few minutes. Just for the fun of it. It's a good thing I make this task EASY by being so horrible that I don't know where to start.

Tonight was meant to go like this: I was to rush all the way home after taking Dad to Evil Chadstone to see *Die Hard 4*, and then do the unthinkable by going all the way back to Evil Chadstone to see *Harry Potter* with Ex-Husband.

(Chadstone, twice in one day!) I don't particularly want to see *Harry Potter*, but it was important to Ex-H, and I wanted to make him happy.

I didn't mean to get home late, and I didn't mean to have a headache, and I didn't mean to seem flippant when I was waiting for the headache tablets to kick in, and I didn't mean to keep talking to Friend A on the phone when I should have been jumping into the car to go to the cinema (but how could I get off the phone when we haven't spoken for weeks?), and I didn't mean for it to then be too late for *Harry Potter* (although, we still could have made it in time), so when he said '*You've let me down'* I was devastated.

I didn't *mean* to let him down. I hate hurting people. I'm his only friend, and that means I should make sure things like this don't happen. I should have shut everything else out, looked him in the eye and said *'Tonight is about you, let's go'*.

First-Born's right, everybody should hate me.

At least I make Dad happy. And Son and I laugh all the time, so I must be making him happy. That's something, isn't it?

———

October 2007

Monday, 1ˢᵗ October, 2007.

Things is Lookin' Up

Today had the kind of humble spectacularness that makes the planet a really nice place to be. It was made up of good thing after good thing, with bonus steak knives thrown in.

I was dreading my Monday morning class, not because I thought anything would happen, but because I didn't see how it could be anything but bleak. Now I have the utmost respect for my [difficult] teacher, because she went out of her way to change the dynamic. I only needed a little bit of friendliness to see her as approachable, and suddenly I was talking to her as though I'm not a timid little flower. I didn't even trip over my words.

And I *like* her. I much prefer that to being scared.

THEN, because I was so happy I went to drawing class and drew a really good... thing. This picture is one of a few that have been evolving in my head for weeks and weeks, so it means a lot to me. It's not great, but it's different and is very much where I was trying to go. My ambition to one day be up-myself is now on its way to realisation. Moody Future Art Collector Chick – after begging me to give it to her (sometimes that's like asking somebody to hand over their first born) – settled for taking a photograph to print up and hang on her wall. I'm now a legend in my own lunchbox.

THEN (and this is the steak knives), I had a brilliant Twilight-Zone twin experience. I've been asking everybody how to send a text overseas because Friend Alice-in-Wonderland is in Europe. People at school used to get Friend Alice and I confused because we have similar features. She's my prettier, more stylish and more polite double, so she always says she's the good twin and I'm the evil twin and '*only their mothers could tell them apart*'. Now I know it's true, because this afternoon we were joined at the umbilicus. I'd just opened the phone to write her a text when I felt it buzzing, and it was from *her*. (Freaky!)

I know I'm getting too excited about silly little things, but what the hey. She called me later and I sat there quietly amazed that you can talk to somebody in London while you're sitting on a train somewhere in Melbourne. Aren't humans *clever*.

———

Thursday, 4th October, 2007.

Jack

I used to think "Jack of all trades" was a positive expression, because it meant you could do everything. But yesterday, after stating that I seem to be doing too many things, Dad said to me that I should be careful because you know what they say; *'Jack of all trades, master of none'*.

What the fuck? Who stuck that negative bit on the end of an otherwise useful expression? You mean you *can't* do everything? *Now* he tells me. And by the way, thanks for the vote of confidence, Dad.

It's alarming that the statement rings true, because I also mistakenly thought that if you put all your eggs into one basket (running with the expression thing here), you'll end up with... lots of eggs? My approach to life is being turned on its head.

Anyway it doesn't matter, because I'm apparently the favourite daughter. That was my not-very-subtle segue into bitching about my younger sister. Not really in the mood for bitching, but let's get it out of the way and defend Dad's honour.

Little Sister and I have a running joke about being the favourite daughter whenever we do something for or with either of our parents. I don't usually make the joke about Dad, because I know she'll take it seriously, but I thought it might be time she grew the fuck up, so I sent an *'I'm the favourite'* message on the weekend. She replied with *'To Dad ur the only daughter'*. That's not actually true, but because Dad's an introverted book worm he and I talk a lot, which is ammunition for anybody wanting to make it look that way for the purpose of self-pity.

A father can love more than one child. He has nine of us – give 'im a break. And actually, twice recently Dad's driven for yonks to visit

Little Sister, take care of Little Sister, and take her to lunch. That's paternal love, right there. REDEEMED.

———

Enabling

A phone call from somebody yesterday saying *'This is a stick up'*, which is a very cute way of asking to borrow a hundred dollars. It made me uncomfortable, because they haven't been calling me much lately (I'm being mildly punished). The humour was rehearsed and insincere and it made my stomach churn, though I couldn't put my finger on why.

So I lent the money, and haven't heard from them since.

It occurs to me that they probably needed it to buy dope. It must have been difficult for them to suck up to me, despite currently disliking my guts. Plus I know they visited Their Usual Supplier the day before, after returning from a hot date. That had to have been an unsuccessful drug run.

I think I've just been used. Blatantly. Makes it very easy to ease them out of my life. Who needs difficult people? Not me, there's too much good stuff happening. Difficult people suck, and I'd much prefer it if they go and suck somewhere else. (Perhaps after paying me back my hundred dollars.)

———

Pulp mill

Just when I thought our government couldn't disgust me any more than they already have, they pucker up and kiss Gunns' arse AGAIN. Economic security is the most piss-weak excuse for a bad political decision. I can't even begin to fathom how they a) do it, and b) get away with it.

Environmental impact of effluence etc aside, has anybody remembered that we have a massive problem with the rampant clear-felling of Tasmanian forests?

And yet, the stupid Australian public keep voting the fuckers in. Sometimes it's like watching a nation full of lab rats fall for the most simplistic manipulative spin. How can so many people be so dumb?

———

Wednesday, 10th October, 2007.

Resurrection

If my fridge is killed in a brutal act of violence and I somehow bring it back to life, does that make the fridge the Holy Entity, or Me? Let's just say it's the fridge. It was dead for a whole night. When I got home from painting I checked its pulse one more time, and then I had a moment of silence, said an emotional farewell, and flicked the switch to *off*. But when I turned the life support back on this morning its pulse started humming, and there was rejoicing throughout the land.

Except, when Son was giving the revived corpse a once-over he found a note from First-Born magnetted to the door. Notes are scary, say what. Especially because he'd only remembered to tell me they were gone when I woke up – I thought they'd just gone to bed early.

'By the way Mum, First-Born left last night.'

I felt concern for a few seconds, until I ascertained that First-Born's actually safe, and then I felt the same guilty sense of relief I felt during the time they spent away over the holidays. After that I felt a bit numb. The note was disturbing, but also contained a sensible plan of action. I read it and got hit with a wave of love.

First-Born's great on paper — I've suggested to them in the past that we never speak, that we just say things to each other in writing so that we never fight. A perfect solution, except that we both talk so much we'd get RSI after two conversations. But mostly they're too lazy, and they love to yell.

So, no paper conversations. Last night the usual yelling started with *'There's no food in this house'*. My response was as-usual *'Are you sure you're not doing drugs?'* because they say it every time they come home, reminding me of a teenage friend's dope-smoking sister.

So I opened the fridge (praise be!) and gave them a verbal list of amazingly good food that they can eat. To overcome this solution-based response, First-Born diverted the crux to my apparent hopelessness as a human being. It's true, I am hopeless – I was supposed to make an appointment for them and kept forgetting because I've got so much to remember these days. In other words, I let them down. Letting people down is a specialty I've got going.

In First-Born's case I'm not so hard on myself, I understand why I keep forgetting. They're lovely for 5% of the time we spend at home together, and angry at me for 95%. Sonic-blast type anger that rattles me with its sheer volume and force. My new strategy is to ignore it and keep out of their way. I figure if I do this for three more years, I can survive my way into their adulthood and we'll all be okay. So their appointment needs aren't held in my brain – I've numbed them out.

But anyway. From downstairs I heard First-Born do a frustrated scream, then I heard loud thumping, then Son called out to tell me they'd killed the fridge, and sure enough, it was dead. I asked Son if he was going to be okay here with them, First-Born said they *'won't hurt him'* (I knew they wouldn't, I was referring to emotions), I went out, I felt sad until I was in the studio with nice people and lots of paint, I came home happy.

Now First-Born's gone and it's quiet. Son and I have a quiet house while they're away and so his life has started to resemble something closer to normal. I feel sad for First-Born, and happy for him. For myself, just numb. A little bit of *see what happens*. First-Born's note said that they want stability, and I'd love to give them stability, but the silly little creature smashes stability to bits. How do you provide for anger like that? You don't. You stay numb, you forget to make appointments, you hold your breath for three more years. And somehow how find a way to write two essays that are demanding your attention.

Effin' essays. Who gives a shit about essays?

———

Friday, 12ᵗʰ October, 2007.

Cabinet of Curiosities

I don't now how to hide it seeing as it's eventually going to hang on a wall, but I can't show First-Born my Death's-Head Hawk Moth because they'll be angry at me for buying it. I showed it to Son, who understands why I find it so beautiful and doesn't ask ridiculous questions like *'How much did that cost?'*.

Maybe when Son grows up and has a serious girlfriend and their anniversary comes around and she's expecting flowers, he'll buy her a framed dead insect instead, because of my bad influence.

This moth is the most beautiful thing. I can't take my eyes off of it; it's gentle and quiet and hypnotic. I can't hang it on a wall yet because I'm not done with carrying it around wherever I go.

What do you do with this kind of love? I might have to write an ode, or something. It's making me think all sorts of philosophical/ethical things about the ownership of dead things. I asked the woman in the shop (a real Cabinet of Curiosities in the middle of the city) if the specimens are murdered, or if they die of natural causes and are just found by innocent passers-by, who aren't really poachers who go around killing little creatures, and she told me *no, of course they're not killed on purpose*. That was over a month ago, and I seriously believed her. What was I thinking?

I still loved the moth a month later so I went back to buy it and give it a home where it would be revered. After we left the shop Friend Boy A (who'd bought a skull that cost five times the price of my moth, making me feel less-bad about gratuitous spending), laughed at my gullibility before assuring me that there's no way in hell the moth was just "found" by an innocent PapuaNewGuinean, in some peaceful patch of forest, where it had lived a long and natural life.

The funny [?] thing is, they put naphthalene in the frame before they close it in, and naphthalene is what old people use to keep moths out of their cupboards. Isn't that like torturing the poor thing all the way into the grave?

I'd never own a live moth because that would be cruel, but gosh I wish I could watch it move. One of the things I love about it is that the death's-head pattern is squashed in a bit, so it's only half visible. It's a good thing I'm not into perfection. But I hope that's not where the murderers slapped it with a swatter. I hope they were at least kind enough to have used gas.

———

Wednesday, 17th October, 2007.

Green Thumb

Today's been a prototype for The Future. I got to paint all day. Then I put down my brushes before I could destroy the stupid thing any further, and took myself out into the garden for the evening.

That's when I discovered how boring I am. Why would anybody with a life stick their garden into their future's prototype? Gardens are for old people. I haven't touched my garden for so long I'm surprised I still have one. The alarming thing is that I've been yearning for it. It's very peaceful out there, and pretty. Having to do gardening is a pain in the arse, but doing it because you want to is different.

I'll shut up about the garden except to say that trimming the little hedge above the steps was like cutting babies' hair, the new growth all soft and downy. I just want to remember it, is all. In my Future I'll be able to spend as many evenings as I want in the garden. I'll be able to do whatever I want.

And the garden's just the beginning. After a really nice walk, I cooked. True dinks, I made lasagna for Son. It's regrettable that cooking lasagna for Son is so rare that it warrants a mention. But still, it's in the Prototype Day now, therefore the future looks promising. With reading, drawing, writing, painting, gardening and cooking all squished into something like sixteen hours, it's proof that I can do many good things in one day. Every day. Soon.

Now I just have to work out how to squeeze friends, chocolate, sex and dancing into this amazing prototype. I might have to remove cumbersome things such as, say, the thesis, in order to fit them in. Wouldn't that be a shame.

———

Friday, 19th October, 2007.

Lost in Translation (Butoh for the Ignorant)

Call me lacking in grace, but I went to see Sankai Juku's *Kagemi* at the State Theatre last night, and from the minute the performance began I found it painstakingly slow. Take tai chi and run it in slow motion – that kind of slow. I should probably say that I loved it before I say why it was a weird and yet fascinating little piece of thingy. Because when something starts off that slow, you sit there waiting for the dancers to move out of their gratuitous little stretch and get jiggy with it, and then after a while you start to panic because that obviously isn't going to happen.

It started slow, it stayed slow. I had to readjust everything I feel about dance and come to grips with a different kind of aesthetic. I was attracted to it in the first place because of the visual quality of the costume and set design, which relies on the simplicity of light and minimal colour to produce striking tonal definition on the body. It's mesmerising. So these more-meditative-than-funky male dancers work their way through series after series of gestural poses and I sat there feeling desperate to draw them, they looked so good.

So in isolation these movements were beautiful, but the bridging choreography was really something like glorified walking. There was a lot of sweeping arm gesture and swaying, which made me think of primary school drama of the "be a tree!" and "be a flower!" variety. Towards the end I heard the woman sitting behind me say '*This is gonna take forever*', as some performers walked in with excruciatingly slow bridesmaid-steps. Even my mum kept checking her watch.

More movement than dance. Pretty much independent of the music, too. If I was a dancer on that stage, I'd want to move my body in synch with the sound – maybe the relationship between body and music is what was missing? Doesn't matter, it was still good. I'd buy the picture book, if there was one. And I'd pay to see it again.

———

Tuesday, 30th October, 2007.

It's Natural, I Swear

I suppose it's time I sat down to have a think, because it's been a while. The alternative is doing housework in my knickers because I just put a new layer of fake tan on my legs, and I can't do that because First-Born's No-Good Bum of a Partner (who's quite sweet) is here.

My tan's looking very patchwork. The bottle lied: all-over *even* tan my arse. Well not my arse, actually. But I have to persevere because I'm going up to Sydney to see the Dobell Prize exhibition, and it's against the law for people like me to wear a skirt without fake tan in Sydney.

I've had lots of idyllic days, screwing up my priorities for the sake of peace and contentment. I don't know how I manage to get so much work done. Preparing my final folio for the year has been fun and surprising. I did the most anatomically incorrect drawing last week, so different from the way I used to draw I had to step back and say *'Wow, did I do that?'*. I can't imagine drawing the way I used to ever again.

AND, the other day I was painting away happily when the key to re-working my thesis came to me accidentally. Like my writing-brain's ticking away on auto-pilot while my art-brain dominates.

AND, the reception venue where I work (past-tense as of three days ago) has just closed, so I'm feeling time-rich now. Sad thing for the community, happy thing for the slowing-down of my life. I can get more work elsewhere quite easily but I'm considering destitution for a while, because I have a lot of work to do and am willing to stay poor to get it done. I can go back to paying attention to what's going on in the world [!], maybe that's why I feel so happy.

I'll use some of the extra time to practise fake tan application. It's much harder than oil painting; don't know how I can think of becoming any sort of artist if I can't even do my own legs.

Banyule Award exhibition = excellent.

Gosh I feel peaceful. S'posed to be painting, but instead following instincts into garden and spending afternoon in shade, tugging at weeds with whole body, mountain goat..

More important than anything to feel content, and to be where you are. Make this place feel like home again. Love the smell of the dirt underneath my window, my connection to place. Beautiful. Surrounded by wasps and probably snakes, echium in bloom. Nice.

———

Slight Omission

You know how you really really want to write about something personal [an unexpected love affair] but you can't because it involves somebody else and it's even more personal [nay, private] for that person because she's not the blurting-things-out type, so you have to write about not being able to write about it instead, because it's also pretty significant and has left you amazed at how surprising life can be sometimes?

Yes. That. I knew I had some discretion hidden somewhere deep inside, but I didn't know I had this much [!!].

———

November 2007

Drawing Euphoria

Don't bother trying to describe how good your trip to Sydney was, because it'll take too long and words will be inadequate. But do mention the Dobell exhibition at the NSW gallery, even though words for that are also inadequate because it was *so good*. I love Art Gallery NSW – they bring art to life by actively attracting excellence and giving it to us. I could have moved in and stared at the walls forever. The only downside is that they don't provide an exhibition catalogue, so you can only take the work home in your memory, which isn't enough.

All of this excitement, I need to channel it somewhere. There's so much to love in the world. But, assessment happens in three days and there's a shit-load of last-minute folio prep to do, piddly finalisation stuff. After that I'll do nothing but watch tv until my head explodes.

Thursday, 8th November, 2007.

And Now What?

I'm so glad it's over with. It's humiliating throwing a folio of student work together for assessment. Invaluable lessons that teach you more than you could've learnt on your own, but it's also your baby poop and you don't really want anybody looking at it. Some kind of pleasant disaster that happens to students on the way to being better.

Instead of feeling relief afterwards I felt lonely. Which is silly because I'm not lonely at all. I have great friends and am never isolated. I mean, I already had good friends, but now there's a group of four of us that fit with a perfect blend of social-meets-workaholism, and we're in each other's daily lives in a big way. When we're not physically together we're continually e-mailing, so even though I still get to spend as much time alone as I need I'm never really alone-alone, and therefore never lonely. It's priceless. I'm allowed to use a fiscal adjective because if I had to buy friends I'd pay good money for them.

If only intimacy wasn't so nice. I think when you've had a romantic interlude you have to re-train yourself to be alone. Especially when you didn't expect it. While you're inside the interlude you spend those days enjoying it, stunned and cautious; it's not until you're back home that you let it catch up with you.

I acknowledge that it's tragic to have looked forward to holidays so that I can spend them doing lots of work. Will start off slowly today, by reading in the sun. I forbid thinking about kissing, and touching is out of the question. Can't let a bit of loneliness get in my way.

———

Monday, 12th November, 2007.

Catching Zees

It's like I've been bitten by a tsetse fly; I keep falling asleep on the job. I curl up with my thesis, start reading and taking notes for the re-write, and within minutes I'm in the deepest, most relaxing sleep ever. I'm trying not to think of that as a reflection of the quality of the work.

I'm awake enough to decree Death to My Manuscript, though. I can't stand the stupid thing. I'm such a show-off, is the problem. The writing's clever all over the place, but ultimately irritating. I seem to have since developed some revolting form of maturity and now have to rub my nose in my immature past.

Luckily my older-wiser self can see what's wrong with it, knows which bits to attack, and there's enough decent writing in there to bring it back to life after the butchering. But being able to stay awake while I work on it would probably help.

———

Sunday, 18th November, 2007.

Discretion: Attempt # 2

I think I'm doing an okay job of not being the Creepy Older Woman. Which has been on my mind, in a don't-let-yourself-know-what-you're-thinking way. I realise that if I hadn't come along her life might have continued along a nice, comfortable path. She's about a hundred years younger than me (although, not so young that it's weird), so I can't help wondering if I've given her a complication she could do without. Even though I'm not the one who made it happen. Initially it happened by sort-of accident, and now it keeps happening by not-accident, which I guess makes it okay? So what's to worry about?

I wanted to write about vulnerability, but it's too hard to write about something and not-write about it at the same time. It's so much easier to just be a big mouth. I might quit while I'm ahead and shut the fuck up.

Other Things to Think About
Thesis. Thesis. Thesis.

Sunday, 18th November, 2007.

Hippydom
Somebody close-by who signs her emails off with the little catchphrase "love and light". Utmost respect notwithstanding, I'm tempted to vomit every time I read it. As much as I care about them both, I've kept a safe distance from both her and her husband.

But I feel sorry for him right now. Ms Love n' Light has confirmed for me and for everyone that people suck, because she didn't return their son to him on Thursday night, and it looks at the moment like he won't be allowed to see his kids again for as good as forever.

When they separated she got custody of The Girl-Child and he got custody of The Boy Child. They've had this dual household co-operative parenting thing going on. The arrangement worked for her because Ms Love n' Light quite openly couldn't handle raising two children at a time.

And now she's run off with the kids, leaving her admittedly weird but not-deserving-of-this husband with very little good in his life. It's very sad that she could do this to another person, and to their mutual offspring. Everywhere you turn, somebody's doing something so horrible it's almost impossible to understand how our species even survives. Apparently the kind of love spread via catchphrase is ultimately self-serving.

How to help a man who says it's not in his nature to fight, and who therefore won't fight? Let me say this loud and clear: sometimes pacifists need a good slapping.

--

Thursday, 22nd November, 2007.

Neverending Story

It's been such a long day, spent trapped inside Chapter One of my manuscript. Chapter One's the motherfuckingest bastard of a chapter to re-write – you have to get the ingredients exactly right, make them unfold as naturally as possible. I've changed a monumental amount of wordage, but after hours of hard slog it still isn't finished. I'm starting to get cabin fever.

Re-writing is usually fun. The next chapters will be faster and funner than this one, and by the time I can see the finished product forming I'll be having a ball. Won't I? If I didn't have art things planned with my peeps tomorrow I think I'd have to cry.

Anyway, I realised as I sat here to write this that taking a break from writing to write something else is an act of stupidity. I need to factor more fun into life if I'm gonna work like this every day for however long the holidays go for. One dog biscuit for every clever trick – I'm gonna earn so many rewards I'll be having too much fun to fit in any work at all.

--

Saturday, 24th November, 2007.

!!!!!!

Did you see him? What a fantastic speech! He's the only prime minister who can speak jingoism and make it sound great. Australia – ya did good. For the first time in years I feel PROUD of my country. [Happy!]

--

Sunday, 25th November, 2007.

Oh My Aching Bones

The best thing I did today was not plummet to my death. I've just spent as many hours as there are between now and evening suspended over the drop beneath my balcony to paint the new timber before the replacement boards get put on. I'm sure that's a man's job – women aren't usually stupid enough to risk their lives for home maintenance. My hanging-on-for-dear-life muscles are killing me.

Whilst manoeuvring around mid-air in a death-defying fashion at about 11:30 pm, First-Born came outside and asked: '*If I ask you a question will you answer it honestly?*'. Naturally I avoided answering that, and just said '*What do you want to know?*'.

I swear they have a sex radar. They asked me if I'm seeing somebody, and I had about four seconds to think up a fat, juicy lie. It went something like "no". Which is true, really, depending on what "seeing somebody" means.

I don't even know what it means. It's been about 46 hours since my last kiss, but I have no idea how they could know that. It's not like I'm walking around all radiant and with a spring in my step. In fact, I'm subdued and distracted by being busy at the moment. Hello – I was practically upside-down and slapping paint onto a raw beam at that minute. Anyway, I'm sure I'm not behaving any differently, and even if I was, First-Born's not here often enough to witness anything significant. So I just told them: '*If I was in a serious relationship I'd tell you. I wouldn't introduce them to you, but I'd tell you*'.

Liar. Even if I was in a serious relationship with somebody I'd avoid telling them for as long as possible. But only because they have a seek-and-destroy reaction to anybody who goes anywhere near me. So I feel mean, especially because they were being so nice. (The benefit of them not being at home as much is that when they are home we get along really well.) (Gosh I love 'em. First-Born really is a good kid, when they're not being otherwise.)

Still, there's nothing worse than your own child asking you about your sex life. I'm willing to indulge in fibbery to protect my privacy. There are some things they just don't need to know.

Vagina-Mite [Not]

Monday, 26th November, 2007.

A Scene

Unfortunately The Carpenter is here working on the balcony and saw the whole thing. I'm not used to this anymore, had to brace myself so that the threats would bounce right off. Like the chopping board, the lunch wrap, the onions, the plate and the phone. (Lunch wrap should be outlawed as an offensive airborne weapon – that one hurt.)

I paused too long before answering a request? Triggering some emotional reflex?

The worse thing you can do is hide things like this, but in saying anything, I've already said too much.

Wednesday, 28th November, 2007.

Who'da Thunk?

Evil Ex-Friend is evil no more. When I first contacted her after she sent that gloriously self-debasing apology letter I was hesitant, wondering what possible value there could be in renewing contact. I thought that some friendships should just stay dead. Then I had other [better] friends in my ear telling me to be careful, and bluntly reminding me that I'm a suck who forgives people too readily. They mean that as an insult, not a compliment, and say I should tell her to go fuck herself. (No manners, my friends.)

Well, I'm glad I'm a suck. The first time I called her I was blah and cautious. I thought my second call was just a polite formality, and I put it off. But I called yesterday to let her know I hadn't forgotten her, and when I heard her voice I felt instantly happy.

These days I'm less easily sucked in by a little human warmth, but I'd interrupted her editing work, and I'd been editing, so we started talking books and writing and we slipped so naturally back onto common-ground. I didn't think I could connect with her again, but when you have a foundation to share the friendship resumes from where you left it, only better because you've survived hardship to get where you are now.

So there you go; I love talking to her, I love writing with her, I feel inspired by working with her. (We taught together at a university – she's brain food.) She's woken up a part of me that's been sleeping, and things are as they should be.

In my defence, it's not about being a doormat or being forgiving. That would put her in a passive or negative role. So she did some shitty things, so what? Losing her was brutal, and it happened not long after Friend Who Died committed suicide in a really brutal way – that's two brutal things that left me winded. That Ex Ex-Friend was a bit nut-jobby at the time is understandable, because Friend Who Died was to her what Friend A is to me, and if anything happened to Friend A I'd probably fall to pieces, too.

Loss is horrible; I'm lucky to have her back.

———

Thursday, 29th November, 2007.

Road Racism

Nothing but jocularity in my afternoon today, which was meant to be spent writing peacefully. Kitchen Nazi turned up with her son, and my first thought was '*Thank fuck I did the dishes this morning*'. Of course, I didn't wipe the benches, because breakfast is just a banana from the fruit bowl. So how was I to know it had Milo on it? Milo is perfectly camouflaged on a granite bench.

Kitchen Nazi walks in with a bag full of afternoon tea, and stands there in the middle of the kitchen waiting for Son to wipe the bench down for her, so that she can sit down to eat. (Well, I wasn't going to wipe it myself. That'd be like licking her boots clean while she watched.) Meanwhile I watched the clock because I had to be somewhere, and she's the last person I'd leave in my house unattended. So I said '*Would you like to come with me? Then we can go for a hot chocolate?*', which I'd promised her recently anyway.

I never remember important lessons, such as DON'T GET INTO A CAR WITH KITCHEN NAZI. I discovered today that it's even worse when she's driving. Whenever she rings me from her car I get commentary about the drivers around her and hear her beeping her horn non-stop (not exaggerating); this time I got to experience it first-hand.

The worst thing was driving along a main road in a school zone – it wasn't 2:30 yet (it was maybe 2:26?), and she'd prematurely slowed down to 40 kph. She beeped every driver who passed us, leaning over me to wave her fists and yell out a commentary about the selfishness of other people, with embellishments about vulnerable little children. Then when we caught up to some at the lights she said: *'Did you see that? He was Asian! I swear, they're taking over, and they get away with it because there're so many of them they have all of the control...'*.

I knew about her aggro problem, but I didn't know about the racism and didn't know what the hell to say. You can't say nothing, so I let her rant for a minute before gently telling her that there are Asian people who've been here for more generations than you'd think, and even if they haven't, I can think of quite a few "Australians" who are worse. She said *'You're not wrong about that – Camry drivers!'*.

No wonder I'm feeling a little tense now that she's gone. After the road rage there was shopping centre rage, escalator rage, and residential rage (at the dog yapping across the street from my house). She even yelled at the yapping dog from *inside my house*. I hope the neighbours didn't think it was me.

Mind you, I prefer the rage to her reading of catalogues at my kitchen table. At least anger isn't boring.

The beauty of it is that when we drove to her other son's school we were running late, so she drove at 70 in a 40 zone. Not a main road 40 zone, where you can see everything, but a more dangerous 40 zone, full of parked cars and unpredictable children. I said nothing. I don't know if it's because I'm gutless or too smart to bother. Maybe both.

Ya gotta love 'er. In small doses. And preferably with a warning phone call when she's on her way over. So that you can scrub invisible Milo from your kitchen bench. Or hole up in the bedroom with a laptop and pretend you're not home.

Just never *ever* get into a car with her again.

———

December 2007

Good Night

First of all, I smell really good right now. If I was out I'd ask me on a date. but I'm home, which is ashame because I'm pised as a fart and should really be dancing. And I would be but there's always somebody in your group who needs to get home to get sleep coz they gotta worjk at 6 am. Anyways, saw BABBA tonight -tThat's gotta make a person happey.

But ya can't sleep if your r'e drunk becuaes you;ll have a hangover the next day. Rule one = sober up before sleep. Sp this is me sobering. I love babba. LOVE THEM. And my friends,. I love them too. And my fiends friends, who I heard calling me gorgeous at least three times, when they thought I wasn' listenng, so my ego is pumped. GORGEOUS ME! Plus friend's frend kept kissing me on sthe cheek . I quite like being kissed on the cheek.. It's nicv to be loved, is why.

So anyway, clearly I scrub up well and now that I'm famous on the babba scene I wish I was out dancing, because wen I was out I looked at the staff who were clearing the tables and they were some of the people i worked with at my restaurant job. so that's where they ended up., we squealed and said *hello hello hello,* and right now they're all out dancing at the irish pub and I want to be there with them but friend's other friend had to work at 6am so here I am at home on abecausehad to share taxi.

I especially feel bad because one of them said *'See you there'* as she was leaving. Fiends frends who have to work at 6am are a pain in the arse.

Iisn't it funny getting sentimental about my old work people now, when when I worked with them I thought I'd never see them again because we had nothing in common? So, who cares if you have anything in common? Dancing is dancing, doesn't matter who wth, it was just surprisingly good to see them all again.

I'm an hour away from sober an that's gonna throw my new schedule out of whacvk.

And the other thing s is that Ex-Husband dropped in earlier tonight and I MISS HIM. he's my friend and I swear, I kept kiassing his cheek (even though I'm the gorgeous one). I seriously I do love him and wish he wasn't so anla. If he wasn;t so anal he;d be a top notch human being. I need to find him somebody ot love, I hate to think of him being lonely. I could practically kiss him , I love him so smuch , but only wen he;s not anal. When I kiss his cheek he turns to kiss me on the lips and that' s nice, really. So I kiss him on the lips, just a little, I'd kiss him properly if he kept that up, but I don't tell him that, because I know it wouldn't be wise to kiss him properly. It's just that whole body thing, when you've known and loved somebody, you fit together by instinct. He was so loved, and he threw it away .Makes me Really, really sad.

I love so many people. How do you love this many people and not burst? I should eat something. We're out of chocoltae, is the thing.

Anyway about smelling good – it's because smokers can't smoke in public venues abymore. !!!! I used to have to shower when I got home after a night out, and the stink of msoke under th water was nauseating, it was so strong. Now all I smell is perfume and body heat. I can't actually tell if it' s my perfume or the perfume of all the women I've hugged tonight. I think it's theirs? Being human is the best thing.

––––

Tuesday, 11th December, 2007.

SHHHHHHH

I'm discovering that the only way for me not to feel tired all day is to get up at 5:30 am. That makes no sense. I woke at 10:30 today because I had a friend over for drinks late last night, and I've spent the day feeling exhausted. What kind of body punishes its owner for sleeping in? (No, I did NOT drink – I sipped a little at the wine and tipped the rest over the balcony when she wasn't looking, so that she wouldn't feel bad. Now that I'm an epicurean wunderkind, the cheap stuff kinda tastes like shit.) (It's possibly there are plants suffering from hangover under my balcony.)

Anyway, I'm going to listen to my body, because I've been getting up early and it feels just like the good old days, when I was a workaholic. I need to anyway – my list of things to do over the summer is spiralling out of control. It's overwhelming. It all has to snap at a sudden point, and after that I'm allowed no interruptions. I think that's why I'm putting things off — if you know your flow is going to be interrupted, there's no point in starting something.

What an excellent excuse.

The peace and quiet is amazing. You can hear a pin drop in this house, because it's just Son and I at home for days and days on end. First-Born's off playing married-couple with their partner (I've given up my gullible belief in their persistent virginity) and that's fine with me. It's like they've moved out of home, so now when I see them I get a fair chance at being able to enjoy their company. I'd like a bit more of them, but they'll come back one day. They're safe and happy, and getting themself more settled into the idea of working towards things. (Like, orgasms and... okay, I'm joking!!) They've even planned their homework schedule for next year. Hilarious from my point of view, but they score points anyway.

The quiet. I love it. I blob about doing my thing, Son blobs about doing his thing, but now I'm wondering if perhaps it's too quiet. Surely kids need some chaos? If we get into the habit of not interacting enough he'll turn into a fusty old man. I'm going to have to resort to Uno. Maybe even Chinese checkers. But not chess, I'm drawing the line there. And then it's back to archery and kayaking. Surely there's more to it than that? It's been so long since our family life has been normal I've forgotten how.

All Work, No Play, Dull Boy

I discovered today that if you're hanging around certain parts of the city with your young bit o' fluff and feel the impulse to pull her aside somewhere quiet to snog, there are very few nooks and crannies to drag her into. Unless you fancy the romantic ambience of public toilets, although the only public toilet around was occupied by a woman who stood at the mirror squeezing her pimples while the tap was running for minutes and minutes and minutes, and we both stood behind her and wondered how you go about getting her to turn the thing off without making her angry, seeing as there's a drought happening. (I considered the tactful saying of *'Are you crazy?'* but decided against it, because she probably was.)

I really really wanted to kiss, and had to wait for hours to be back at her place (since when have I been so discreet?), and even then I knew I had to pick First-Born up on the way home so I couldn't be too late. The lecture First-Born gave me when I finally picked them up was... deserved.

So now I regret not spending the whole day kissing. Being half-naked and digging around under clothes for a hasty fuck (please excuse tactless French = it's late = I'm tired = I had a bad brownie experience = no manners left), knowing that I'd have to make a quick getaway, seemed like such a shame when I didn't really want to stop.

Which is me being greedy and also being reluctant to shut myself away from the world for the next million weeks, even though shutting myself away to work is what I most want to do.

Really it's okay because we're both about to embark on an uninterrupted working glut (I'm finally in "the zone") and am therefore not allowed to think about distracting things like kissing. Although, my lip's swollen with that nice bruised feeling which = a pleasant physical memory, so maybe I'll think about it a little bit.

It's so late now my up-early morning isn't likely to happen, and I'm going to have to plan tomorrow very carefully to make it work. It's all business and pure business from hereon in. Here goes nothing.

———

Wednesday, 12th December, 2007.

Brownie Trauma

Only about three weeks after it started, my love affair with Max Brenner is over. That's fine, because the hot chocolates are too sickly sweet anyway, as opposed to chocolatey, which just goes to show you can't buy me with sugar after all. The tragic deal-breaker is the brownie. All day I looked forward to that brownie. I travelled far and wide in search of etching supplies and oil paints, and I visited galleries, all the while knowing that my aching legs would be sat at a Max Brenner table for the reward of a brownie.

You can imagine my disappointment when I found out that Max Brenner people are scumbags. Price went up a little, but that's not the worst of it. The waiter brought my brownie out and the first thing I noticed was that the little bowl of melted chocolate was NOT THERE. I said something intelligent like *oi, where's the chocolate?*, only to be informed that it's no longer offered, and if I wanted it I'd have to pay $2.20 extra. What the? It took me a while to recover from the shock of such a blatant drop in service. What's the point of the brownie without the chocolate? It clagged my mouth shut. I'm so writing them a letter.

Anyways, I vowed never to go there again, but had to break my vow because Friend Boy A called us later to say that he was about to arrive in the city with his kids and could we please please all go to Max Brenner's for a hot chocolate. So we did, but that was the LAST TIME. Ya just don't fuck with chocolate, Max.

———

Saturday, 15th December, 2007.

A Touch of the White Rabbit

Don't panic. DON'T PANIC!!! It's *nice* that First-Born's home. (Don't panic!) It's mature, even, for them to say they've decided to spend the week at home. A WHOLE WEEK. And it started really well; they came home yesterday afternoon and demanded that we all '*spend time together*' watching a movie. I love it when they're like this.

So now I have to change my motherhood technique from fend-for-yourself to I'll-look-after-you. (Panic! Panic!) And give up that time I was going to spend alone. It's okay if they stay this nice for the week, because we'll have made progress. But upstairs right now the sound of screamo music is a bodily assault. I'm very "delicate" and really don't want any noise, so I'm rattled about the hard-won peace evaporating.

Even that's okay, because it's just family life. What's worrying me is that I have soooo much work to do, and no mental space in which to do it. Forget getting up at 5:30 am; I'm going to have to get up at 3:30 am. So I can have those quiet hours in the morning for writing? And use the afternoons for art? Then I can enjoy noisy old family life all evening... ?

Rational! I'd love one whole day alone, though. Just one day. The phone calls and visitors and more visitors and logistical things needing my attention = driving me crazy. One day, that's all I want.

Deep breath. If I find a way to feel peaceful about all of this I can make it work. And maybe lose that silly attachment I have to the act of sleeping.

———

Sunday, 16th December, 2007.

Dictation

It's taken me all morning to realise that I'm feeling grumpy. I just don't do grumpy, so I'm enjoying the novelty. I've been propped up on my bed with my laptop working solidly, and when the kids come anywhere near me I'm like a dog guarding its bone.

For example, Son stands in my doorway with his visiting friend (the smelly one) and asks *'Can you drive us to Kmart so that we can buy a new Xbox controller?'*, and I say *'Do the words* fuck off *mean anything to you?'*. Then I give him a really evil smile and he backs out of the room slowly.

Now I'm eating bread and honey, just like the queen, and am enjoying seeing the house through grumpy eyes and growling at my ungrateful children. I've decided to run our life like a drill sergeant from now on. It's the only way. All fun has to be pencilled in at something like sixteen-hundred hours and can only happen after duty inspection. The rest is business. No joking, I've made lists.

Then there are the rules they keep breaking. Ya gotta love 'em. Anyway it's all under control. When First-Born disobeys me after I tell them not to use the internet on the other computer, I disable the computer. Under an oppressive regime my children will learn humility. And good manners. And to bow to my every wish.

Monday, 17th December, 2007.

Idyll

First-Born's gone AWOL again. How can I be a drill sergeant if I don't have any troops? Despite the prospect of peace on earth inside this household for the next few days, I wish they hadn't gone back to their partner's place, because I miss them. I mean, I miss them *a lot*.

We all had dinner together last night, and it's amazing how a family can bond over a bottle of Maison. It was *fun*, I tell you. My kids are hilarious when they're together; I just sat there laughing and soaking it all in. So when First-Born said later that they were going back to their partner's I was disappointed. How could they give up such nice family life for insubstantial frivolities like rampant teenage sex and complete freedom from draconian parental oppression?

Parenthood can be no-win sometimes. So I'll send them a text today telling them I miss them and can they please come home more often.

Last night's insomnia (first in a while – these days I sleep like a log) had two sources. One was that the door between my left and right brain hemispheres wouldn't close and I was being bombarded by project thoughts. Way ta go, brain; make me so excited that I can't sleep and will be too tired to do any of the things you're excited about.

The other was thinking about my kids and wanting us all together. On Friday I drove First-Born to a friend's and remembered a news bulletin they'd told me about the night before, about a cat being tortured. Thoroughly disturbed by this, I'd looked it up that day, and without thinking informed them *'That cat was sexually abused, too'*. They burst into tears and said *'Don't tell me things like that – you can't tell me things like that!'*. It reminded me of what they were like when they were young and always trying to solve the world's problems. I felt incredibly guilty, and lucky that they'd interrupted me before I could tell them about what the perpetrators did to somebody's pet rabbit.

As much as I hate to see them upset, it's good to see that they're still the same person, and suddenly I feel like I know them again. And the way they followed the election with admirable extremes of dislike for John Howard and his policies – they're going to be a wonderful adult. What a nice thing to see in my hostile teenager. That sweet little thing, of course I want them home. Rose-coloured glasses rule.

Thursday, 20th December, 2007.

Wonders Never Cease

My spies have informed me that Feral Friend now has soap, shampoo and conditioner in his shower. AND he has deodorant (!!!!!). This is good news for an up-coming annual dinner, for those of us who may have to sit next to him. Just goes to show that all good hippies come to their senses sooner or later (note that my definition of a "good" hippy applies exclusively to hippies who are hippies no longer), and realise that it's worth risking a little bit of accumulative aluminium poisoning for the sake of smelling nice.

On the Outside

I have to write about my haircut because it's the only thing I've done all week that isn't work. Plus my hairdresser is hilarious, she's so bad at her job. I love that I just watched her hack away without asking her to stop. I should probably try to care, but I'm just amused.

The best thing is that my hair bounces, because it's much shorter and she was over zealous with the tapering, giving me half a bob on one side. I now look like a cross between a middle-aged woman (which unfortunately suits me) and a kid who's been playing with scissors.

Still Thursday.

Grunge

If you wanna re-write a novel you've gotta put your head down and make like a mushroom. I've been spending anywhere between ten and fourteen hours a day buried in an old manuscript, and I'm going to stay inside that manuscript until it's fully revised.

I'm having a ball, except that I didn't realise the writing style was so brutal. Possibly vulgar. And slightly confronting. My eyeballs are getting bruised just reading the thing, and I'm beginning to suspect I might have been a real bitch when I wrote it. An articulate bitch, but a bitch nonetheless. Except, I don't remember being a bitch. I remember it being inspired by softness and fluff. I must have some serious communication issues? (Actually "bitch" is a bit harsh; tough, maybe. But like a cornered animal.)

So anyway my mission, if I choose to accept it, is to tidy it up. This one's really important to me, so I can't just throw it away. I have to soften it up and lose about fifty percent of the longwinded middle chapters. That's what I'm up to at the moment, the icky part, and it's so challenging it's actually fun. I can't believe how easy it is to recognise the crud when you come back to it after a couple of years, and how good it feels to axe whole chapters at a time.

The amount of sex in the manuscript is making me squeamish. I don't like that it's essential to the plot – I hate it when I meet people who are obsessed with sex (and I may be blunt but I'm nowhere near obsessed), so one of the characters just makes me feel dark. It's putting me off sex altogether. I'll have to regress to childhood for a while to get over it.

Now I'm stuck because I want to get away from the ballsy voice, which I've decided is not a good thing, despite the nature of the work. I swear, sometimes I write like I'm covered in tattoos. What I really want is to finish it off and then cleanse my brain by writing something gentle. (With no swearing in it, even.) I've done it before and I can do it again. Just as soon as I remember how.

Wednesday, 26th December, 2007.

Porky Pies

To my credit, I've tried honesty on for a while and it doesn't work for me. Many of my friends tell me I shouldn't have to lie. This makes them puritanical dumbarses. My conclusion is that only stupid friends encourage honesty, and I'm going to blame them for every wasted minute I've had to spend with people who just don't understand why I'd choose to be at home working rather than doing sweet fuck-all.

Nobody listens to you if you say you're busy doing something that doesn't pay money, and they turn up at your house without being invited and then don't leave. Make up a lie, though, about not being home or having to go out, and you're socially acceptable.

I wish I'd remembered that on Xmas Eve; if I'd lied about having to be elsewhere I wouldn't have gotten stuck at a huge motherfucking shopping centre for two hours longer than I'd planned. I had to watch somebody else shop! I'm way too polite. It was excruciating, I might not get over it. (*And* she bought me the worst hot chocolate *ever* – some people have no standards.)

I've since sworn off honesty and have already told two big fat fibs in order to protect my work time. As a result I've had plenty of time between myself and my computer, making mad passionate hard slog. I've managed to cut a huge amount of words from my manuscript – so many I'm not going to mention the figure. It's in the five-digit range and revealing it would be like advertising the extremes of my verbosity. I might as well scream out BAD WRITER and be done with it.

Nearly done. I'm freight-train-ing my way to the end, and then planning to leap right into the next one. It's not that I don't love my people, but I should perhaps put a "Wrong Way, Go Back" sign at the top of my driveway? That's not as honest as a plain old "Fuck Off" sign, but at least it won't upset the neighbours.

Seriously. I give them bits of time here and there and I love [most of] them to bits, but if my people knew how much I don't want to see them when I'm working on a project, I'd have no friends left.

Thursday, 27th December, 2007.

Finito

Aren't I supposed to feel joyous, or something? I backed up my files, tidied my desk and danced around for a bit. Said a bit of a *whoo-hoo*. But now I'm... I dunno. I suspect I hate the manuscript. And of course that makes me think about how I just wasted so much time on the revision. I know it's technically one of my offspring and everything, but there's no way I'm entering it into any bonnie baby contests.

Now I'm going to work on a painting and will go back to the manuscript after a few days, give it one more read (with slashing tools ready), and send it off for assessment. So sensible. So financially *crippling*.

I suppose the good thing is that once I'm working with oils I won't give a toss about the writing. I'd better start painting tonight, before I sink into a self-critical funk. Oh whoops – too late!!

———

January 2008

Nice Start

Been painting. Been obsessed. Been very happy. Been socialising with likewise obsessed friends. Been neglecting everybody else. Been sometimes kissing. But often not kissing. Been too busy. Been spending every last cent on paint. And more paint. And then some. Been discovering how expensive it is to be me. Been thinking I need money to ventilate workspace properly. Been thinking that if I don't ventilate properly fumes will kill me. Been thinking work harder. Neglect people more. No problem!

Thursday, 3ʳᵈ January, 2008.

Legend...?

You know how somebody comes up with a really good storyline and makes a really good movie that's gripping despite the too-far-from-human screeching creature sound effects (cheap scare tactic – not necessary), and then they almost ruin said really good movie by making it all god-ish at the end, thereby perpetuating the anti-intellectual-evolutionary belief that human scientific intelligence is Bad and will inevitably end in our self-destruction, and that only dog-spelt-backwards – who is unscientific and therefore Good – will be able to save us from extinction? Well, dog-spelt-backwards *and* the Will Smith character under divine guidance in *I Am Legend*. Yey Americans and their pro-xtian bandwagons. Nothing like using gawd to fuck up a good plot.

Very good movie, despite.

Chris Fontana

Thursday, 10th January, 2008.

A Fraction Less Ignorant

Old movies are hilarious. Because I was stupid enough to think that *I Am Legend* was an original thing in this age of recycling old stuff, I had to undergo re-education by watching *The Last Man On Earth*, and then *The Omega Man*, and then listening to the audio book of *I Am Legend* (by Richard Matheson). Funny how following the same story four times in a row isn't even boring. In fact, after watching all of the movies, the audio book was gripping. Especially because I wanted to know if the original conclusion was rampantly churchy or not.

That's witch-hunting on my part. The answer is: NO; the original is an intelligent narrative that applies a speculative scientific foundation to a history of supernatural horror (vampire myths). The whole point of it is to debunk religious crap and look at humanity as-is, and in extremis. Which makes the godishness at the end of the most recent movie even worse, because it means the xtians are at it again.

This is where sociological (and historical) awareness is important, because it's in the subtle narratives of culture that religion asserts itself and becomes this insidious pestilence (i.e. xtianity was originally spread by poisoning existing cultural stories with the virus of its own ideology, ultimately erasing existing value systems by absorbing and overriding/replacing them). Every self-respecting atheist in the world has been watching xtianity infiltrate contemporary culture by appropriation like this over the past few years, and it's alarming.

I still love the new movie, but with a caveat. If you try hard enough you can look at it as cautionary, as opposed to science-bashing. And I like that it downplays the vampire aspect by sticking to reptilian primality, because vampire myths are dumb. I still think the title no longer fits the story, because the word "legend" has been hijacked by dude terminology. But what a whopping good story it is. Times four.

———

Tuesday, 15th January, 2008.

Bad Thing I Did

I don't know how I've come so far in life, having known so many old

147

people who have eventually died, and still not learnt the equation of old-person plus sick-person equals practically-dead-person. Sorry, I'll make that clearer:

> IF THEY ARE [very] SICK THEY ARE [probably] GOING TO DIE.

I might've been helped overcoming my lack of foresight had my uncle – who I adore but at whom I'm really angry right now – had called me and said something along the lines of '*Oh by the way, I have something sad to tell you, Aunty E has leukemia*'.

That visit I kept putting off and putting off and putting off because I was so busy? And that time on the way home from Bairnsdale in September when I said to Son *let's drop in on them please please please* but Son said '*No*', and instead of doing some parental overriding I said '*I suppose we can come back soon and do a proper visit*', and then promptly didn't drop in even though it would have made them both so happy? Well. Too late. She's dead. Ask me if I'll ever get over how bad I feel. No matter how many amendses later, this will haunt me forever.

They thought I was the ants pants. Especially because they were usually feuding or conspiracy-theorising about Rest-of-Family. I was spared being conspiracy-theorised about because back when I was the black sheep of the family and living in sin with my "wife" and baby in Warragul, Uncle and Aunty would visit us often. We bonded over our mutual black-sheepness and grew very close.

I don't feel so ants-pantsish now. I haven't called them for a while, obviously. Maybe even not since the end of May. She was sick then but they didn't know what it was. I thought nothing of it because they both always had something wrong with them. Mum discovered her death in the newspaper death notices. I suspect Uncle didn't let me know she was sick because they thought I'd tell Mum; they weren't talking to her over some stupid quarrel and therefore didn't want her at the sick bed.

Hence they leave me out of it, and he tells me over the phone on Saturday (when I call to see if it's true) that he loves me and we have '*something special between us*'. That's all very nice because I love him too, but in the meantime Aunty E has died and I didn't get to be there and say goodbye.

Stupid humans and their stupid fucking feuds. It occurred to me to be angry about this during the funeral today. Everybody else finished their crying and I couldn't stop. Fact remains, if I hadn't avoided calling him because I felt so bad about not visiting, I would have found out for myself, and I and my children could have been there at the end. It's all my fault.

It's his fault, too, but it's my fault more. Busy my arse – I'm pathetic. This is the pinnacle of all the neglect of loved ones I've ever committed. (That's a lot of neglect to be the pinnacle of.) I watched Little Sister with him today. He was saying '*Let's not let anything come between all of us ever again*', and she was so good with him. But the way he hugs me, it's clear to everyone that I'm his favourite, and all I can think is that she deserves his affection more than I do. She should be favourite. I'm too selfish to be this loved.

Lesson: fear of letting people down makes you let them down more. Don't love anybody. Especially don't let them love you back.

———

Worse Thing I Did

I'm a bad mother. Really, this time I am. I didn't take First-Born to the funeral. By their age I was an expert funeral attender, but I think First-Born has only been to one so far, so this not only denies them an opportunity for emotional reflection and sharing, but I'm failing at fact-of-life education stuff.

I didn't quite know what to do. I'm overwhelmed, and not comfortable having to deal with these things. So I didn't try very hard to contact them. I'd told them about Aunty E dying, because even though they haven't seen each other for years, they were fond of each other. First-Born said it was sad but didn't express any interest in the funeral. Well they couldn't, I didn't offer the information.

Then First-Born had a party here and it got ugly and we were upset with each other, and I forgot to ask them about the funeral before they left on Monday morning.

After that, I assumed they wouldn't want to go. I knew I shouldn't make that kind of decision for them but I did it anyway. I tried to call them, couldn't get through, got distracted, didn't try again. Thought of it this morning, was going to call, got distracted again. (By what? Well I'm selfish = I got distracted by painting.) Then it was too late and I was scared to call them.

I have the most ridiculous fears and they make me do the most ridiculous things.

I think deep down I didn't want them there because of how they spoke to me on the weekend. I knew I'd be a mess at the funeral and didn't want them to see me vulnerable. That wouldn't have stopped me taking them, but in the end I just didn't know how. Throw-back from childhood: they get mean, my defences go up. Part of me also thought it'd be false to be there in death when towards the end we hadn't all been there in life. (That's so screwed up.)

I dropped some jelly beans at their partner's house on the way home and when I mentioned where I'd been they said '*Oh, I wanted to go to that!*'. I felt so, so bad for not trying harder. And for assuming they wouldn't want to anyway. And for dreading being emotional in front them. In a car. For four hours plus the service. And now, because they're at their partner's and not here, I don't know if they're upset about it or just accepting. If they're angry at me they have the right to be. And yet, they might not be giving it much thought, or their thought might not carry the same weight as mine, because so much time has passed between visits.

Why oh why is it that when I make a mistake I make such a BIG one? If I just did what I had to do instead of being busy and distracted and fearful, life would be easy, everybody would feel loved and I wouldn't be such a schmuck. I really over-think this shit. I have to toughen up.

———

Less Bad Thing

My mother has bionic eyes. She got those implanty things and now doesn't need glasses and it's disconcerting. I think she's looking at her thousands of offspring and seeing them properly for the first time in years, and thinking '*They're so wrinkly – when did they get so old?*'.

She visited on the weekend, was sitting opposite me at the kitchen table, a fair distance away. Stared. Said, '*You've got some grey hair!*'

I said: '*It's white. Grey is for commoners; redheads skip straight to white. But yes, it's been there for a while. There's only a little bit,*' and I pointed to where it is.

She said: '*No there's a lot, look at all those strands on the crown of your head!*'

I said: '*I think I liked you better when you were half-blind.*'

———

Still Tuesday.

A Really Good Thing

I've been redeemed! Or am just off the hook. First-Born dropped in to pick up chocolate and toilet paper supplies, so I got a chance to say sorry for today. They said '*Meh, oh well*', which means I was right about them having the nice memory but the connection being so worn that their not-going to the funeral was an okay thing. (Women's intuition – I should never have doubted the mechanics of my presumptions.)

This means I haven't accidentally [carelessly] fucked with my child's head, and First-Born won't grow up needing years of therapy to cope with my emotional incompetence.

Also I got to tell them about the funeral, which was Catholic. Because I was raised Catholic, when people started making the sign of the cross my hand went to do it automatically. Close call! Luckily my brain realised what my hand reflexes were about to do and I stopped just in time; if I'd made that holy gesture the skin of my forehead would have burned like it'd been doused in acid. Plus, Little Sister would have laughed at me for the REST OF MY LIFE.

During the service I looked at Dad and noticed he wasn't saying all of the saying things, and I was very proud of him. I think we were the only two in the chapel courting damnation. The rest of them did the rapture thing and I just waited patiently for all of the ho-hum to finish, so that they could get to the good bits.

First-Born left here tonight feeling quite happy and relaxed, and was well supplied. I'm not a bad mother after all. A bad niece, but not a bad mother. I'll take that as a half-win.

———

151

Friday, 25th January, 2008.

Confidence: Under/Over/Temporary?

I might need slapping over the head to separate myself from this thing I've done. As it is I have to peel myself away from the staring-at position in front of my painting to write this. I'm glad it's not a self-portrait, because that'd make me narcissistic as opposed to just plain up-myself. Because, you know. It's good [?]. I'm as surprised as anyone about this, but I'll say it out loud before I change my mind and start hating it again: it's *good*, like a real portrait, likeness n' all. If it was smaller I'd make mum hang it on her fridge.

I just added the final touches (the real final touches, not the pretend-final touches I added when I finished it on Wednesday morning), and now I feel strange. I want to keep working on it but there's nothing left to do. Except to stop and think nice things at myself.

Ex-G-Not-G used to ask me why I never use art to make something beautiful (as opposed to political), and now I have – I did a beautiful thing. I'm relieved, and the future's looking bright.

My thoughts are out of kilter, but I suppose I should add some self-consciousness to balance things out. Because although I knew in a nervous way that I could paint like this if I followed my instincts, I also knew (and have confirmed) that it's not the way I want to paint. It even sucks. I suspect that any goodness in my work is counterbalanced by the boringness of my vision. As in, will the things that obsess me please other people? I don't know. That doesn't mean I'm not pleased, but frankly, beautiful is for pussies. I want to be rough and spontaneous. And fast, that wouldn't hurt.

So I have this style, and I need it to evolve. That's okay, because I love the process of starting somewhere tight and loosening up. It's all-consuming and nothing else matters when I'm working. I don't like that I neglect important things (like people) (and thesis), but if that's the way I am then that's the way I am. Deal with it.

The reason I'm so happy with this one regardless is that even with it's illuminating faults, it's a good starting-point.

Up-myself, I did warn you. I had friends over for a "viewing" on Wednesday and they make me feel lucky and love the world. Their enthusiasm plus my relief equals a temporary confidence that'll either change or worsen according to my subject's reaction when she sees the portrait. I think I'll cry either way, because she's a close friend. Painting her makes me emotional.

Anyway, in this moment I'm happy. I guess if your work doesn't measure up to your own expectations, it means you don't have enough skill to justify the obsession. I may only have beginner-skill, but it's there. My happiness is of the thank-fuck variety.

Okay, enough. I left the real world lying around here somewhere and now have to re-enter it. But not for too long; I want the euphoria of that involved-project-headspace back. Within a day or two my confidence will slip away, but confidence is irrelevant when you're just doing what ya gotta do. I know what I want, now. 'Bout time.

Sunday, 27th January, 2007.

Ego Stroking and Beyond

Lucky I didn't write this entry yesterday, because I was floating on air and it would've been full of intolerable syrup. I guess Portrait Subject's reaction was the finishing touch. Moved to tears, yes; called it beautiful, yes; pandered to my temporary up-myself-ness with many comments (such as *'It's an honour to know you'*), yes (that one's my favourite). Funny how working on something like that becomes a huge event in your life, and reactions that meet the intensity of your own exhausted emotions inflate the magnitude of the whole thing.

So that was yesterday, lots of inflated magnitude. And time to relax – I can't even remember the last time I did something quiet and unhurried. After she'd gone I put on a sun hat and light shawl, and took myself off to one of my favourite cafes to sit alone with the Saturday paper and a hot chocolate, and enjoy being in the heat.

I *love* summer.

I feel outrageously content. Something important has fallen into place. And now that the magnitude is deflating I'm back to thinking about work and what I'm going to do next. Which is humbling, because it means going right back to Square One, all of the floating replaced by labour-intensive weeks and long-winded bouts of uncertainty. Art-making is the nicest knocking-about you could ever give yourself.

But first, let's think about people. I like them again. Love them, in fact. Suddenly they're not demanding pains-in-arses anymore. There are still a few I'm-in-troubles I have to face, because of all the phone calls and days-out that I promised and never delivered (I meant well). I deserve the reprimands, so I'll just grin and bear it. They must be so sick of my apologies, but I don't feel guilty anymore. Feeling this good now makes it all worth it.

————

Monday, 28th January, 2007.

Weird-Arse Housewifery and An Inappropriate Mind-Fuck

Men really are shits, aren't they. (Deliberate lack of question mark.) (No offence.) Although I have to be careful saying that, because my friendship with Friend Boy A has made me quite fond of the gender (and all of its glaring shortcomings).

So here we go; writing this out is an attempt to make sense of it.

Ex-H has been here for a few days now, and we're getting along well despite his apparent belief in my endearing inferiority. We're tired because we were both up before the sun, committing hard labour upon our hillside garden. This is a hillside that you struggle to climb up and down if you happen to be removing about a million dead branches in an overdue tip-run, involving a truck and an excessive amount of effort. (Honestly, who needs a gym – I should sell membership to my garden as a natural work-out venue.)

Amicable teamwork, that's us. So his attitude tonight is surprising. After the tip I wandered into the city to visit first Reformed Hippy, and then Friend Girl A. I had the nicest afternoon lolling about in cafes, completely forgetting that when Ex-H had wanted chicken for dinner last night I hadn't said '*Cook your own fucking chicken*', because I'm so graceful. I'd said instead '*I'll cook it for you tomorrow night*'. Meaning tonight, this being a kindness I was willing to endure, seeing as over the past few days he's been doing more gardening than I have, and he's my friend, and I wanted to do something nice for him. My halo glows.

I meant well, but as with everything I do my afternoon took longer than expected. That's fine with me because I love my friends, and I haven't seen them properly for so long I had no intention of cutting the visit short for the sake of cooking chicken. Plus I forgot. Plus I'd planned to see them long before I even knew he was going to be here. So I was surprised when I rang to check on Son, and Ex-H asked me *'What about the chicken?'*, at which point I was quite tempted to say *'Cook your own fucking chicken'* after all, because what was he waiting for? If the tables were turned I'd have started cooking without him.

Amused by the situation and too tired to wonder about how weird it is that a man I used to be married to was wanting me there to cook his dinner for him as though it's my duty, I went home to cook. And I remembered how much I hate cooking, especially cooking food I don't have enough appetite to eat. And yes, wondering why he hadn't cooked the meal himself made me hack a little bit harder at the meat, but I cooked like a good little woman. HALO STILL GLOWING.

Then I sat at the table with my men and assorted houseguests, but all I had myself was a glass of pineapple juice, because I wasn't hungry. It was fun. I had a laugh with the boys and waited with my best manners until Ex-H had finished eating before I left the table.

The weird thing is that I heard Ex-H doing the dishes I'd left soaking in the sink (I'd already washed everything but the pots n' pans), so I went upstairs and hugged him and said *thankyou*, thinking it was very sweet of him. That's when I found out he was actually pissed off.

I asked him why he was grumpy. He said that I'd ruined the evening by not coming home to cook before 8 o'clock, and then by not eating, and then implied that I was slovenly for not cleaning the pots (stating that he had to do them because *'no-one else would'*), even though it was quite obvious that I was intending to return to finish them after a decent amount of soaking time had passed.

I have to say, I love him to bits, but his household martyrdom is getting on my nerves. He seems to find guilt-tripping an effective way of asserting his superiority. Which is stupid, because I'd grant him superiority for free if he'd just stop being such a shit.

I dunno. It seemed funny a day ago, but after tonight his attitude seems almost sinister. Is he trying to control me again? Why not just enjoy me? I'm very enjoyable [!] and give him no reason to do anything less than smile all day long, because he encounters pure friendliness when he's here. I don't understand. He does so many nice things for me he must like me at least a little bit, so why the meanness? Really, if he was planning on staying here any longer I'd probably have to kick him out a third time. I swear, officer, he *made* me be a bitch.

I much prefer it when he's being my friend.

I'm uncomfortable with him being here tonight, not just because I hate the unnecessary negativity, but I find his expectations disturbing. Dunno, dunno. I welcome him here, but he wasn't invited, so why does he want me to cancel all of my other plans as though he's my guest?

There I was feeling friend-love for him. I'm so dumb. Now all I feel is disappointed. And maybe hurt.

———

Or...

Maybe I'm accidentally a bitch? Maybe he just wanted to have a nice evening meal with us, and was hurt that I didn't realise this? Even though if he wanted me to realise, he should have told me what he wanted? Then I could have told him my other plans get priority, '*Don't wait up for me*', et cetera.

Technically, did I let him down the same way I seem to keep letting everybody down these days? He made the salad, by the way. And he really does do a lot of nice things for me and the kids.

What's a bit of cooked chicken between friends? It was the least I could do. That I always seem to do the least is perhaps the problem, but I really do mean well.

Anyway, the criticism about the dishes was mean. Try as I may to find a way to blame it on myself, there's no getting around that. The bright side is that even though he did the dishes to be mean to me, it meant I didn't have to do them, and not-doing dishes is one of my favourite hobbies.

If only people were mean like that more often.

———

February 2008

Friday, 1ˢᵗ February, 2008.

Blast from Past

The good news is that Friend Who Does Nothing has wrinkles. Not many, but her skin looks tired just like the rest of our skins, probably because she's an outdoorsy type and tanned to pre-leather stage. The first thing I did when she was distracted for five minutes was text another old friend to say *'Wrinkles! She has wrinkles!!'* (I repeat – I'm happy to grow old gracefully, just as long as everybody I know grows old gracefully with me).

I half wanted to see her, but I half wanted to turn her away because I was busy. Well I *was* busy – wasn't I busy? Plus I was (by necessity) a bit dismissive. Which means I was almost a bitch again, and had to learn the don't-be-a-bitch lesson for about the millionth time.

It's just that Friend Who Does Nothing really does do nothing. I found this out when I contacted her a couple of years ago for a "what have you been up to" phone call. My list of things-done was very long, and her list was empty. She didn't work, didn't study, didn't do her art, didn't see movies, didn't visit family, and many non-et-ceteras to that. She lived with her boyfriend in Sydney and he was earning enough for her to be a kept woman. Still does.

'But what do you do all day?' I asked her, and she said *'Well, I go to the beach and blade around...'.*

That's a lotta long years of nothing. I decided then that we had nothing left in common. When visiting Sydney I would happily have run into her if I'd run into her, but would probably have been suffocated by an empty feeling if I'd gone to stay at her place. I can't even imagine doing nothing – I can't think of anything worse.

That's how dumb I am. I know her better than that, which makes me twice as dumb. When she said she wanted to come and stay here, for a visit, I was dreading it. Not because I don't love her, but because I didn't want to be sucked into The Nothing. I still guard my time like a bulldog, and when you're guarding your time people who are never busy are your worst enemy. Plus she'd chosen a *really* busy night. Plus, when I suggested we wait until we could get all of our friends together, she said she just wanted to see me. No conversational back up for when the nothingness took over.

Twice as dumb? Try a hundred-fold.

When I first saw her in my rear-vision mirror I couldn't stop smiling because she was decked out in her blading gear, and she was so *her* I nearly screamed. I've changed my mind about people who do nothing – they're wonderful and *I'm* my own worst enemy. This is exactly why I should hate my life; the things I miss out on because I can't squeeze them in just happen to be the best things.

She's amazing, and now that she's gone I miss her. More than that, I can't wait to see her again. She fills her nothing with so many things, and none of it's ponderous or serious. She just drifts through life via physical experience and it's gorgeous. All of that going-to-the-beach she does involves snorkelling and foraging, and making things out of what she finds. When she tells me about being under the water, and the not-well-known places in Sydney, it's like I'm there. She's more than amazing, and when she's not talking to a human she talks to herself ALL THE TIME. Next time my friends remark on how much I talk, I'm going to introduce them to her and they'll think I'm a complete mouse.

I feel very happy now, having learnt my don't-be-presumptuous lesson. I'm never going to dismiss anybody again. And no more being overly cerebral – I need to go snorkelling. She taught me how to snorkel at the Black Rock pier when we were teenagers. She's good for me. She is *life*.

So; I should probably burn books and go running naked into the wilderness, but it might be enough to worship the people I love, and visit them with enthusiasm in the future, instead of dreading being dragged away from my own garbagey busy-ness. Thank you, Friend Who Does Nothing – what a wonderful residue to have left behind in my life.

___

Conversely...

...it's safe to say I taught Friend Who Does Nothing *nothing*. Instead I left two bad impressions.

Firstly, I'm trying not to bond with First-Born's kitten. This is extremely difficult, but I've insisted that First-Born feed the thing and keep it with them as much as possible. When First-Born goes to their partner's house, they take Kitten with them. Kitten's sister lives there; when they're reunited it's a truly joyous thing to behold.

I never call Kitten by her real name. I will NOT bond with her. We have three other cats; my loyalty is to them. But the main reason is that First-Born's been accusing me of stealing Kitten's affection from them since they brought her home (against my ineffectual wishes). For the sake of First-Born's emotional security, I must not *steal their cat*. (Artist/writer = works quietly all day = cat-magnet.)

Friend Who Does Nothing LOVED kitten and played and played with her. My [disciplined] failure to interact with Small Creature might have left Friend WDN thinking I'm cold-hearted.

Secondly, I had to spend the morning wrapping the portrait, hiring a truck, and delivering it to an art depot (busy!). That meant having to drop her at the station in a mad rush. As though she's not important enough for me to put my roller skates on and roll around the local streets with. (So much for learning a better way to be.)

___

Saturday, 2nd February, 2008.

Off Target

I'm talking about Target stores and yes, they're *off*. This afternoon I discovered a giant sign posted onto the wall outside the local store – I assume it's at every store – and it's nothing short of vulgar. It says:

> *Every Australian has the right to look good and feel good about how they dress and live.*

Do they really? Beyond the shallowness of the statement, let's get to the crux of the matter here; propagation of an obscene sense-of-entitlement. Most items sold in department stores are affordable by so-called *deserving* Australians because they're produced off-shore in sweat shops by low or underpaid workers. Who the fuck are they trying to kid? (Ah; the willing many who don't give a flying fuck about where things come from.)

Obviously I'm angry. It's bad enough that we ride smoothly on the desperation of other people, but to declare it's our *right* to do so is blatantly selfish. Are we so special? We're a selfish country full of citizens who collectively protect their own ignorance in order to continue benefiting from corporate exploitation of other nations, is what we are. Why on earth would a store attempt to foster and perpetuate such a revolting notion of personal merit?

The buck stops here. There. It's a shock to be undertaking the odious task of shopping and then have your sense of morality offended in such a big way. I feel like I've just been called to battle. I have a good grip on the theories behind capitalism, false-consciousness and notions that challenge the way false-consciousness is used to justify abhorrent behaviour, but I don't know how to use that knowledge/theory in a practical way. (This is what my thesis is/was about). Other than to stamp my feet. I'M STAMPING MY FEET NOW!

How do you educate people when this kind of attitude is so rampant? One little statement posted onto a wall in whopping big text, and the society we live in just got uglier.

———

Thursday, 7th February, 2008.

Hiatus

I have a crick in my neck because there's a kitten sleeping across my shoulders, and some stupid genetically programmed nurturing instinct doesn't allow me to put it down and walk away. I think this is what it'll be like when I have grandchildren. Or maybe worse – you can arrange for your grandchildren to be babysat elsewhere. Shove them into a crèche or lock them in a cupboard or something. But they don't make crèches for grandkittens.

I painted a whole undercoat onto a large canvas with her sleeping across my neck. And it's taken me about an hour longer to get into my workroom every day this week, because I can't take her in there with

160

me, and can't stand to hear her lonely mewling at the door. It's like I have SUCKER tattooed across my forehead, in cat language.

Anyway that's probably a good thing, because my current canvas is hideous. Being stuck here under a sleeping kitten means not having to look at my own cruddy work. I hate this part, where you get the undercoat on but have to wait for it to dry before you can start on the second layer and make it vaguely presentable. I look at it and shudder.

Funny, it seemed like such an important thing to do at the time, and now it seems like indulgent rubbish.

This kitten is so cute. How am I going to get back to work now?

Erasure vs Vanity

The best thing I've done since finishing my last painting = I painted over some old half-finished works. Apart from saving me hundreds of dollars on buying new canvases, it means I've erased the worst parts of my old way of painting. It took courage, actually, but felt good. Now I want to paint over everything. I would have painted over some old finished ones, but I had a photographer document some work last week and while he snapped pictures of one of them I made the mistake of telling him my plan. He said *'That's a shame, it's really pretty'*.

I don't really do pretty, but it made me put it back where it came from. I'll do that one when poverty gets so bad my desperation for canvases makes painting over it a necessity.

Saturday, 9th February, 2008.

And Then There Were None...

I love being home on Saturday night. Weekends are for folks who have weeks that need ending. Obviously I don't work hard enough for that.

In keeping with my now repetitive routine (fun for me, boring for everybody else), I've worked on a canvas all day. One small break at my favourite café again for some quiet with the Saturday paper. I needed to smell people. Saturday café people smell so nice.

Apart from that, painting. Which means I'm still stuck in my underpainting funk, but getting closer to emerging with something

decent to show for my efforts. (Or not.) But anyway I have a worse
funk to deal with – I've run out of Robin Hobb.

I know! Disaster. And I had such a good stash of her. When I
finished my last painting I was one book short of finishing *The Liveship
Traders* on audio, and it had me on the edge of my seat. Every single
chapter was tantalising, and combined with the act of painting my days
were a complete trip. So I waited until I was well into the painting stage
of this one (and past the planning, which takes too much think-work
to make audio books acceptable in the background) before starting the
third *Liveship* book.

A proclamation: Robin Hobb is the best storyteller ever. She's
good on the page and she's even better on audio, because the human
brain is so wonderful you can paint using one cerebral lobe, and
concentrate just as fully on the story you're being told with another.

I was breathless by the time it was finished, and then bereft.
Because what can live up to that kind of excitement? Poor old Haruki
Murakami. Desperate for more story I started listening to *Norwegian
Wood* today, and it was dead boring after Robin Hobb. Not Haruki's
fault – it's my fault. I shouldn't have switched genres so abruptly (RH
is Fantasy). But I gave it a go and after a few hours it started to grow on
me. I might even be liking it.

Still, I have a feeling I'll have to go back to Robin. When I read
the *Farseer* and *Tawny Man* trilogies years ago I did so in book form,
but I have them on audio. Seeing as her books are about 30 hours long
they'll keep me going for a long time. And there I was laughing at Son
for reading them twice in one year. He's having the same problem I'm
having – the next book you read (after ROBIN HOBB) has to be a killer
to break your habit. The woman is pure crack.

———

Still Saturday.

Just Go, Already

I'm such a suck I'm going to miss him. Eventually. Not yet, though.
My consistent advice to Ex-H is that he shouldn't spend more than a
couple of days at a time here, because he doesn't tolerate family life.
But he keeps coming back, even though his patience has run out.

I said it again over a week ago. I bit my tongue when he made some petty insult that made my blood boil, and welcomed him in anyway. I suspected he was gonna blow.

I wanted to go to bed early that night, but was being thoughtful. I was also shit-scared, knowing that if I went to bed too early he'd complain. The rule is – and he knew this in advance – that if he stays here he goes to bed when I go to bed, so that he doesn't keep me awake. I get up early and nothing-but-nothing is allowed to interrupt my routine when I 'm working on a project. That's just the way it is – I'm a mother, time is gold.

If he lived here a more flexible routine would be negotiated by consenting adults. This isn't me being bossy, I'm trying to say. When he lets me know in advance that he wants to stay over and stay up late, I usually say yes. So I decided to have a word with him, because you don't just turn up at somebody's home and tell them to shove their routine up their arse if it doesn't suit you.

The thoughtfulness = I waited until 10:10 pm before giving him the wind-up. I said *'I'm going to bed in a few minutes'*, in a friendly way. He didn't budge. He was sitting at the table reading the *Green Guide,* so I went off to get ready for bed, wondering why the fuck he wasn't making a move. At 10:50 I went upstairs again and asked if he could please go to bed, because I was knackered and ready to fall asleep on the spot. He said *no.* He said he was going to finish reading the *Green Guide* for however long that took.

A stand off. A childish battle of wills, just like a teenager. Even First-Born has gotten over the bedtime crap.

I'll interrupt myself here to consider his perspective, because I feel sorry for him. We (the kids and I) are chaotic, messy, intense. I can see why he isn't happy being among us. He's calm, controlled, austere. Wants to live peacefully. I respect that. But this is why we're separated. I live here, I don't have the means to up and leave to escape his moods, when his routines are imposed on the household. He doesn't live here, so the onus is on him not to impose an impossible standard upon us.

Anyway. I said *'What the...?'* and he started an argument about my [alleged] selfishness. He said unkind things about how I do everything wrong (same things he said when I kicked him out last year after he'd overstayed his welcome). He said things – word for word – that First-Born used to say when they were being rebellious.

So I was firm with him. Pointed out that I *never* speak to him like that, resorting to insults and character disparagement. The attack was unwarranted. I reminded him that owning half the house doesn't entitle him to take over or judge us; that he knows the rules, and could he kindly oblige without causing agitation before sleep.

When he does this very deliberate sort of thing it's clear he has unresolved issues, that he's arrived with an agenda and a goal, and that is to assert authority. He doesn't realise that this is inappropriate.

I'm not being flippant when I say he frightens me a little. He wants the friendly contact – which is good – but hates the parts of me he can't control. When he insults me for things other people like, I know he's trying to make me feel like shit. I don't understand why. He doesn't want us anyway; how can he love what he hates so much?

Naturally he waited until I went to bed before he stormed out and drove off into the sunset, never to be seen again.

He'd made a comment a few days before about us being lucky that he *wasn't the type to bump himself off and take everybody with him*. I'd laughed and batted him on the arm, saying *'That's horrible – don't even joke about it'*.

He was trying to illustrate how much suffering I've caused him, chosing that particular hypothetical scenario to describe extremes of unhappiness he can't otherwise express. He wants me to understand how serious this feeling he has inside is. And I *do* understand; we were good together, until family life became a nightmare for him. *I* became a nightmare for him. Being around me is *still* a nightmare for him. I don't pretend to be so perfect that I'm not a nightmare to him or anybody. But, do men realise when they say something like this that it comes across as a threat? Saying that I'm *lucky he didn't do that* implies that it was on the cards, so I should be careful not to upset him?

Is he saying that's what he thinks we deserve?

I removed myself from his life to protect us all from having to endure these bad feelings. I try to keep him in our lives, but he needs to go. For a long time this time. Find himself a girlfriend and come back when he has us out of his system.

His words surprised me, probably because he's such a gentle man. And intelligent. And funny. And my friend, I thought. How sad that he can't just laugh [affectionately] at our differences, say *phew, we escaped each other*, and think *nice* things.

———

Here We Go Again

When I was watching *So You Think You Can Dance* I leapt about the couch, gesticulating wildly and calling out '*Oh come on*' to the judges. Like a bogan barracking for the footy.

My inner-bogan should be okay with the way my sometimes-bogan First-Born speaks, but I'm not. Tonight I'm [allegedly] the C-word. I haven't been the C-word in such a long time. Also I'm [allegedly] pathetic and [allegedly] the worst mother in the world, but it's when they use the C-word that my body stiffens and I think *could you please not?* Anyway, it's funny how I can be travelling through day after day so happily, just working away and keeping to myself, then First-Born gets into the car when I pick them up and starts hurling insults and suddenly I'm sitting here like a vegetable, unable to think. It's like they and Ex-H have teamed up, both criticising me for these things:

Writing; Painting; Drawing; Studying.

It's possibly what upsets me most, that I really am happy being left alone to do things that are quiet, industrious and ultimately harmless, but get yelled at when I least expect it. It's like sneaking up behind a grazing rabbit and yelling out *BOO!*

The problem is First-Born's personality is so *big*, their voice so *booming*. On one hand I'm getting plenty of love thrown my way on a daily basis, because I have sweet people in my life. On the other hand, these two people have direct access to my equilibrium and are quite prepared to crush it. And I'm trapped in a house with one of them. All the love in the world doesn't make that any easier.

What do they want me to do? Never draw again? Never read? Never write? It's not like I'm sitting on my arse all day drinking beer and dragging on a bong. It's cruel picking on things I can't change. Like saying *what you are doesn't suit us: curl up and die.*

Same old same old, I guess the school year has started. Getting my timetable this week and dreading things getting hectic. Especially if First-Born's doing this again. Makes me feel so tired.

I should say something nice about Ex-G-Not-G, because I sent her a birthday text with a don't-reply instruction tacked on, but she replied anyway. She made me think of a dog wagging its tail at me, all stupid and friendly, which was kinda cute. A long text full of conversational details, squeezing a whole chunk of friendliness into one short breath. She's okay, at a safe distance. I'm sure she sucks close up.

———

The narrator of *Norwegian Wood* does women's voices so well. I'm loving it now. Which is a pity, because it's nearly finished. Still, philosophy thinly disguised as fiction is probably good in small doses. Worried at this stage about how depression/mental instability is presented (deliberately or inadvertently) as an admirable symptom of deep thinking. Haruki's angle on that will be clearer when the novel concludes, I guess.

———

Tuesday, 19th February, 2008.

Please Turn Down the Volume

Life's gotten so loud I can't find a bit of quiet anywhere. I'm feeling the effects of the weekend, when I said *yes* to Son inviting a handful of friends over to sleep in tents down on the back lawn. I wasn't even tempted to say no, because tents are outdoorsy and outdoorsy is a good thing to encourage in adolescent computer-game addicts.

Clearly I forgot how much adolescent boys smell. Worse – when Son's Annoying Friend arrived he asked me if there was somewhere safe to put his medicine. I pointed to the bench by the phone, and then later looked at it casually, not even curious, more just because it was there. I was horrified to see that one of the boxes contained an ointment for toenail fungal infection, and the other a drug that I later discovered (gawd bless Google) was for tinea and nail infections.

Fuck! Keep your diseased feet out of my house, you flea-bitten little... *thing*. He kept his socks on, even though it was hot, but was that enough? I don't know, that kind of thing makes me paranoid. I had this impulse to disinfect EVERYTHING, but I resisted. For once I was happy that you can rely on boys not showering, because it means he didn't go barefoot in our shower.

It's a bit weird, anyway, that a kid leaves his medicine where you can see it, as though he shouldn't be embarrassed by his fungussy feet. Not all mothers are nurturing and understanding of these things. Apparently. Some of them are easily grossed out. Shouldn't his mother get his feet amputated, or something?

Double anyway, it gets worse. He took his fungus-infested feet out onto the neighbour's trampoline before 8 am on a Sunday morning. To my horror. I staggered to my window, after three hours of sleep (was up painting until a million o'clock), to call out '*Too early!*'.

Instead of translating that effectively as '*Go back to bed*', he banged bamboo sticks together to wake the other boys, and then they were knocking on the locked front door [mwahahaha] to come inside. They gave up when I didn't answer, went away, then came back. Eventually they just kept knocking. What's the point of sleeping in a tent if you want to come inside so early?

So, no rest. So busy. So much to think and no time to write it all down. Would love a day alone, but that's not gonna happen. First-Born split up with their partner, which is very mature of them and I'm kinda proud. They cry so loudly and unabashedly all over the house it's bizarre. I'm a quiet cry-er, I don't know how I bred somebody so vocal. I could hire them out for mourning. Point being, the end of quiet as we know it. No more weekends off. Everything's going to be really weird (in a good way) for a while, I think.

Thursday, 21st February, 2008.

Airing the Dirty Linen

I just committed bathroom-rage. Which is funny in itself, because I wasn't even angry, I was just disappointed.

I was going to wind down by writing about books, but all I can think about is how good it feels to be throwing things again. Throwing things when overly stressed is satisfying, especially if they break. If I was teaching at Parenting School, it's the first lesson I'd pass on.

No winding down for me tonight. This whole First-Born-leaving-their-partner isn't gonna work for me. It means they're going to be home all week, and ALL WEEKEND, EVERY WEEKEND.

How's it going so far? My maternal instinct runneth dry. I may love them, but I'm realistic enough to want to send them to boot camp. I can ignore teenage rudeness to a certain point. I've let a lot of it slide this week because the break-up might be making them tetchy, but biting my tongue is getting difficult.

Also, they've stayed home from school for two days so far. Also, non-co-operation. Also, et cetera et cetera. We have to go through a period of adjustment, is all. Re-learn how to survive each other. In the meantime, things happen, I throw things. End of story.

Thought I should let it be known that I'm no saint.

———

Wee Medium-Sized Hours

One of those nights where you're really tired and want to go to bed something like three hours ago, but you can't because your teenager is having a standoff upstairs and you can't be fagged going up there to fight it out. So you let your brain go vegetable and start googling people you know, because anything less than inane activity won't do, and then you realise that if you can google them then they can google you, so you google yourself to see what they'd find.

I get less hits than I used to, and that's only with my full name. One of them's a me in LA; same name, same age, and is a writer (except, she has a proper job). She's quite a suck. Is it unkind to say I'd rather be less successful than be so big a suck? (Got my wish there.)

As I sit here passing time while the teenage angst dies out in favour of sleep, I'll think about good things.

First good thing: this week I finished another large portrait. A large head and shoulder image of Son. It does what I wanted it to do, so teenage arguments aside, I'm feeling good. And dazed.

Second good thing: *Medium* was on tonight. I love it because I get to watch She and He being married, and they're my favourite married people to watch. All of those harmless bed scenes with their bodies overdressed in elaborate pyjamas, and pecks on cheeks n' such. I think I like watching people sleep.

So ends my list of good things, and so ends my day, with no noise from upstairs = teenagers are in bed = finally, I can go to sleep.

Monday, 25ᵗʰ February, 2008.

Face-Ache

I don't know if I was sitting with my head in my hands at the doctor's because I'm a woebegone diseased old thing, or because I was desolate, having forgotten to bring my mobile phone, my pen, my notebook or something to read.

That's because pain drives you to distraction. I had to do *nothing*; it was excruciating. I eyed the National Geographics with longing, but you never know who's touched them with their phlegm-smeared fingers. It's bad enough signing things with somebody else's pen. Gawd knows what people cough up onto stationary at a doctor's surgery.

Anyway I'm here both to praise a book and to extract sympathy, because I'm experiencing what we refer to in patient circles as *fucking agony*. My chipped tooth must have an exposed root, because the whole right side of my face is killing me (i.e. infection).

That was my weekend; a bit of parental sadness (understatement), a bit of pain (understatement), and a lot of literary/artistic swooning (understatement). Sometimes the euphoria of art makes me suspect I'm half dipsy. The light in your brain = sublime inspiration, or the result of a blow to the head with a blunt object?

It's like I have a split personality merging into one, somehow managing this year to work on books and art at the same time. That's been my struggle for the past – what? Eight years? Something like that. It's deeply personal and I'm floating around dazed by the niceness of it all. A feeling you wish was caused by a drug so that you could give it to other people.

Now that I'm getting worse at multi-tasking than ever before (I especially suck at parenting when I'm trying to do art), I've broken my focus down to three projects this year. On top of that, I'm letting myself read. At first just on the train, but that wasn't enough so over the weekend, for the first time in I don't know how long, I did little other than sit on my arse and read another book.

I almost hated *What Was Lost* by Catherine O'Flynn. The initial narrator shit me up the wall, not quite convincing as a child voice. I generously persisted because I was eager to get to the social commentary aspect, focused on the microcosm of a shopping centre, and it was so worth it. A beautiful book. The sort of book you hope gets read by a lot of people so that it doesn't end up only preaching to the converted (the converted being anybody who laments the empty nature of life within consumer-driven society). Once she hits adult-narrator's-voice she takes off and her observations made me wilt. Definitely a writer I could fall in love with.

Although, like Haruki Murakami, she writes characters whose lives are peopled by very few... um, people. It strikes me as odd, and yet also probable and therefore sad. But then, maybe having a life not-too-full of people wouldn't be so bad. An interesting consideration either way.

After that, in the sunken couch of my café on Saturday, I started reading Geraldine Brooks' *People of the Book,* hence my trance-like state all weekend. (Well, that and the painkillers.) The kind of trance you go into before doing a lot of hard work. Books, art and medieval history, right up my alley, and so beautifully written I'm the proverbial pig proverbially wallowing in the proverbial mud.

Remind me not to go too long without reading ever, ever again.

———

March 2008

Woe etc.

There I was going about my business, occupied by interesting things, and suddenly I was hit with this overwhelming feeling of pointlessness. Where the fuck did that come from? It's revoltingly self-indulgent to feel this bad, so I'm trying to get a grip. But I guess it was bound to happen; I can't pretend to be useful forever.

I think it's partly the clean and slightly perfumed smell of Ex-H's car upholstery. Driving his car (which I now have in my evil clutches because he's started his new job and is based in Perth, leaving the remnants of his old life here with me until he returns, which he will do periodically so don't get too comfortable) reminds me of what it feels like to be secure. Maybe even looked-after. That I don't feel that way too often is a no-brainer.

Solution: breathe through mouth and stop smelling car.

Also it's this stupid multi-tasking thing. I can't do it. I'm a disgrace to womanhood. I thought I could reduce my focus to two projects, but there are so many other subsidiary projects and I piss-fart around them, not knowing how to divide my attention between one thing and another. Before I know it I'm taking more time to do less work than ever, and there you go: useless.

Failure Day happened last week, notable for the official not-handing-in of my revised thesis. I had a choice: finish the revision, or paint. Doing those paintings over summer changed everything for me, so I'm not about to regret my decision.

Maybe I'll go back to it later, maybe I won't.

Also last week, I had an idea for a short story that accidentally became an idea for a novel that I know I have to write soon. At first I was excited because it hasn't happened in a while, but now I feel deflated because it's just one more thing I can't fit in. The research alone will be too much.

I've somehow got myself believing that because I can't do *everything,* I can't do *anything.* A million years of studying and the only thing I've learnt = my limitations. And now I have to make decisions. Have I ever mentioned how much I suck at *that*?

———

Survivor

I'm writing this today because I *can,* because I'm *alive,* despite having travelled in a car with Kitchen Nazi Friend during the week. I know I've mentioned her road rage before, probably somewhere inside a list of all her other rages. I realise [again] that I mostly experience it when she directs it towards other cars while *I'm* driving. And that it's so much worse when *she's* the one behind the wheel.

She offered to help me take my paintings in to school (show and tell) with her tank-ish four-wheel drive, and I delayed saying yes because I feel guilty for needing help.

For the friends who occasionally ask me why I remain friends with somebody so aggressive, I have to say she's the sweetest person. When I eventually said *yes please* to her offer she was thrilled, saying she wanted to do it so that she could see another part of my life, because she loves spending time with me and wants to get to know me better. In fact she said she loves me (don't we all) and the usual head-inflating stuff (such as how beautiful I am), and it's very humbling. I'm not *that* good. It's weird being so loved and respected by somebody who scares the shit out of me.

Although, to get this fear into perspective, I'm not scared of telling her what I think, and if she's doing something "wrong" I'll be honest with her in a way I guess other people might avoid, because she bites. I mean I'm scared because you can spontaneously find yourself in trouble for something you either did or did not do, depending on her mood. I never *am* in trouble with her (although I sometimes should be), but the way she is with other people makes me worry that she's gonna one day decide [discover] I'm not as nice as she says I am, and *then* bite. Or maybe she just rattles my bones. As nice as she can be, it's terrifying sitting next to her in the tank while she weaves in and out of traffic at full speed, shouting abuses at just about every car we pass.

One poor woman driving ahead of us got a blasting through a closed window when we caught up to her at the lights. Not only was Kitchen Nazi Friend screaming and gesticulating wildly, she made shooting-pistol motions with fingers to her temple. I was shocked.

Despite this, she's so sweet on the inside and has an innocent enthusiasm that's kinda touching. I don't think she realises what she's doing, like a crocodile who occasionally eats a human being without knowing that eating people is bad manners. So I can't really hate her for it. I just need to not-be around her when she's hungry. And as long as I hold my breath and scrunch up my face while I'm sitting in the car with her, I'll be okay. If I allow five minutes to stop shaking when we reach our destination.

Which I'll do because I have to get my paintings back, and she's offered to help. (Is it too late to stop being an atheist and start praying?) I really need to stop working large-scale. Or just get rich so I can buy myself a van.

———

Monday Night, 10th March, 2008.

silencio, per favore

Deep breathing and soaking in some quiet before bed is just what the doctor ordered. Because nothing to be alarmed about, but I'm probably *dying*. This is a self-diagnosis job; it doesn't take a genius to work out that I'm very stressed. Even though I'm outwardly calm. It's just that waking up with an irregular heart beat – a bit of hopping and skipping where there shouldn't be hopping and skipping – has me wondering what's going on inside. An indicator that me nerves are frazzled, happening more often now.

Well go figure. After two weeks of utopian parenting during which some alien freak invaded my child's body and made them behave with outrageous normality, First-Born is back with a vengeance. So a quiet minute before bed probably *isn't* what the doctor ordered; any self-respecting doctor would order me to fuck quiet moments and just *run away from home*.

Friday morning was the worst because I wasn't expecting it after all the niceness. Then with stupid optimism I thought they'd be fine when they got back from Ex-Wife's on Sunday, but no. Not.

I hate to admit it, but I let them do things I don't want them to do just so they'll leave. They say they want to go somewhere and if I say *no*, they say they're going anyway, so I drive them to the station (aiding and abetting), letting them get away with disobedience just so that I can get a few hours of peace.

All the while I wander around feeling otherwise happy, except for the crying, which I don't even realise I'm doing until I notice tears streaming down my face. Then I think '*Wow, am I crying? Isn't that funny!*', but of course it isn't.

Crying's stupid, especially repressed crying. So I've made an executive decision to stay home tomorrow and draw in close to silence while the kids are at school. Healing, in a Band-Aid-on-brain-tumour kinda way.

Doesn't matter. A solution will present itself. In the meantime I'll just have to make life calm so that we can both survive when they're here. And see if I can get this over-zealous heartbeat caught on ECG while it's so frequent. I'm very healthy, so it's got me curious. Especially because it only happens when I'm stressed. Makes saying '*First-Born breaks my heart*' so much more theatrical.

Friday, 14th March, 2008.

Two Days to Get Through

In a minute I'll write about a book. So that I have something good to think about. But first, I'm in defeat-slash-recovery mode. I was wondering how to offload my troubles without whinging, wishing I could remember the nice things I wanted to write about, when First-Born stopped halfway down the stairs to inform me that they *do* respect their environment and they *do* respect this house and they're going to *prove* it, and then have their 16th birthday party here [!!!!]. They'll start by cleaning their bedroom, but they're doing it for *themself,* it has nothing to do with *me.*

I wish they'd decided to respect their environment more *before* damaging bits-of-house.

They're wrong about the birthday party. Little Sister warned me that they're planning a big one, and this evening they finally told me about it. I told them *no.* I said they could take their friends out to a restaurant, but not a party, because the last one was full of vomit and they left the mess for me to clean up.

There were words said. I tried to keep it calm by explaining that we don't live well, and can't invite anybody into this. No parties. No nothing until we get it right.

A plea. A verbal battering. And so on, and so on, and so on.

At least I had my day of drawing on Tuesday. It was nice. If I can get some mind over matter happening I can shut everything out and draw again tomorrow. But lately I think of my friends and their lovely lives with their loving children, and I look at my own and wonder if I'm poison and don't deserve to be around them. If I shouldn't be going to school, because try as I may I have something always pulling me back.

So many things I love doing, but when First-Born accuses me of uselessness I think they're right. Look at me sitting here recovering while other people are out in the world, being politically active, being in love n' such. Where are my biological imperatives?

———

Poor Ex-Husband. He does so much for us, and in return he gets his half-house broken. I'm glad he's in Perth now. He's glad he's in Perth now. I hope he doesn't come back for a while, just so that he doesn't have to walk into this.

———

Still Friday.

About That Book.

I've been reading *Harpoon* by Andrew Darby and it has my head spinning. History of whaling: fascinating, distressing, thought provoking. Will change your life. Will make you hate human beings. Read it.

A Really Good Thing
Some shocks are pleasant. During an art theory lecture this week the lecturer started reading from *Ulysses,* and as soon as I heard '*that rusty boot*' it was like falling in love again (with James Joyce, not the lecturer). I sat there in rapture and if anybody had seen inside my head I'd have been very embarrassed. It's intellectual sex, that is. Another part of myself that I'd beaten back with a stick = suddenly wide awake and hungry for it (reading, not sex).

After studying Joyce I stopped reading him because he messes with my writing voice. That was a million years ago. Now I don't mind being messed with. Just for a bit, just to feel that way again.

How do you forget something you loved so much? (And now that I've been reunited, how do I squeeze something so monumental back into my little, tight-fitting life?)

Interesting
First-Born choosing to go to school so that they could sit a Literature essay test.

Interim report: perfect grades for Philosophy.

They've already told me they love Philosophy, sticking it to the xtians. My subjects, my field; their future, my present. As much as they don't want to be me, they're going to be me. A bigger, better version. Mind's awake, there's no escaping it now.

Sunday, 16th March, 2008.

You Say Something? *What?*
It's hard to type when you have Alannah Myles singing *Black Velvet* on the headphones. I HAVE TO SHOUT THIS JUST TO HEAR MYSELF THINK. I'm trying not to wear ABBA out so I'm recharging my iPod for a while.

Headphones are, as planned, my new strategy. I'm giving up parenting for good, shutting them out by wearing headphones when they're home. My brilliant idea is that I provide food and bus fares, maybe drive them to the bus in the mornings, and beyond that they're on their own. With headphones, I needn't speak to them again until they've grown up. How many years?

It's working already. No work done this weekend, but I cleaned out the garage and laundry and pretty much everything else.

I have a swatch of colour on sample paper that keeps catching my eye when I walk into this room. That swatch is my next drawing. I started this morning but couldn't continue. Tomorrow am wagging school and damn the consequences. I'm staying home to draw.

Elvis loved *his* mother, by the way.

———

Also...

I'm itching to get my canvas stretched so that I can start the next portrait. Got my references sorted yesterday, what with Kitchen Nazi coming to pick up her first son and her second son being my next subject. I took a lot of photos. I'd love to paint him from life, and will keep observing his features casually when I see him, but I felt intrusive even taking photos. It made my skin crawl, because I know that I'll be scrutinising his face, invading his privacy.

It's just that he's so beautiful. The poor boy was willing but awkward in front of the camera. There I was telling him to relax and act natural and pretend I'm not there, while he listened to his mum telling him to smile, of all things. When I asked him to please not-smile he got plain old confused. What can ya do but keep talking and wait to catch him off guard?

I was showing Kitchen Nazi the photos later, pointing to the ones I want to work with, and she kept telling me to use the smiling ones. I now realise that painting your own son is easy, but painting somebody who belongs to somebody else comes with icky obligations. No-way no-how am I painting a cheesy image that might as well be a blown-up photograph. People are weird, the way they want sunshiny utopian images of their kids.

Don't they know that all kids are bastards? (Joking!)

Before sleep last night I looked through the photos, and without KN looking over my shoulder I was able to relax and see what it was that made me want to paint him. At that moment he stopped being a person, and became my object. There's something private about painting somebody's face that has everything to do with them and yet nothing at all. I love that vision, it's mesmerising and will be in my head for weeks now. So I'm off with the fairies for a while. Thank you, headphones.

Monday, 17th March, 2008.

Giving Up the Ghost

Of course, in theory it's easy to shut them out. In reality I'm so profoundly sad it's an effort to lift a water bottle to my mouth to drink. I can't walk it backwards. Let's call it an epiphany just to sound smart. The final realisation that I've failed. Not a temporary failure that you can fight your way through. That kind of failure is for amateurs. This is a thorough, permanent, something-died you-can't-revive it failure.

First-Born was always intense, but now everything's a battle, and I know I'm not going to win. There's no prize. I've lost them.

I've lost Son, too. Just by the wayside. He's the civilian casualty. I think we get along, but really I don't think he even likes me. An irrational thought, I'm aware of that, but it doesn't stop me thinking it. If I'm not home he calls me, so he must be aware of me. But we don't go on holidays together, or even day trips anymore. It's a struggle to get him to come anywhere with me, so we have very little shared social life. When I'm out with friends I'm the only one who doesn't always have her kids with her. Neither of them want to be involved. And why would they? What can I offer them – my company?

When I painted Son I was painting the last signs of his youth. It was an emotional experience, actually, and it's all there in his expression.

The sad thing is that people ask me what he thinks of it, expecting me to tell them he's proud or excited or even interested. The truth is he's hardly looked at it. I know he thinks I've done an okay job of it because he hasn't said otherwise. Even First-Born praised it. But that's all. My own kids don't care much about what I do or how I do it. We just exist in a dead house and I sadly have the memory of when it was alive. They used to draw with me and there were always people around. I miss the chickens. Little bits of life everywhere, when you have chickens.

It's just sad, is all. To have put so much love and optimistic energy into something so dead. It's a shock to suddenly see things as they are. What I want to know is, how does somebody who did all the right things still suck so much at making family life work?

This wallowing isn't getting my drawing done.

———

A Good Thing
Red Symons putting the sound of his front gate to music on ABC Radio this morning. Made me wake up smiling.

———

Tuesday, 18th March, 2008.

Brain Rot
Eighties' storytellers have a lot to answer for. I just watched *Transformers* with Son, and really, I need a bucket. Isn't it crazy to resolve to give up parenting and then do something as self-sacrificially parental as watching that movie? Where are my *balls?*

Not my fault, anyway, that they had a pupil-free day at school and he woke up asking to *'do something'*. When I realised he meant something other than computer games I was too stunned to remember to be heartless. He's too ace. I tried suggesting great things like kayaking or a bike ride, but in the end the options got whittled down to hiring a DVD. Universal forces and all that. Maybe we can work our way back up to kayaking some other time.

So now my brain 's empty. Worse than empty. Kinda soiled. You know – losing four work days in a row to debilitating woebegone maternal emotions, and then filling the void with crapola autobot fiction. I feel like washing my head out with soap.

On the bright side, Son watched a movie with me!! Without being forced!! Maybe things will be okay again after all.

––––

Cooking is for Masochists

The roast is in the oven and so far the only cooking injuries I've sustained are a cut into the tip of my finger and a burn to the elbow. It's annoying typing with a Band-Aid on, but considering my cooking injury history, this time I've come out on top.

I figured I could cook properly because I'm not getting much work done these days. Every day this week I've set myself the same two tasks, and every day have avoided them. (Well, I got half of one of them done.) The plus side to that being that I've instead gotten some novel research started. And some television watching. And today a trip to the city to see a printmaking exhibition that was CLOSED when it was supposed to be OPEN.

Doesn't matter, I suppose, because it was sunny. I'm less forgiving of my favourite café being closed on the way home. Café's should be like police stations and hospitals and just never take a day off.

Sweet thing = that a few times this week, when Son was offering me his cheek for his kiss goodnight, he hung around for a bit like he wanted to make sure I knew he really meant that offered cheek, and one night he even offered me his cheek *twice*. I think I'm allowed to call that affection.

Also, he at first turned aside when I went to hug him one evening, after I got home to find he'd cleaned the kitchen, then let me hug him properly, remembering that he didn't really want to turn away. Although he made it clear that he didn't clean the kitchen for me; it was because of my new rule that nobody's allowed to invite friends over if the house isn't clean. Then he said *'No offence'*. Still sweet, but with conditions in the fine print. I think I'm allowed to call that...? I don't know what to call it.

First-Born's trying to be friendly-ish, but I think that's because they need me to drive them places. They told me a couple of days ago that they're not going to swear at me anymore. They're going to achieve this by replacing profanity with the word "SMURF". I wonder if that'll make me laugh, or hate smurfs?

They mean well, but I'm not dropping my guard this time. I don't trust that anything good will last for very long.

So I'm not sure where I want to be right now. Here or not-here. Mostly not-here. I don't want to work at home. It's too full of whatever it's full of. What I'd like is for there to be something to look forward to. But there's not, so I'll just do my work and wait for something good to present itself, the onus being on me to make good things happen. Out of thin air. Pity about the resources.

Roast dinner out on the balcony, that's a good thing. But first thing's first – let's see if I can turn the meat without drawing blood or scalding my delicate flesh.

Someone to Look Up To

I finally finished reading *Harpoon* and have so much admiration for Andrew Darby. He presents the story of whaling with an obvious anti-whaling bias, but that bias is rational and informed (i.e. very well supported by factual information), and he conveys emotionally charged content without any cheap tugging on the heartstrings. This allows the reader to make up their own mind and experience their own emotional response, no manipulation. It's very decent.

Despite exposing the dishonesty (for want of a more motherfucking word) of pro-whaling operations, he also shows respect by presenting the "other side" with understanding, as opposed to pure judgement.

I'm about to read a couple of books on anti-whaling activism, and although I think they'll be good in their own way I can't say I'm expecting the same level of rationality from them. I hope I'm wrong.

Monday, 24th March, 2008.

When the Cat's Away…

…the mice will, um, stretch a canvas? I've really gotta get a life. I'm no good at partying at the moment and am wasting some unexpected freedom by spending it alone and sober, but at least I've enjoyed the peace and quiet. (Ohmigawd, how *old* am I?) And it may have taken me a week to do what I'd planned to do in one day, but at least I've finished my drawing and stretched my canvas, and I'm feeling pretty good about it.

Drawing is [still] a euphoric thing. When I'm drawing I can't imagine ever painting, and when I'm painting I can't imagine ever drawing. The two things fill me up, so I'm heading towards a decision to simplify things by focussing solely on both for a while. And writing. And research. But apart from that, only both. Everything else can wait.

First-Born's rebelling against teenage stereotypes by being nice again, so apart from being full of visiting teenagers the house has been calm. I'll join it in that feeling soon enough, I'm guessing.

Anyway it hurts to type because I have canvas burn on my fingertips, because I'm too poor to buy canvas stretching pliers. So excuse me while I go and listen to the silence. (*Sweet.*)

Friday, 28ᵗʰ March, 2008.

Gilt

I'm *swooning*. After months of waiting with not-much-patience, *The Medieval Imagination* exhibition opened at the State Library today, so I was there with bells on and was practically crying, the manuscripts are so beautiful.

Now my brain's short-circuiting from too much input. There were so many people there, and everyone was bouncing around expressing their joy to anybody who'd listen. You just couldn't keep exclamations inside, it was that exciting. And so many people to exclaim with!

There was even a conspiracy theory being spread by a crackpot old German woman about these manuscripts being fake, with the real ones allegedly locked away in Europe, being valuable where nobody can see them. No end of drama in a scholar's world.

Anyway I'm a bit mean. Kitchen Nazi was helping me drive a canvas around again yesterday (this time she jolted us over three curbs and one substantially bumpy median strip, but both passenger and canvas are recovering nicely), and when I told her about the manuscript exhibition she excitedly said she wanted to see it with myself and the kids, because she loves my company and *'Thanks for bringing me into your world'*. (She's very sweet). I said *yey* but then went in to see it without her. I'll go and see it again, with her, but I wanted to see it alone first.

I took her to my sacred café yesterday and she loved it, but she looked around and asked *'Why would anybody come here to read when there's so much else to see?'* (referring to the imported things they sell on the shelves, i.e. shopping).

Afterwards, when we were at a local library, she was talking to a librarian about how great books are even though she never reads them, and *isn't the history of language fascinating*, and it turned out that he (the librarian) doesn't read books either. I was pissin' meself laughin', because out of the hundreds of people around us, the two most non-book-reading people had managed to find each other. In a *library*. What are the chances?

It's technically silly of me not to have taken her to a book exhibition where you don't read, you just look at the pictures. (To contradict myself, I'm hoping I can find one written in Middle English so I can read it, which'd be a real buzz) (inconspicuously, as opposed to ostentatiously, depending on how much I remember.) But still, I got to take my time, is the point.

Sunday, 30th March, 2008.

Fireside

It would've been good to sit around a fireplace while First-Born told me the story of their closest friend's mum yesterday. They started by telling me they were going over there to stay the night because Friend's Mum was going to a swinger's party. I asked *'She's going to a what? How would you know a thing like that?'*, and First-Born said *'We just know, duh – that's where she goes with her boyfriend'*.

Then the story, starting with a list of Friend's Mum's venereal diseases: hepatitis; herpes; gonorrhea; *'Oh, and crabs'*.

The most I've known about Friend's Mum's vices to date is that she's a leopard-skin-underwear-wearing smoker-alcoholic who drives all the way through the penalty periods of her lost licenses. Wow – I've never met people with venereal diseases before.

The story continued with how First-Born's Friend's Dad (no longer married to the mum) told his child how the mum once found crabs on his pubes (can you imagine somebody telling his own child this?) and went mental with accusations of him having an affair. Of course he hadn't (I hate to be shallow, but he's dead-ugly and pale as a vampire, there's no way he could have), so then they inspected the mum and found out that *she* had crabs, and had given them to *him*, because it was *her* having the affair after all, the dirty little strumpet.

Turns out the pale-as-a-vampire father has also had hepatitis, but from drugs (hence, pale), so the family history is looking [ironically] pretty colourful. And yet First-Born's Friend is well-balanced, studious, intelligent, into human rights and politics, and is going to be a kick-arse non-drug-addicted non-slutty adult.

Needless to say, the summary of First-Born's family background is starting to look less sordid now. Just as well I look good in a halo. And that halo is *definitely* not leopard-skinned.

———

April 2008

Zen

Pesto is the elixir of life. How I forget these things is beyond me. I made myself some pesto for the first time in months and it's like spinach is to Popeye; now, every day, I'm super human.

Also swimming – how did I forget *swimming?* You see what happens when you drop a subject at Art Skool? Even though you love that subject and will go back to it eventually, once you've dropped it the pressure is off; you can make like a hippy and start living properly again. So I swam laps today for also the first time in ages, then came home and ate pesto on my toasted salady thingy, all of this after a long morning's hard work, all of that after a long week's hard work, and I feel *wonderful.*

It helps that I've had lots of time alone, and the house is clean. Now'd be a good time to fall in love; it's a waste not to share this feeling.

To summarise, the best recipe for good living is obviously: pesto, chocolate, love, a 50 metre pool, and a sauna. (And money, the secret herb-n-spice to this recipe. No wonder I can't cook.)

Dog Eat Dog

As much as I love 'em, kids are bastards. I won't talk about the state of the house when I got back from a lovely day out with my peeps at Heide, other than to say my kids are learning that if they don't do anything, I don't do anything. In other words, cook your own dinner, piglets, because I'm not stepping into that filthy kitchen.

It feels good to not-care about not caring. Parental guilt is so yesterday.

As for Heide, we went to see the Rick Amor exhibition and it was... I'm running out of words for good things these days. Apparently I'm not allowed to say *I loved it*. I keep being told-off by certain art-appreciation-vocabulary-police for putting personal opinion into my evaluations of art. And yet, *fuck off*; if I loved it, I loved it. And I did.

Rick Amor's work makes me feel good for so many reasons. And the book by Gavin Fry, with beautiful colour reproductions, pisses all over the catalogue, which looks like somebody "corrected" the darkness of the images in Photoshop. Don't know how it passed proofing. So if you go into the bookshop afterwards it's like seeing two exhibitions.

And you get to frolic in the gardens. In *sunshine*.

Then if you happen to go back to a friend's house so he can show you a book about another artist from his amazon-addiction stash, and your brain expands so much you can hear it creaking, well. Makes for a great day. So much to think about I don't know if I'll have time to sleep.

Kitchen. *Pah*. Who gives a shit about the kitchen?

———

Monday, 7th April, 2008.

Dog Eat Cabbage

My not-caring strategy isn't going to plan. I'm stuck at home today because I have to take Son to the dentist later, and I'm finding it hard to concentrate with the kitchen being the way it is. Although the kitchen isn't the heart of the problem, it's definitely the front-line of the battlefield. I want to build a house without a kitchen in it and then see them try to sabotage our life.

I've been following the path of a piece of beetroot First-Born left on the kitchen floor two nights ago, and it's making impressive progress. It started near the pantry door and is now next to the sink. Needless to say I lost the beetroot battle, which went like this:

Me: *Can you please clean that up before somebody steps on it and walks it over to the carpet, First-Born?*

First-Born: @#% %^&$$ %#@%!!!

Time to review my parental techniques. Lately I've gone back to minimalism, using the lockable chocolate cupboard (what – you don't have one of those?) to hide plates and glasses and mugs and cutlery. I leave one of everything out for each of us and that's it, so when they trash the kitchen it's at least not as bad as it could be. And it's worked pretty well, except that I keep losing the key.

But anyway, "pretty well" is relative, because what you can't trash with an abundance of dirty dishes you can trash with carrot peel, celery stubs and super-glue-esque Milo powder. In the end I still look around me after my kids have been home for any amount of time and wanna slash my wrists. (Figure of speech. If you really wanted to slash your wrists in my house you'd have a hard time finding a knife.)

Unfortunately First-Born has finally, after years of trying, learnt how to pick the chocolate-cupboard lock. Plus they've been raiding the curry bowl cupboard, so it's all way out of control. I love my curry bowls and they're for special (i.e. curry). They're not priceless items but they represent happiness, so I hate seeing them strewn across the house. I stood in a large curry bowl last night as I was crossing the loungeroom floor. It contained leftover bolognese, which is now all over the carpet.

If I get home after drawing this evening and find any more of them, I'm quite happy to smash my happy curry bowls all over the driveway. Try eating out of them then, you little bastards.

I'm thinking of spending an hour today packing all the dishes away in boxes and putting them in the garage, where the kids won't look. Then buying two dog-food bowls and writing my kids' names on them and leaving them in the cupboard. A pig's trough would be better, but it'd be too hard to store between meals.

Plus I'll get even stingier with my shopping. I'm already buying nothing but the basics. The kids hate it but I think it's great. They can't litter my lounge room with wrappers anymore because I only buy fresh food. They get to choose between fruit and vegetables and not much else. Just like in the olden days. I have this absurd fantasy about being alive during the depression and having to survive on eggs and cabbage. I'd like to see them take things for granted after *that*.

First-Born's demanding that I buy juice and chocolate, but I'm unmoved. I'm developing a sadistic streak, their pointless commands making me experience a kind of joy matched only by twelve year-old boys pulling the wings off flies.

Parenting's not so bad. First-Born may be winning the war, but I'm still all-powerful. Mwaha. Ha. Ha ha.

_____

Salt of the Earth

I just remembered seeing a strange thing on tv last night. The government's running an advertising campaign to encourage people to move to "provincial Victoria", showing scenes of a happy community gathered around a backyard picnic table, living the rural idyll.

One of my favourite scenes on *Sesame Street* is of a farming family gathered 'round just such a table, eating corn on the cob. Doesn't the government know that country idylls don't work without corn cobs? Also, seeing as we're smack bang in the middle of a drought, and have a current investigation into food pricing that involves corporations undercutting farmers' livelihoods, shouldn't they have added images of rural poverty? Some thirst, perhaps? And don't they know that for a lot of rural Victoria, isolation is a fact of life?

Bush-Dwelling Brother told me recently about one of his social work jobs, spending time with a young boy from an isolated town in East Gippsland. The circumstances of this child's life are extreme and representative of struggles suburban people couldn't even imagine.

Will an influx of the targeted wealthy help eradicate existing social problems in less fortunate areas of our state? I don't think so. I doubt a series of (expensive publicly funded) images like that will work on even the most optimistic imagination anymore. Not while there's so much wrong with the world.

Perhaps John Brumby should do something radical about social and agricultural infrastructure, earning the right to promote this imaginary idyll? Worth a try.

_____

Jack Ass

I ran a red light again. The third time in about six months. Just like the other times, I was talking so much I didn't notice until I was passing through. Had to say '*Sorry I almost killed you, Passenger*'. My inability to multi-task is getting extreme.

I feel like a very bad person. I'm sure people who run red lights don't get into heaven, for instance. It could have something to do with stress levels wreaking havoc on my body. Stress bad enough at the moment for Mum to be worried about my health (Little Sister told me), and for me to be worried about my health. I have to concentrate hard while I'm driving and thought I was doing okay until now. Time to avoid complicated trips for a while.

I'm becoming a useless human being, so wholly focussed on art and stories that I'm alive when I'm with my arts friends, but to everybody else I'm as good as nothing. I didn't get home that late, but the kids were already in bed, the house the same. I might as well not be here. How can I be anything to anybody if I can't even make a home, when home is something I put so much energy into? I love my kids but really, what am I to them? I don't think I've ever been enough. Maybe they'd be better off without me.

A self-flagellatory mood. If this is my sum total, what an absolute bummer. And yet, hanging on the wall in front of me is a drawing that is I guess part of that sum total, and it embodies my instincts, and I'm craving to go back to them. Behind me is a painting that also embodies those instincts, and I want to paint so badly it hurts. I've done all of the prep, so tomorrow I'll do both, and then being nothing won't matter?

The bright side is that when I have these epiphanal moments where I just suddenly "know" I've always done everything wrong, and that's why I am where I am, I at least have a practical plan of action to improve our life. Just draw a lot and don't drive.

The craving to use graphite again is so *strong*. But it's just a feeling, isn't it. Is that enough to justify being useless? Probably not. All the same, it's time to put my head down and work, and be invisible for a while. (Red light cameras won't catch me if I'm invisible, correct?)

––––

Wednesday, 9th April, 2008.

Seriouser and Seriouser

I'm still shaking, not a sensible bodily reaction to something that wasn't physically threatening.

First-Born did something extreme, because I took their internet access away, because they called home sick today. I gave the school permission to let them leave before lunchtime, but with the proviso that they come straight home. My only way of knowing if they were genuinely unwell.

Two and a half hours later they weren't home yet. I called and discovered they were at the shopping centre, hanging with friends. Flippant about it, as though there are no consequences, and why should I be bothering them et cetera.

When they later discovered their internet access was cut they rang my mobile to get angry at me between lectures. I hung up on them, the anger was too much. I rarely do it, but removing internet access is the only disciplinary option left. They don't care about anything else.

Now I'm sitting here breathing in oil paint fumes, coming from my bedroom, where First-Born painted a wall full of messages for me to discover when I got home. Using my good paint. Cadmium red deep, such a beautiful colour, from a big and expensive Michael Harding tube. So smooth to paint with they probably felt real joy when they did it. They'll grow up to be an artist now that they've experienced how good it feels. A paint euphoria.

They wanted me to feel shock, and I did. Hence, shaking. I don't know how vandalism can hurt your insides, but it does. At least they didn't swear at me on my wall. The things they wrote are awful, a couple of them concerning. One makes me think that for whatever irrational reason, they feel genuinely hurt. Another is a bullying tactic. I suppose I should be most disturbed by the largest, central comment, which reiterates their disapproval of my '*selfish*' art habits.

It's so pretty. So striking I want to touch it.

Anyway, I yelled. First-Born was in bed when I got home and I went in there to wave my precious paint tube at them, and yelled '*You Fucking* Idiot*!*'.

I never swear at them like that. I hardly ever yell. I raise my voice when I need to, but I don't yell-yell. Whenever I yell it's because I've been pushed over the edge and I start crying, which ruins the effect. This time I gave it to them. I spelt out how much the paint cost ($265), how oil paint is gonna be a bastard to remove, how they've probably poisoned themself by using it without gloves, how I can't sleep in my room for I-don't-know-how-long because of the fumes, how they got paint on my bedding, *you fucking idiot* (such an ugly expression) *x 3*.

All of this because I didn't have words for what they've really done. The money and the work I'll have to do to repair the wall is nothing, but the personal relationship consequences are huge. What am I supposed to do with them? What do they even *want*?

Tomorrow's going to be horrible, I'll have to send them away. Maybe temporary foster care, maybe my mum. I hope my mum. It's going to be devastating, but what else can I do? Ironically, First-Born doesn't like being away from home. Is this where they learn how much they have to lose? I'm scared for them. It's all my fault, because every little decision I've made has led us here to this point.

Whatever I do is going to hurt them, but this time I can't do "nothing" and hope it goes away. I'm worried about them. I'm worried that they're up in their bed now feeling depressed, because they know they've gone too far this time. That after this, the only way forward is ugly. I'm worried that they're going to feel rejected when whoever comes to get them leads them through that door.

I love them and I can't protect them if they're not here. I can't protect myself if they are. If I do nothing it'll get worse and worse. I hope I die in my sleep so that I don't have to make it happen, but I know I'm not going to sleep tonight.

There. I've written it, so now I don't have to talk to anybody.

Her kitten is sleeping on my lap and keeps farting.

(Question: why's the hammer sitting next to the computer?)

I'm so tired. Maybe if I watch TV I can fall asleep on the couch.

This is the first time I've ever felt uncomfortable writing something personal. I wish I could write all of the good things about them. Because they *are* good. They're great. They're just so lost, is all.

―――

Thursday, 10th April, 2008.

Afterthought

At least they didn't write REDRUM. Now *that* woulda been funny.

I miss my bedroom. I grabbed a cosy, unused doona from my cupboard and curled up on the couch with GrandKitten and eventually fell into a fitful sleep while watching an old movie about Thomas Jefferson on ABC. Which is a bummer, because I was enjoying the movie. Then in the morning when Son was coming up the stairs I heard First-Born say to him *'Be more quiet, Brother – Mum's still sleeping'*.

What a strange bit of thoughtfulness that was.

———

White Out

I dunno. I go into my bedroom to get something and forget what I went in there for because I start reading my wall. Little Sister said she couldn't understand all of the big vocabulary (*'First-Born gets that from you'*). As far as vandals go First-Born's on the intellectual side. I think there's something wrong with me, though, because when I read it I want to get in there with the oil paint and correct the three spelling mistakes. Reminds me of the "Romans Go Home" scene in *Life of Brian.*

Maybe it'll end up being funny after all. Something to show on the powerpoint at their eighteenth birthday party. Gosh, won't we look back and *laugh.*

———

Saturday, 12th April, 2008.

Thoughts One Two Three

Son has a friend over, so I have to stay awake for another three hours or so. Bugger. Being awake at all is being awake for too long today. Goodness knows I tried my damndest to catch up on sleep while I was driving, what with all the lovely sunshine, and the car being so warm.

Big deal, listen to me with my blow by blows. Today I breathed in, today I breathed out. Some kind of boring catharsis that's supposed to make me feel better before I try to draw.

Alright then, what's on my mind.

I don't want my new job. I wanted to stack supermarket shelves, or something inane and physical where I could be 90% brute and no brain. Also, being anonymous would be nice. But I have a weeny little teaching thing and I don't want to do it, because I have nothing left to give anybody. I went to the interview on Thursday, in the wake of First-Born's vandalism. I had to fake my own personality, some quick thinking on my part, for an uninterrupted hour of conversation. Smiling, even, as though my guts weren't churning.

I love teaching, but I got back to the car afterwards, put my head down on the steering wheel and just sobbed.

Friday was lovely. Friday was school studio and I didn't want to go home. Even though at school people come and talk to me every ten minutes. Literally – I timed it. I was trying to draw and listen to an audio book and had to keep pressing pause. Half driving me crazy because I just wanted to work quietly, half making me feel loved. People are so nice to me.

I was right about the graphite. Quiet concentration – I can draw with it for hours and just not stop. Perfect for the way things are now.

What else. I miss my bed? It's hard being in my room. Like it's not really mine anymore. I wonder if I'll be able to sleep there even after the fumes have dissipated. The couch is as comfortable as a bed, but it makes me sad.

———

Thought Four

Ex-Wife to the rescue. As is obvious by now, I couldn't send First-Born away. Thursday night and the "it's going to get worse" prediction Little Sister had been making all day was already coming true. The dollar signs on the extra-curricular cost of living in this house are getting pretty exhausted right about now.

I was worried about my child, who was distraught after saying things out on the driveway that left me stricken. So I called Ex-Wife and handed the phone to First-Born. Then I eavesdropped. Son passed me at one stage and in a disapproving voice asked if I was eavesdropping, but even he backed down when I whispered that it's the only way I can know what's in their head without it being yelled at me.

Ex-Wife is a beautiful person. So I continued to listen, First-Born gradually calmed down and I followed the conversation as best I could.

A few things hurt. For example, First-Born kept saying that I tell them they're the worst child in the world. I never, *ever* say that. I don't even get close to saying things like that. They kept saying that I think they're crazy, that I'm making other people think they're crazy, but the truth is I'm the one telling First-Born and everybody else that they're *not* crazy. What they're doing is extreme, but that's not the same thing.

For the record, First-Born also said that they know what they did was wrong (they'd been saying up until that moment that I deserved it and had it coming), and that all of the things I say they do are quite true. Big of them, and validating for me, for what little good it does without a court of law there to witness the conversation.

But anyway, that's not the problem here. The problem here is that Ex-Wife solved one of our problems with some brilliant lateral thinking. First-Born is now in charge of the kitchen. They're the boss, so there'll be no more fighting because Son and I don't argue when we're told to do something. Problem solved.

The catch is that Ex-Wife is buying First-Born a laptop computer as a reward for this new responsibility they're taking on. The good thing about this is that First-Born wants to write, and will write, so the laptop will be useful. The bad thing is that they'll have wireless internet access that I can't control, and I'm still the one paying for the internet. The trust system doesn't work – they use up my download quota in five seconds flat. I can't afford it.

The biggest problem is that Ex-Wife, although sweet as all heck, has just given my child the message that vandalising their mother's bedroom wall is a good way to get a shit-hot present. *You did that because you were sad, Princess? Don't worry, Daddy will buy you a Porsche.* The whole consequence thing I'm trying to teach them isn't going to work now. I don't want them to be buyable like that.

Plus if the plan doesn't work, First-Born will have a laptop anyway. I'm supposed to call Ex-Wife and ask her to take it away if First-Born doesn't fulfill their role, but that's asking for trouble, because it makes me the bad guy all over again.

As much as I want Ex Wife to feel comfortable exercising independent parental rights, there are some things she should discuss with me first, and that was pretty much one of them.

Thought Five

Social workers "not" to the rescue. When I asked them the day after if I should send First-Born away for a week they said *no don't do that, they might feel rejected*. Of course. And part of my problem is that I can't stand the idea of First-Born feeling hurt, especially because of something I've done. But it surprised me, too, because they've just done this serious thing, and it happened to be a very personal attack. First-Born doesn't quite get how serious that is, and nobody's willing to show them.

Aren't these little cries for help?

So we're going the passive route with an in-home counsellor of sorts (does this service exist?), and a youth worker. That's good. Or will be, when it happens. In the meantime there's no immediate solution to the immediate problem.

They're well-behaved today, post laptop promise. But what about tomorrow? And the next day? As the object of both their love and their hatred, I'll say it quietly: there's nobody there to help. I'll continue to fake it by passing myself off as cool, calm and collected, because too many people are worried about me and I don't want them to worry. Reality is, I'm a mess.

Thought Six

Six is too many, blah fucken blah. Let's pretend for a minute that I'm actually being interesting here and have gotten the catharsis over with quickly. Beyond catharsis, today I went to the city to buy canvas. Stopped at Heide on the way to buy a book I wanted. Was going to go to the Sudanese festival at the Immigration Museum, but turned around at the last minute because I figured going to a festival alone would be tragic. Tomorrow I'm supposed to draw, but I don't think so. I think I'll be driving to the quietest country town I can think of. I've been wanting to go there for a while now. To have lunch in the old cemetery on the hillside.

There, a whole paragraph without any crawly emotion. Life is better as a list of simple I-did-such-and-suches. See Spot run. The end.

———

Sunday, 13th April, 2008.

Resolution

A rearranging of furniture will do the trick. I woke up optimistic because there are ideas floating in my mind, itching to get out. I resolved to give up all misery because there's art to be had and books to be written, but then I got up and looked around and the house was holding bad memories. I know I have to find a way to exorcise the little fuckers before they drag me down.

It's like Rodney, whoever he was. Rodney hung himself on a pine swing-set at that house on the corner on the other side of the foothills. A long time ago I was walking towards it at about six in the morning, wondering why the small crowd gathering, why the woman screaming '*RODNEY! RODNEY COME BACK!*', why the little girl crying on the nature strip while a woman from across the road was trying to lead her away. Then the screaming woman pointed while she told the neighbour *'He's in there'*. I followed her pointing finger to this rope on the other side of the fence, and thought *oh fuck*. Pine swing-set becomes gallows.

I eventually changed the route I walked because I couldn't handle how bad it felt to walk past that corner and see the white rope mark on the pine swing-set on the other side of the fence, even after the house had sold and months and years had passed. But I walked that way again a few weeks ago, drawn to the killer hill I used to climb every day, and somebody had renovated. Old fence torn down, swing-set gone, memory erased, RIP Rodney.

Similarly, bad memories haunt this house. Also good memories, and the promise of a good life that's been disintegrating bit by bit, which makes the bad feelings worse than they would've been if there'd been no hope to begin with.

But there's all this space, so if I rearrange things, I can leave it uncluttered and ready to work in. Then, oh joy, if Ex-Wife's great plan works and the fighting dies down because First-Born starts writing more and clearing their own cobwebs out, there'll be no more unhappiness haunting us.

Now: *where the hell do I start?*

———

Monday, 14th April, 2008.

Slow but Steady

The longest ever thing to read is *Stuffed and Starved*, by Raj Patel. First it takes me forever to get around to it, now it's taking me forever to get through it. Even though I'm hungry for it (GREAT PUN), and I'm taking it with me wherever I go, some of it's just so difficult to chew on (I'M ON A ROLL!).

I'm getting less from it than I want, but only because there are passages that just aren't clear enough for a[n] ~~dumbarse~~ ignoramus such as myself to follow. I thought I could follow just about anything, so this is doing my ego no good.

For example, there'll be a great anecdotal build up to some great point, and then the chapter will finish and I'll have missed it because the point was implied rather than spelt out. I get the people-are-dying bit, but sometimes can't quite tell why. I re-read, but it does no good. Which is such a shame, because I'm fascinated and moved, I'm just coming away from some of it as uneducated as I was when I started. Like I've walked through an impoverished farming community but forgot to look around me while I was there.

So if anybody were to ask me what's happening with food distribution in the big bad world, I'd probably just look at them stupidly. That's no good, because I'm a soap box person and like to punch my fist in the air, telling people to *do something, dammit*.

Having said that, I'm getting to some clearer material and figure if I can memorise some key terms the information will stick in my head more tenaciously. It just needs to stick long enough for me to process it – if I can process I can understand and then I can preach to all and sundry and the world will change for the better.

Things everybody needs to know. Which is why it matters when an author writes a book like this – it needs to be accessible to us commoners or it defeats its own purpose. Fingers crossed that it all falls together, because if we don't understand it we can't fight. Not-fighting is out of the question.

———

Friday, 25th April, 2008.

Top Notch Man-Hating Tantrum

Instead of listening to an audio book while I paint the balcony railing I'm listening to my own mind repeat the mantras *you motherfucker* and *you motherfucking cunt,* over and over and over and over. I don't mind skipping lunch while I take this little break to put it in writing. *Motherfucking cunt and a half.* This is as close as I'll ever get to hatred, and from now on, whoever stands between me and my oil painting is going to get unreserved hatred, no holds barred.

Needless to say, I did NOT want to paint the balcony railing today. That I'm doing it would have happened soon anyway, because the weather is about to turn cold. I should have done it gradually over the last month or so, but when I've had time it's been raining or I've been distracted or there's been something more important to do, or I've just plain forgotten. So with the weather changing I would have worked it out for myself: it must be done.

But I don't like being told what to do by my ex-husband. I take back all of the he's-lovelys I've said to my friends, because when he waltzes in from wherever, he *always* expects me to drop what I'm doing to do something that suits him. As though I've been sitting around on my arse doing nothing while he's been away.

I even yelled at him last night, and I just don't do that. I called out *ALRIGHT I'LL DO IT!* when he was throwing his negative comments at me from every corner of the house, forget that I have a schedule that's sensitive to interruption, forget that every interruption seems to set me back a whole week.

The thing about the balcony is that he's poisoned it with bad feeling, and I've had enough of bad feeling. He seems to think the fact that it cost so much to repair and replace was my fault. As though replacing a railing over a seven metre drop (railing full of missing posts and rotting wood that swayed when you leaned against it) was an extravagance. Somebody could have *died,* for fuck's sake, if it had given way. Or if a small child had wandered out there when nobody was looking. But he criticises me every time it's mentioned. He wants to punish me for getting it repaired. Therefore he won't help me paint

198

the railing or oil the new deck. The job will take at least three days, more likely four or five, and that's with one coat.

So while he's down there mowing the lawn, which I could have done myself and only takes an hour and a half, I'm up painting and hating his guts, because of the way he told me to do it, and because of the way he refuses to help.

Mainly, I hate doing it alone. I do everything alone, and this is a big place to manage without cooperation. To do this alone is to remind you that the box you live in is just a box – it stopped being a family home years ago. Just another reminder of what a fuck-up I am. I have mixed feelings about the house and what it represents, and what I can't make it represent. And then this paternal fucking godhead comes in with his motherfucking guilt trips and tells me that there's this whole other part of my life where I just don't cut it.

Fuck the hell *off*.

———

Monday, 28th April, 2008.

Presage

I don't know why people think you have to grow up to get married. Our ex-marital conversations tend to go something like this:

You're mean to me.
Only because you were mean to me.
Oh yeah, well you were mean to me first.

Meanness aside, for an MFC Ex-H is pretty saintly. I do like it when men cop a bruising to their ribs and have the flesh ripped down their backs for my benefit. While I was off drawing with friends he spent all day Sunday loading some WHOPPING BIG plan drawer units onto a truck and bringing them back here. Having helped him unload them as soon as I got home, I know just how much hard work it must have been. (Free plan drawers!)

But now I have this fear of dying, because there are still more to be carried in from the garage and last night the steep brick steps down the side of the house (leading to the french doors to my studio) tried to kill us. Before we lived here some genius had an idea to put a ramp down the middle to make it easier to push and lug wheelbarrows while they were landscaping the garden. (Note: it doesn't make taking wheelbarrows down the steps any easier whatsoever.)

First Ex-H slipped on the ramp and got a little crushed, then when I manoeuvred to help him I slipped and my fingers got crushed. After rolling around under heavy furniture laughing and calling out *'It hurts! it hurts!',* we gave up for the night.

I'm serious about the fear of dying. I feel like if I use those steps I'm going to die this morning. So, goodbye cruel world. On the off chance that I don't die, though, I'm going to have a very neat studio. This is me eating my words – forget all of those mean things I said about Ex-H. He's been redeemed. For now.

———

Wednesday, 30th April, 2008.

Spring Cleaning

I feel lucky, and housework is giving me no end of joy. I'm not even being sarcastic. I would have felt lucky with one set of plan drawers. Well, no; maybe with two. Three. But now I have six of them and those battered old things have changed my life.

Is that all it took? I think I feel lucky because they were promised to me a long time ago and I was wondering if I'd ever actually get them, being the kind of person for whom promised things don't always eventuate. So first I pinch myself to see if it's real, and then I start tidying up.

The reason this matters so much is that it gives me a way to reclaim the house as a place I like to be. I spend my whole life struggling to make things run smoothly so that I can work, and suddenly I feel unhindered.

To prove how kick-arse I can be with new plan drawers in my life, I finished a couple of drawings yesterday. But I'm behind my own intentions by about three weeks, so I can't get too excited.

Finishing them felt good, even though I made the stupidest mistakes. The kind of mistakes you know you're making while you're making them but you go ahead and make them anyway. One day I'll learn the lesson that makes me stop.

Every-now-and-then I open the door to the workroom and flick on the light quickly, hoping that when I look at the drawings I'll suddenly catch them not having mistakes in them anymore. Doesn't matter – three more pieces and I'll be caught up to where my wise old head tells me I should be, and then I'll be footloose and fancy free (except that by then I'll be behind on three more pieces).

Reformed Hippy Friend is suddenly obsessed with drawing, also. I receive texts all the time about how great life is with drawing in it, and until now I had no idea that somebody as sucky as me was out there and this close. We're both running around with rapture dripping from our tongues, because this is what everything was for.

This is the place I've been working towards for years, making it possible for things to happen. I wouldn't call it smooth-sailing, but I'll make do with happening at all, and hope the smooth-sailing will just eventuate one day. It's all good.

———

May 2008

No Worries

This week there were about three days where I did five major things between sunrise and sunset – you get to the end of days like that and feel like you're trying to live three lifetimes.

But I'm still managing to slow down a little and have removed all pressure. So instead of giving in to the eagerness to start on the next phase of the portrait I'm working on, I held off, working on one section and then stopping to do some lesson planning, so that by the time I got to the classroom to teach I was very relaxed.

This is so uncharacteristic it's spinning me out. Did you *know* it's possible to not have to rush through one thing to get to something else? That if you don't push too hard you can just amble along? I like this new me, who still seems to be getting everything done but doesn't fret over any of it.

New mantra: *I can do everything*.

I love teaching. My classes keep running overtime because as with life there's just so much to squeeze in. Perhaps pretending to slow things down means you can trick yourself into being calm in the middle of an information-processing frenzy? I am actually calm now, aren't I? So calm. If five-things is this good, then I might drop down even further to doing only three major things a day. I could probably manage three things really well. (*Everything!*)

Bonnie and Clyde

I partook in criminal activity over the weekend, and Ex-H was an accomplice. It was so geeky I'm almost embarrassed to admit it. It's just that in a fit of magnanimity Ex-H had not only made us all a nice dinner, but he'd also cleaned the kitchen afterwards. I mean, really cleaned it. Like, *really*.

I'm still not sure why. He'd witnessed another scene between First-Born and I the night before, one where I was pushed to raising my voice (therefore, inevitably, I cried, and a plate got broken). It was a very emotional scene. (First-Born did finally ask for my lovely company by saying they wanted to spend more time with me).

So the next night this dinner and this clean, clean kitchen, and I was going to go for a walk after I finished painting and invited Ex-H to come along. We were passing an uphill house when he produced his laser light and said *wouldn't it be funny to shine this on their ceiling?* But of course he wouldn't, because he's sweet. And has no balls.

When he got the laser light a few weeks ago he told me they've been banned in Victoria because people have been shining them at aeroplanes when they're trying to land. He said he had to order one because soon nobody would be able to. If you ask me that's twisted geek logic. Because once you have one, what do you do with it?

I begged him to let me use it and shone it on the ceilings of people who were watching TV late at night. So much fun, because you then have to run away. It was as I was hurrying away with the contraband item, with Ex-H beside me saying '*I told you you'd get into trouble; they're probably calling the police!*', that I realised it was Saturday night, and whilst I was getting my juvenile kicks other [normal] people were out dancing and getting laid.

Put my paintbrush down. Get out more.

Still Monday.

Christopher Hitchens is Great

Even his title is a ballsy up yours, innit? I've been listening to *God is Not Great: How Religion Poisons Everything* again while I've been painting, and it's just as good the second time through. It does what Dawkins didn't do with *The God Delusion* in that it doesn't rely on science as an [inadequate] foundation for the battle against "faith".

Dawkins is like pre-school, something to prepare you for the real stuff. In the main arena he's nothing next to Hitchens. This is because there is no battle; you can explain faith away without mentioning science at all and still make sense. All you need to do to understand (and then discredit) religion is to study history and you'll see it all there before you. The mystery behind the unfortunate phenomena of religious belief will be exposed, and buggered if Hitchens hasn't done what needed to be done. A little bit irreverent, but only semi-arsehole about it really. More like a *'Come on youse guys, you can't seriously believe in this shit, can you?'* tone of voice. He reads it a bit quickly on audio, but if you're listening to it at all you're probably smart enough to listen at light-speed. Yey you.

I'm also going to read Raj Patel (*Stuffed or Starved*) again, and now have to buy a copy to dog-ear. Also it'd be bad manners to spill Milo on a borrowed copy, so if I want to show it some serious lovin' I'm gonna have to invest.

It's less densely expressed as you read on, but if he were to read it aloud he'd have to go really, really slowly for my feeble brain. I was right in thinking that the content of this book could change the world. TRULY. If your thoughts happen to have been on finding a way to emphasise regional produce in local markets as a way of saving society from itself, then he's your man. I'm so excited by the book it's a wonder I haven't drooled all over it.

In the past when I've tried to wax philosophical about the decline of community being a result of not knowing where our apples come from, I've sounded like a bit of a moron. Possibly because I couldn't make it past the apples, and people gave me a kind of *apples-what-the-fuck-?* look. Now I have a non-moron to quote to explain my back-yard sociological fears, and we all know that if you quote a book you have automatic clout.

So: by showing us what's happening in the world he makes change seem possible. Not easy, but possible. Raj Patel is an underwear-on-the-outside-of-his-stockings kind of author. Another piece in the enormous jigsaw puzzle of the world. I want to *thank* the man. *Thank you thank you.*

Tuesday, 6th May, 2008.

First-Born is Also Great

We're doing happily-ever-after at our house now. I got home late after drawing tonight and First-Born had just started cooking the chicken for dinner, so I was able to be there for some picture-perfect happy-family life. (Normal !!). They cooked the chicken, Son cooked the potato, and I fed the cats and did the bins, because it's frankly much better that I don't cook.

My kids have beautiful skin and lovely natures. We sat down together to eat, and afterwards, when I thanked them, they let me give them a long cuddle. I think I'm a mum again. It's been so long since I've been allowed to just love them.

Unlike all of the bastard pretend turning points of the past, I think the other night was the real turning point. It just feels different this time. I didn't even know you could get to such a significant turning point with only one broken plate. A bargain.

———

Stunned

I was looking forward to writing more happy stuff tonight, with life being such a bed of roses. In fact, First-Born said the funniest thing today, but it'll have to wait until tomorrow because I've had such a shock that I have to write this other thing out before it eats at me.

It's something Ex-Wife said to me over the phone, after a productive session with a family mediator this afternoon, where I had to summarise the-story-so-far from a pretty good place (things being on the way to being better).

Obviously, parenting is a huge aspect of my life. I may be obsessive when it comes to doing art or writing, but that's just part of being somebody who does art or writing. And I may be a complete ditz and forget important things sometimes, but mostly only under extreme duress. I'm even inadvertently neglectful when I'm in survival mode, and given the circumstances I've floundered quite a bit here and there. But I adore my kids and would do anything to fix this mess up.

I'm allowed to say that there are things I suck at, and being a good mum is occasionally one of them. BUT – that's because I know that

205

when I do suck at it there's usually a very good reason. I also know that I don't really suck, I just feel guilty a lot for being inadequate. I give myself a right proper beating over it.

Ex-Wife, however, is *not* allowed to say that about me. Absolutely *not*. Especially now, when I'm feeling bad about not being the mum I used to be. I know I'm not the mum I used to be because one of my children has pushed me so far away I don't know how to get back. But now, having been given permission, I'm back to running on pure maternal instinct. It's like my kids have just been born and I wanna tell everybody how cute they are – *that* kind of maternal instinct. Be thankful that I'm keeping it to myself. So far.

So I was telling Ex-Wife that all's well, and marvelling at how First-Born had believed [mistakenly] that I never think of them or put their needs first. I said something like: '*You know what it's like as a parent – every decision we make is centred around our kids*'.

Ex-Wife replied with: '*I disagree with you a million percent – more than a million percent. It's true for me, but not for you*'. She then repeated the million figure a few times. So that's an unequivocally accusatory statement that I live life without ever considering my kids.

Even when I'm being a crap mum, I'm considering my kids. I don't even go out at night anymore, because I want to be at home with them. Sometimes I'm just a presence, but I've known that while things aren't perfect my presence is the most important thing in the world. Anybody who's invited me to something social over the past year or so will attest to that. Unless it's an artishly important thing, in the end I just say no. (Hence, First-Born now thinks I'm socially backwards, even though my social life is sometimes quite active in daylight hours.)

I said something like '*What?*', then was too gobsmacked to speak. She replied with '*You don't; we'll just have to disagree on that*'.

I changed the subject, to keep it friendly. Moving right along. I faked my way through a few pleasantries and then escaped the call. But in that one sentence, she just lost all of that nice, warm and fuzzy friendship I felt for her.

Firstly because *she wouldn't know*. I speak to her a few times a year, and it's always pleasant. But she literally just doesn't know that kind of detail. If a closer, more involved friend had said it, I'd think it through with them and ask for advice. But not her. She assumes that because she knew me intimately once she could know me intimately now, only without the access to my thoughts she once had.

Secondly, she's been talking to First-Born. A lot. She was one of the people I called upon when First-Born did the bedroom thing. I *trusted* her, as an adult, to help. Not to ignite a blame game. What shocks me now is that over the past few weeks First-Born has said some things that made me wonder about whether or not Ex-Wife had said something to them, because they were drawing from some invisible authority and had gotten something very wrong. But then I thought *nah, Ex-Wife wouldn't do that now. No way.*

Has she been fuelling the fire? Little Sister has been talking about how duped she gets by First-Born and how she now knows that being there for First-Born means treading a fine line, because helping them can sometimes end up hurting me. Not First-Born's fault, it's just where they're at. They've had such an angry viewpoint for so long their brain is wired to interpret my words and actions in the worst possible way. I think Ex-Wife has missed the subtlety. So what the fuck, 'scuse my French, has she been saying to our [very impressionable] child????

A lot of the things First-Born wrote on my wall are about parental responsibility and neglect. Has Ex-Wife been validating that idea? The more I piece this together the more serious it is. She may have been doing very serious damage without even realising it.

And what kind of person, exactly, does she think I am? Is it possible that an Ex is just an Ex? That they can tell you they love you and tell you you're wonderful etc, but when it comes down to it the Ex Factor is the dominant part of your relationship with them? You'll always be the person who left them, and that makes you inherently evil in their eyes? I had more respect for her than that.

Things are going to mend because First-Born has somehow finally managed to see past their anger, and I can now fix my own behaviours (I do do some things wrong). This is our chance to start again. But there's this other-mother out there who might be poison, and I had no idea. I just lost my trust in somebody very significant in our lives and I am, quietly, devastated.

—

Wednesday, 7th May, 2008.

Retaliation

While I'm here I should embark upon a smear campaign of presidential proportions. Not that I'm brooding over it, but I realise that I protect that silly Ex-Wife woman. I protect her all the time. When asked what she is to the kids, I say *'she means well'*. I did it just yesterday, to the mediator. I say she's their Other Mother, hesitate, then say *she's in their lives, but kinda casual about it*. In the nicest possible way.

Seeing as Ex-Wife said that thing about me, let's talk about *casual*, on accounta one of the things I get into trouble for from First-Born is that I haven't given them other people they can rely on. They have three other parents, one of whom rejected them outright (Ex-H). The other two are so often absent they might as well not be there.

In Ex-Wife's case, I'll provide two examples. 1) A buyer of many things, last year she promised the kids a Wii for Xmas. For the third year in a row she not only failed to see us over Xmas, but she sold the Wii to somebody else who wanted it. Materialistically that doesn't matter, but the message to the kids is that they're not important.

2) Most recently, as in last week, she'd arranged to take First-Born out for lunch. But she FORGOT. This at a crucial time for a struggling teenager who's trying desperately to feel loved.

Ex-Wife gives First-Born sooo much love – that's not the problem. The problem is it's mostly verbal. She steps up when we need her, and that's invaluable. It's why I hesitate to criticise. It's just that she also lets them down in significant ways. Because she's human – we all are.

There's more, but I've said enough, more than I would've had the insult not been leveled at my head. Let the record state: *so there*. She can stick her judgemental opinion up her jacksy. Let the record also state that despite my faults I have been, and remain, holier than thou.

Thursday, 8th May, 2008.

Fetish

You know how you buy your new-favourite paper in bulk and you can't wait to get it home so that you can touch it? And you go to a lecture and all you can think about is how your paper is in your car and you want get back there to touch it? And you get it home and wish you could take it to bed with you because it's so utterly beautiful to touch?

I had to buy it in bulk because it's cheaper that way, though bulk isn't *that* bulk because even when it's cheaper it's still too expensive. But it's bulk enough and will keep me going for a good few serious drawings. The sheets are so big and so heavy I'm swooning. Son helped me carry them in from the car and asked *'What is it with you and paper?'*. Gosh, ya just don't ask a woman such personal questions.

Art Supply Shop Owner said as I was paying that this paper is addictive, because once you've used it you'll always want to use it, and he's not wrong. The good news is that he therefore keeps it in stock. The bad news is that the way I use paper, as far as addictions go heroin would be more affordable.

I sense a week of not being able to afford train fares ahead.

———

Sunday, 11th May, 2008.

Feijoa Heist

It may *seem* that I've let myself go, but it was actually fortuitous that my evening ensemble consisted of camouflagable black jeans, black top, black combat boots and a combat jacket, because as I was leaving my parent's house I happened to look over at the feijoa tree in Neighbour-Who-Died's old house and realise that I was facing my big opportunity.

I opened my mobile to see if I could use it as a torch, because it was dark and I couldn't tell if there were feijoa's on the ground or not. It looked like there were, and I looked up at my parents (who were waiting to say goodbye to me) with my eyebrows raised. They answered my raised eyebrows with *'NO!'*. I've told them before about my great plan to sneak in there in the dark to steal the fruit. The house is being rented and the tenants don't eat it.

If I was boss of the world, it'd be a crime *not* to eat feijoa's. I *LOVE* them. One of the only seasonal fruits left, you can't just buy them any old time; they only ripen for a few weeks during autumn. Last year was my first year without a feijoa, because my parents would rather let them rot on the ground than let me thieve under the cover of darkness.

Well this apple fell a long way from the tree. I have no scruples. They said *no, no, sorry but no,* and looked at me like I'm scum of the earth. I pretended to be uncharacteristically obedient, said goodbye, and drove off. But they're right, I am scum of the earth. Turning to the kids, I said *'Let's park round the corner and walk back'.*

They said *no, Mu-um, no,* but I pulled over around the corner, nagged them until First-Born relented, drove around the block just to be sure I'd fooled my parents, and parked a little distance away from their house. The kids wouldn't help, but they let me tip-toe to the house next door and crawl around on the ground in the dark, picking up as many feijoa's as I could before the yappy little dog in the back yard started barking.

Then I said a quiet *fuck,* and tip-toe-ran back to the car, fully expecting my parents to run out of their front door having suspected their dishonest daughter of fruit-thievery all along. Thank goodness they didn't. I wouldn't have cared if the neighbours had caught me, but if my mum had I'd have died on the spot.

After we'd made a clean get away Son asked *'Mum, haven't you been telling us never to steal?'.* Yes, but, *shut up.* I hope my kids don't end up with the same moral fortitude as my parents. I like to think I'm raising them more proper than that, with a clean sense of respect for seasonal fruit that overrides legalities.

And anyway, Son helped me eat them, so he's an accessory after the fact, or a receiver of stolen goods, or both. Some were bruised inside (too late in the season), but the nice ones were *extremely* nice. And it's true that stolen fruit tastes nicer.

The world didn't used to be this full of fences. Fruit was there for the taking, once. Within reason. (I'm old enough to reminisce?) I should always walk around in good camouflage clothes, just in case.

———

Wednesday, 14th May, 2008.

Prehistoric Soup

This week I care about two things – painting, and feeding my offspring. I've got it easy with this renewed fit of maternal piety, because when I did a spontaneous defrosting of the freezer the other night (so I could make a snowman in the sink with the ice), I found two tubs of three hundred year-old soup buried at the back.

If this soup wasn't frozen it would have fossilised by now. I know I didn't make it last year, and I know I didn't make it the year before. Admittedly it's sad that I can remember not-making vegetable soup for whole years in a row, but this does prove I was, once, a very good soup-making mum.

It's damn good soup, by the way. You'd call it a bisque if you were into using stupid words to describe something that already has a perfectly good name. So when I was opening the container, ready to tip it onto the garden to nourish the earth, I thought it looked potentially good and decided to experiment.

We didn't die. Or even get stomach aches. And it was so nice we're going to have the other tub tonight. All of those rumours they spread about frozen food having a limited shelf life must be wrong. I bet if you thawed Walt Disney out and ate him you'd be okay afterwards. Except for your obvious psychological problem.

Being a mum is easy, especially if you can pull a motherhood you prepared earlier out of the freezer every now and then. Now, I wonder what old food I have hiding at the back of the cupboards...

p.s. Snowman lasted a day and a half. In case you were wondering.

———

Friday, 16th May, 2008.

Let There Be Light!

If the light of autumn is this bad, then winter's gonna be a complete motherfucker. I've gone over the dark side of the face I'm painting at least four times now, and it's still wrong, because the light changes every five seconds and then your vision goes to shit.

Yesterday I thought I'd solved the problem by taking over Son's old bedroom, but I was going hell for leather thinking *this is great!* and being generally amazed at how easily I paint when the light is good, then in the afternoon discovered that the glossy bits were so obviously not blended well with the matt-ish bits that I had to suppress a scream. With swear words, which it turns out are a great scream-suppressant.

I've had no end of trouble with the light since I started this painting. I have to solve this problem NOW, seeing as I'm not likely to ever be able to rent a studio, being a dirt poor single mother. And as a good friend pointed out recently, I ain't ever likely to end up in a relationship where I can start afresh in a better-lit place, because I'm just not marry-able material (thanks Love, for crushing all romantic aspirations). This house is it. It's big enough, so I have to make it work.

This is very modern of me, but I think electricity might have to be the go for winter. And damned if I didn't just discover that my lamp had a mere 40 watt globe in it. That makes me an official idiot. Except that I learn from my mistakes, have bought 100 watt globes, and I can *see* with them [!!]. There's a possibility they're tricking me as much as the window light has tricked me, but I'm pretty sure the Dutch masters used 100 watt candles, so fingers crossed.

----

p.s.
Electricity is so overrated.

Monday, 19th May, 2008.

Trial and Error
I'm getting good at the error part of that process, but tonight I get a reprieve because I won't be able to see the full extant of today's error until I have daylight. I finished my painting during early afternoon, hated it by late afternoon, attacked it again in the evening when it was way too dark to see, and now it looks temporarily aces.

A love-hate relationship. I think my painting and I need a few days apart. A bit of breathing space. See other people. It needs to set me free, is what.

Monday, 26th May, 2008.

Resurrection
If you're not lucky love can knock so many years off your life. You know the scenario: wife dies, husband dies two months later. Or Husband

dies, wife dies two months later. Fretting. Or something more like devastation. (Insert wife/wife and husband/husband variations as appropriate.)

My uncle's a trooper; it's been four months since we lost Aunty E and he hasn't snuffed it yet. He's not far behind schedule because 'round about now it's starting to happen. It's sad in one way, and amusing in another, because he's in hospital and clearly losing it [sad], but having the funniest delusions [not sad] [ok, sort of sad].

The main funny delusion is that Aunty E has come *'back from heaven'*. He's sustained this delusion for quite a while. When we visited him in hospital yesterday [sad] he was telling us how she's come back shorter [not sad]. Also she's come back in a really bad mood, and won't talk to him. And she took off with his car.

You try answering a million questions about why somebody would come back from heaven [eww] with a different personality. He thinks that because Mum has worked with the elderly for years she should know the answer to this, as though it was covered as part of her training. I'm personally more curious about why she's shorter. I wonder if that happened to Jesus.

The lesson here is that in the early stages of dementia the guts of your personality starts getting out of control. Both Uncle and Aunty were grumpy old conspiracy theorists who were estranged from the bulk of their relatives [sad] and cried poor a lot more than they needed to [irritating]. It makes sense that she's come back in a foul mood, and that in his dotage he's worried about money money money, and having his car stolen. It's true to character. (In my dotage I'll be running around making wild exclamations about how I've overdone the highlights and can't see well enough to blend the paint.)

Back to the point, my poor uncle. He's losing his faculties, losing his freedom, and has lost his wife. When hugging me goodbye he said *'Your hair smells really lovely'*. At first I thought *great!*, he can't be too far gone if he has such excellent taste in hair product fragrances (damn right it's really lovely, I practically snort the stuff when I wash my hair). But then it struck me that he's all alone, with nobody to hug. The smell of people is a thing of closeness, and not nice to be without. (In my dotage I'm gonna also run around sniffing people.)

So I'm worried about him and need to make sure that however long he has left is as un-lonely as we can make it. Which is hard because he's far away. Also it's hard to break somebody's innate conspiracy-theorist habits, goodness knows I've tried. I've thrown so many look-on-the-bright-sides at him I make Pollyanna seem depressing, but so far to no avail. That's the worst thing – being an unhappy demented instead of a happy demented. It's like being an angry drunk instead of a happy drunk – a waste of good alcohol, a waste of good deteriorating brain cells. I hope I'm a happy demented when I grow up.

I'm being flippant in order to manage the awful understanding that Old Age sucks. There's the graceful, wise and fluffy-white-haired side of it, but the rest just leaves a big sad lump in your throat.

———

Bright Side:

I did, however, manage to rescue the cake, which he picked up spontaneously and waved around. That was First-Born's entertainment for the day, we were sure it was going airborne and couldn't stop laughing.

That and visiting the maternity ward, where sixteen years ago they were about to be born. Except, there's no window full of babies anymore, so there was nothing to show them.

———

Friday, 30th May, 2008.

Ego-Stroking

What's the etiquette on this one? Are you allowed to laugh at your own jokes in polite society, or do you have to be modest?

For weeks my students were asking me to show them some of my work, and I carried the most tame story in for them but somehow never managed to pull it out. Apart from bald self-aggrandisement I couldn't see the point of sharing it. Until this week, when I was teaching them the hows and whys of using dialogue. Even though it's not entirely full of the stuff, the plot of this tame story was driven by dialogue. So I dusted it off, and made it our read-aloud-in-class story for the week. I was, for another twenty minutes of my life, dead famous.

They each read a page, and as it was going around the room we couldn't stop laughing, because it's *funny*. I'd remembered it being devastatingly clever [!!!!!], but I'd forgotten it was funny, and buggered if I could stop myself. It's weird laughing at your own work, but how do you not? Especially if you wrote it a hundred million years ago so it's like it belongs to somebody else. And if you don't laugh you're just gonna look wooden.

I'm being well and truly grounded in up-yourself training, which is bound to happen because having students is like having your own personal fan club sometimes. Somebody tells you you're wonderful every second week. Which is balanced out with me thinking *they're* wonderful; it's one big love-making-the-world-go-round riot. Truth is, if they weren't telling me I'm wonderful I'd probably be self-conscious and worry that I wasn't entertaining them enough. Yes, I really am that insecure. I think I have to change the tattoo on my forehead to LOVE ME, PLEASE?.

I know this makes me a dickhead, because my teachers at Art Skool aren't like that. They're cool and self-possessed. I can't be mature like them because I get too excited by... *everything*. That's why I love teaching, especially writing, because we're constantly discussing the world and it's like hanging out with friends. You inevitably fall in love with your class. It's very personal. If you happen to be immature.

Also, though, it's so nice to be working with words again. Back in the saddle and all that. Feels like home, and I'm so, so close to having the best of both worlds. *Any minute now.*

Freak Show

Let's not get too carried away with the up-myself business. There's plenty wrong with me, and I'm up for a bit of psychoanalysis of my ticking technique. Which is funny if you're into puns (I'm not), because my ticking technique is influenced by my motor tic. Oh ha. Ha ha.

The hardest thing about teaching, for me, is marking the attendance roll. I can draw you the most delicate and complex image if you ask me to, but ask me to make a single stroke on the page, in a specified column, and I can't do it. Or I can, but only with a lot of effort.

I look at it and consult with my hand, and my hand has this malicious motherfucking grin. I try to wrestle with it to make the stroke quickly, but I go over it compulsively, probably three times. Four. Is it stressful: YES IT IS.

Shits me up the wall, but at least I've improved. When I was a teenager I did this every time I wrote and would nearly rip through the page. My full stops could have poked your eyes out. One particular teacher was always giving me lines (I am my child's mother, and was also in trouble a lot); he thought I was making them messy on purpose. Actually writing lines for me was utter torture, and his accusations really compromised the placement of my halo.

The good thing is that as a grown-up I can almost train myself out of it. My daytime class roll has had the fat, overworked ticks for weeks, but I noticed this week that the most recent columns contain easy, single strokes. Not only did I win the battle, but I did it without noticing. Mind over matter. Although, I guess that's the point – to make it not-happen, it has to not-matter to me.

So tidy, such freedom. So *normal*. Administration will check the rolls and say to themselves *gosh, look at those neat ticks – that's one very relaxed teacher*. I tried to replicate this freedom of penmanship during my evening class, but the evening class roll is doomed because I'm carrying the contents of Day with me by then. I couldn't do it.

I'm like my own lab rat, keeping tabs on the stress levels. Obviously they're abating, and I have the daytime roll to prove it. They're just not abating enough. (*Freak.*)

———

Still Friday, 30th May, 2008.

Peace on Earth
The moon's always blue, pigs have flown backwards, the sea's frozen over and the grass is definitely greener on *this* side.

How many weeks now? So many I've lost count. But however many, First-Born has stopped attacking. It's like we're living on a different planet now, and this time I'm not being naive or inappropriately optimistic. No dupes where I'm standing, we're all rational beings here.

On top of all this goodness, we went to a mediation meeting yesterday and I was impressed by how it went. The mediators were witnessing Happily-Ever-After in the flesh. We practically did their job for them. In the end what came out of the discussion was that this time we both let our guard down at the same time, and it can't be reversed.

Very happy. We have our "us" back. A bit of stabilising and relationship building to do, but it's all sweet.

———

June 2008

Wednesday, 4th June, 2008.

Saving the World

Sort of. The supermarket has become a battle zone, but now I have a weapon. I bought *The Guide to Ethical Supermarket Shopping* at Readings a couple of weeks ago and have become a consumer warrior.

When I go in to shop I skulk around soldier-like, eyes darting sideways. All of that supermarket trickery. Saving the world isn't easy, but I thought this'd be a nice starting point, changing my consumer habits bit by bit. Only, it's hard to find substitutes for some of the products I need. Want. Need. For example, I didn't realise that the Nestle boycott is still on, and that means NO MILO!!

How to stop people from buying badass Nestle products? Proselytizing about the wrongs of the world works with some people and not with others. Son, for instance, doesn't care [yet]. First-Born does, and now our shopping experience isn't just about making a list, it's considering what we're allowed to buy and not. No questions asked, they just accept that ethics overrule everything else. Big brand chocolate companies = listed as bad = no more good chocolate.

I feel guilty for not having known these things earlier. This little book has just about every possible category of grocery covered. I'm already trying, buy all of my fruit and vegetables from small F&V stores. Okay not bananas – I buy them too often so I go for easy there. OH THE GUILT. But it's not enough to do small things. How do you encourage everybody to make the effort to change?

Famous Breakfast Spread made by Big Company is bad = no more Breakfast Spread. And after years and years I now discover I have to change my washing powder. That means changing the smell of everything (don't panic!). I've made a guinea pig of myself for the public good; after an intrepid new purchase I've discovered that Planet

Ark's Aware Eco Choice is nice enough, though I don't recommend sniffing it when you open the box because it'll make your head spin. Trust me, it smells okay.

If you have cats and you're too poor to buy fresh meat, [allegedly] only Snappy Tom is okay. It costs more but that's the point, isn't it? If something's inexpensive, chances are somebody else is being ripped off and you should feel bad about that. If you want things cheap you're probably a motherfucker.

Speaking of motherfuckers, I'm buying this book for all of my friends' birthdays. When I visit their houses they'll be hiding all of their unethical products, to avoid my impending lectures. I can feel myself morphing into one of those annoying people who tell everybody how to live. They'll thank me one day, when the world doesn't spontaneously combust, and their consciences don't shrivel because of the exploitation they no longer inadvertently perpetuate. (*My pleasure.*)

Thursday, 12ᵗʰ June, 2008.

Consider the Lilies, Consider the Birds

I was driving along Doncaster Road today when I noticed a church with one of those message boards that offer pearls of wisdom out the front. This one said '*Persevere – even snails made it onto the ark*'.

Two levels of interpretation for that; one that made me really angry, and the other extending the first in such a way that I get to laugh at the morons who put it there.

First interpretation: the statement works only if you don't expect a snail to be worthy of being "saved". If this is you, you're surprised by the generosity of the good lawd in rescuing such a revolting creature. You believe that if the good lawd saves a snail, then of course he'll save you because humans are so much better, thus reinforcing the appalling and ultimately detrimental belief perpetuated by [most] religions, that humans are superior to all in the creature hierarchy, bugger ecology.

You're the reason the planet's going to shit.

Second [extended] interpretation: if accepting the first message, you'll be comforted by the statement most if you yourself are as revolting as said revolting creature, because it's telling you that gawd loves you even if you're no better than the slug-equivalent of a human being, so hang in there.

Makes me want to spread snail pellets around the entranceway to churches. Joy and salvation to all.

———

It also makes me nostalgic. When Ex-Brother-In-Law lived with me during the time of our totally platonic but intensely emotionally-involved friendship, we bonded over xtain signboards whenever we drove home from uni together. I feel like telling him about it, but can't because he's being such a prick.

———

Wednesday, 18th June, 2008.

Anti-Ahabbing

Up yours, KRudd PM. Up yours with a [metaphoric] razor blade. I started reading *Ocean Warrior* by Paul Watson, expecting it to be charismatic but on the annoying I-am-hero side. Well – not. It's well written, informative, and not nearly as arrogant as I expected. It both inspired and made me angry. Especially because I was halfway through when sitting in a waiting room with Me Lovely Mother (being her post-operative looker-afterer), and saw a harpooned whale on the front page of somebody's copy of *The Age* newspaper, with the announcement that Kevin Rudd has backed down on his promise to fight the Japanese whaling operations. A front page that'll make you cry.

It's devastating that we – being our country – *could* do something, are one of the few countries who *can* do something, but we – meaning our motherfucking prime minister – have decided to do nothing at all. Did the Japanese say *please* and he was too polite to say no? The more I read, the more I realise I need to learn before I'm ready to summarise and preach. (Hold that thought.)

I also read *Breath*, by Tim Winton, and was in awe of the dynamic he creates between his characters and the sea. Pity about the ending. All of this immediate action, and then suddenly this flat, inactive prose that goes something like '*and then this happened, and then that happened, the end*'. If I was editor I'd smack him on the wrist and send him home to finish his story properly. The novel's still brilliant. I magnanimously forgive him for the ending because he took me somewhere I hadn't been. It's beautiful.

Enough, let's get back to being angry at KRudd PM.

I don't know why but ocean ecology is foregrounded in my psyche. I read these books and it goes through my mind as though I have gills. A matter of suddenly realising what the ocean means to the world, and how it's everybody's business.

I then read *Whale Warriors*, by Peter Heller, and couldn't put it down. It's not just ethically sound and inspiring – it's full-on high adventure. It's an account of his (I refuse to use the worn-out word "journey") experience on the Sea Shepherd ship (Farley Mowat) during an anti-Japanese-whaling expedition to Antarctica, and reading it is like being there. Except that if you're reading it on land you're probably not about to die every few pages.

Read it read it read it. Especially good because he doesn't fawn or hero-worship, doesn't have mother-earth tattoos, worship Gaia or change his name to Riversong – he's rational and observant. Down to earth. And not a vegan. (Sorry.)

Gosh, I've been to sea three times in two weeks. I more than admire these people. The world would be awful without them. Look at me in this safe little house on this safe little hillside, knowing what's going on in the world and doing so little to help. [So far.] But my mentality's shifting in every way possible. I was raised to be *this*, and I'm training myself to be *that*. As soon as I figure out how to get beyond thinking so that I can start *doing,* I'll be onto it.

I give myself three weeks to make myself useful. Preferably without risking my life in the process. Now *that's* a deadline.

———

Friday, 20th June, 2008.

Two-Leaf Clover

That's two leaves short of good luck. And sort of always being left behind. If certain friends throughout my life had to evacuate a burning house, I wouldn't be in the must-grab pile with the photographs. (Be warned – today I'm wearing my victim hat.)

I heard from Evil Ex-Friend again yesterday, and it's completely undone my carefully cultured toughness. I haven't mentioned that I heard from her again a while ago. I was walking that morning and had started thinking about her. Not nice things – more like being un-surprised that she'd sent her lovely apology and plea that we catch up, and then disappeared again. In fact, I was swearing at her in my head. Even though I hadn't expected much from her.

When I got home that day I found a new text msg on my phone, from her. Very Twilight-Zone timing. Of course, being tough doesn't mean I'm not a desperate idiot who misses her. I jumped on the phone immediately and we had a long catch up. She told me where I could apply for teaching work, and that she was moving to Northern News South Wales. We slipped straight back into friendship mode. And I was stupidly happy for five whole seconds.

I applied for the job, got it, remembered how tough I was, didn't trust her much yet, so didn't even tell her about it, not even to say thank you, not wanting to ever put myself in a submissive position with her again. Plus I thought what's the point? She was moving states and I expected never to hear from her again.

One thing I had told her was that our other colleague (three of us had been sessional teaching at a university together) was also living in Northern NSW, not far from where she was going, and that I'd only just found that friend accidentally, there's the luck of it. To be able to move to the middle of nowhere and find there's already a friend waiting there for you. Bully for her.

So yesterday I received an excited text from Evil Ex-Friend saying that I hadn't told her Other Teaching Friend was pregnant. Well, I didn't know at the time. As I replied with this fact before class, one of my students (who used to be her student) asked me *when's Evil due?*. That's when I found out that Evil Ex-friend is pregnant, too, and hadn't told me. I queried, she replied: she'd wanted to surprise me with it, and say goodbye before she left.

I would have loved that. It was really nice of her.

So now I'm profoundly sad. My students didn't quite get my full attention during that class. I'm really happy for her, that's the problem. Because what's the point of making me feel all warm and remembery

222

if I have no way of spending those emotions? This is a happiness that comes with such a sense of loss, and a memory of a helluva lotta pain. Raw-wound variety.

It's taken me a long time to feel lonely, but now that I'm changing the way I live I've got plenty of time to notice I don't have anybody to share things with. Loads of friends, but they're all over the place, and this year's project work could leave me very isolated if I'm not careful. The lesson her friendship left me with is don't-need-anybody. I take it seriously. What a fucked legacy.

There's a not-so amusing irony in spending more time with more and more people but feeling lonelier and lonelier. The more you step into the outside world, the more you need your people from the inside. (The inside world being art and books and art and books and art and books.) Which breaks the not-needing rule. Which is a recipe for disaster. Being human is hard work, innit?

Sunday, 22nd June, 2008.

Calamity

Oh heck, I swore in public. Does that mean I'm turning into a bogan? It was terrible, and I was about to cry. Because not only have they installed self-service checkouts at our local Safeway, but tonight they made me use them.

I didn't even want to go to their stinking Safeway, too knackered from working hard and working late, but the kids wanted me to get milk. And chocolate. So there we were, Son and I, about to go through the checkout, when I realised there were no checkout staff. I was confronted by the changing world and so distressed.

I cannot stand machines talking to me. Of course I know how to use the stupid things, but I looked at it dumbly, looked at the overseeing Safeway woman less than dumbly, and in my best this-world-sucks voice (which doubles as a cracking about-to-cry voice) I said 'I hate this – I fucking hate it'.

Then I did the stubborn child thing by banging things around more than was necessary. I also childishly said 'I'm never shopping here again'. Removing the human element: sacrilegious last straw.

If corporations won't stop logging in Tasmania because it would cost people their jobs, then why are Safeway allowed to give human jobs to machines? *Thank-you-for-shopping-Safeway* my arse. I told the machine to fuck off. If sentient machines ever do take over the world, I'll be on their hit list. Especially if the self-service check-out machine talks to the automated telephone-answering machines, which probably have me on record as a serial swearer.

No, I *don't like it*. I need to join a Luddite collective and hang out with the kindred. I wonder if they advertise online.

———

If I only know the things I know because I've spent years reading certain books, how can I possibly convey the amount of information that needs to be conveyed to non-reading individuals, to show them why so many things are fucked? I can't stop panicking about this.

———

Also: when I was supposed to be doing something else, I spent a few days working on a drawing. Very quietly, didn't even show it to anybody. It seemed like a private activity, something to be self-conscious about. But I followed my resolve to enter it into a competition. Then cringed and thought, *what am I, crazy?*

Surprised, then, to be informed that I'm a finalist and selected for the exhibition. Welcome validation. I've been working away without feedback from the outside world for so long, I've started to feel guilty for being so caught up in these obsessive thought patterns. For producing work that potentially had no value to anybody.

Oh lawdy hallelujah, the world wants me after all; makes my garret a less lonely place in which to work. It also gives me permission to neglect people. That's all you need, permission. I am *allowed*.

———

Thursday, 26th June, 2008.

Paint. Poetry. Et al.
Life's not slow yet, but at least I'm making time to read, and this gives the illusion of slowness.

I'm currently addicted to poetry, having fortified my stomach against the unpleasant stuff you have to read through to get to the good stuff. Although at the moment I'm reading Craig Sherbourne, *Hoi Polloi,* and am so excited by it I can hardly sleep. He plays with language the way a singer plays with voice, controlled but effortless, a natural way with rhythm. I can feel the way he thinks as I read. I can feel him write. I think I'm in book love.

Also I've been writing. Also painting. Also doing research. And drawing. And not-neglecting my people. Hence the slowing life down thing isn't really working.

As Friend Boy A pointed out to me yesterday (having taken on the role of Destroyer of All Self-Delusion and Wielder of Brutal Honesty, complete with evil chuckle and evident delight in his naysaying): when I slow things down, I look around me and see a gap in time that I immediately fill with something else. Or as he expressed it, my life will never slow down because the minute it gets even a little close to calm, I say something like *'Ooh, look at all that free time, here's my opportunity to learn quantum-physics'.* (That's a joke by the way. As if I'd take on quantum-physics.) Then I turn around and wonder where all of the lovely slowness has gone.

So I need to drop at least one of my pseudo-slow things. What really isn't working is the not-neglecting-my-people business, so the people have to go. Just selectively. Because man, do people take up too much time, or what? It's lovely seeing them more often, but they take time out of your control without meaning to.

Eg. Drive Lovely Mother to visit Uncle at hospital. I say *let's go later rather than earlier,* so I can paint for a while first. She says *'Oh, we can't go late because I have to get back'.* (To what?) She barters my proposed time backwards until my painting time is eaten away. I get offended because if I was doing paid work she wouldn't have expected me to give the time up.

Even the people you love spending time with suck sometimes. But I figure most of my people love me even when I'm neglecting them. Technically I get away with it, therefore I should insist that they work around me. (Except, I love Mum and want to make her happy. I make an exception for her; also because she's so persuasive I can't say no.)

Never mind. My body's shot with stress, no respite from my motor tic (a trusty barometer). I have to find a way to relax. But this painting I'm working on – with time so limited, I painted the eyes three stages earlier than usual. Usually eyes are for almost-last. They're so strong they're spooky and I'm so excited by this I practically can't breathe. (How do other people paint portraits without hyperventilating?)

———

Saturday, 28th June, 2008.

Cat Out of the Bag

Young people shit me. And you can't even hate them for being young and stupid because it's in the job description. If they were smart they'd be old.

Dad turns eighty next week, so we had a big get-together for him tonight. I was sitting at a fairly large table with half the family, Dad included, and his sister and a cousin I haven't seen for about a million years. It was fun, but early on my niece called a question out to me across this heavily populated table, and this particular question revealed possibly the most personal and most secret thing about me in the whole wide world.

I was stunned into a this-cannot-be-happening state, gave her a desperate *please-don't* look, and damned if she didn't say it again, just in case THE WHOLE WORLD didn't hear it the first time.

First-Born's eyes met mine and sent me a shitload of helpless empathy, because they knew as well as I did that that moment and those words were irrevocable. I sat there watching my life change before my very eyes with this enormous violation of my privacy, wondering if there was a possibility that people didn't understand what she was saying, and then [not very] discreetly crossed the room to whisper into her ear '*Don't you ever say that in public again*'. Not even a please, just plain old firm.

I'm regretting that her mother (Friend W-L) tells her daughter everything. I warned her so many moons ago that kids have stupid big mouths. If they proposed a law insisting that all teenagers be de-barked, I'd vote for that government.

226

Anyway, I managed to keep my chin up and let my personality run on auto-pilot, but the quiet is catching up with me now. I'm glad I didn't go to the after party at Baby Brother's house. Even though being asked to the after party is like being invited to sit at the back of the bus with the cool kids. Really, though, that only ever reminds me that I'm not actually cool, so I came home to get an old-womanly early night, so that I can paint for as long as possible tomorrow. I didn't have time to paint today and it kills me not being able to just keep going.

What I did do with my very small amount of free time today was swim. Swimming is good medicine and I think it's going to save me, because a kilometre in soft water relaxes me like nothing else. I have to approach relaxation as a therapeutic thing now. Violation of privacy notwithstanding, tonight is nice. My body feels both alive and peaceful, GrandKitten's nuzzling very beautifully into my neck, and there's nothing to stop me from working quietly tomorrow. Life is good.

Monday, 30th June, 2008.

Oh My Aching Bones

Thirteen hours is too long to spend painting in one day. Somebody needs to remind me: I enjoy this, why... ? I mean ya wouldn't, in ya right mind.

I didn't even finish what I wanted to finish. Sometimes I look at my work and feel self-conscious because *anybody could do this*, but during days like today I'm reminded that no, not many people can. And if I'm not careful I'll fall into the not-many-people category, because being tired could've made me sloppy.

Days like today also remind me that there are some things I'm still awkward with. It's humbling. I liked it better when painting was just plain difficult, instead of monumentally difficult. Sometimes I'd like to be one of those not-many people, because if I was other-people I wouldn't spend thirteen hours a day slaving away over a canvas. I'd probably have a life.

227

July 2008

Sunday, 6th July, 2008.

Just Thinkin'

In an alternate lifetime, I wouldn't have had a banana and some wasabi peas for breakfast. I would spend this sunny day painting the balcony railing, oiling the deck, weeding and pruning the front garden, sweeping the steps, and then have wine and cheese on the balcony while the sun sets. After having removed the flapping white linen from the clothesline. Of course.

This is the best daydream I can come up with while my kids are sleeping in and all's quiet. I hope they sleep 'til a hundred o'clock.

I haven't painted [art] since Monday, too busy with people around here. But I've spent a lot of time writing, refusing to accept that I couldn't make an ugly thing beautiful by adding the right kind of human element. (Did I succeed? I don't know.) And yesterday I went to a distant art gallery with my mother, who happens to be a great person to do exhibitions with because she looks at works and says things like *'You could do that, V-M'*, and *'Yours are much better than that, V-M'*. (I do correct her, for the record.)

It doesn't look like my social life's going to abate for a few days. Finally went out with my L-P-B-bitches, had the funnest time. I *love* them, and need to go out more. I don't because I'm more café than pub, and pubs are where everyone goes, but in the end once you're a little pissed who cares where you are? I just love my people. And dancing. Talking to strangers. Watching friends have their heads shoved into tranny crotches during drag queen performances.

I could probably learn to get over the feel of other people's cigarette smoke rasping its way out of my lungs the day after. And I could learn to live with the distance between home and city (not as bad now that I've met my new best friend, Eastlink). All in the interests of not becoming prematurely old. That danger was lurking; I could've forgotten to go out forever and just slipped into nursing-home mode before my time, without knowing what I was missing. I can't believe I forget these things. How do you forget to have fun? That's just dumb.

———

Effort

Gosh, did I ever have to get my hands dirty today (sweeping, weeding, pruning the rose garden, pruning the potato vine). And isn't it a good thing that ~~that silly man~~ Ex-H keeps ~~all of that annoying cardboard crap~~ useful old refrigerator boxes and such-like up in the rafters in the garage. And even though I miss having ~~a slave~~ somebody do these things ~~for~~ with me, there's nothing like a good, hard day's work to make you feel ~~like you still wish somebody else would do all of your menial dirty work for you~~ a great sense of job satisfaction.

———

I also read *Muck*, by Craig Sherbourne, and he's so damn good but the love affair's over because he forgot to give out reader rewards. His adolescent self makes a shitty character, and I don't care how beautifully written it is, it was depressing to be inside his head. You have to give out sunshine if you're going make your readers stand in puddles. A bit of a chin-up here and there. I even had to put it down halfway through the week, and today forced myself to finish.

I'm not sure I can forgive him for the calf. It's too sad. A bully of a way to end a book. Still, I somehow can't wait for the next one.

———

Writing, Reading, Writing

I'm a hypocrite. When I say an author has failed to reward their reader with light moments, forget it. It's time I start thinking that's acceptable, otherwise I'll have to criticise my own work. Hell forbid.

The new novel I want to write has no manners and is pushing itself to the front of the queue. *I don't have time for you, Project.*

And yet, it's there, so I'm getting ready for it, which means clearing all unfinished projects out of the way. Especially the ones I've already finished, which need some spit n' polish n' tying up with string before I put them back on the shelf to collect dust. Which is how, a couple of days ago, I picked up one manuscript and started to read. Well not really, this is the computer age; I propped myself up on pillows with my laptop and started to edit.

I discovered that I'd done exactly the same thing as CS (all darkness, no light), except less famously. For a whole half-manuscript the novel's as clever as fuck. Yes, I say so myself. But it's also too grungy, so being *clever* doesn't make it *good*. I took a break, did some family things, went back to see if I could finish it in one day. Taking a break didn't fix anything. No rewards for the reader. Who forgets to reward the reader? Only an idiot. There are light moments in there; just not enough. (I did finish it in a day, improved it slightly, but it's not even nearly a cleaned-up copy.)

A few days ago I started reading *The Spare Room* by Helen Garner. Unfortunately at night, which equals no sleep because I couldn't put it down. Hers isn't roadkill, even though it's full of blood and guts. It's just a beautiful, sad story. Notice how other people don't wreck their novels? I should try to be more like them.

Now I'm wrestling with rhythm, I just can't get it on this other piece I'm working on. It's all there except for the rhythm. It's like being out on a dance-floor and not being able to dance. Which probably means it's time to get back to the painting. Belonging to two guilds instead of one is sometimes a good thing.

———

Tuesday, 15th July, 2008.

The Miracle of Technology

Now I've heard everything. The Pope sending a text message to "the pilgrims" at Youth Week is too worldly. Catholic upsucking is such a class act.

Don't let the fact that they're using technology fool you into thinking this is anything less than medieval. If only people would read history, they'd be so much less stupid. But at least all of the Catholic youth are up in Sydney and not down here in Melbourne. Makes the air feel... I don't know. Cleaner, or something.

———

Monday, 21st July, 2008.

I Love a Sunburnt Country

I really do. I just spent a few days on a road trip with me Dear Old Dad, and we're both such exceptionally nice people we had an exceptionally nice time, getting along exceptionally well with our exceptional degrees of politeness and consideration for each other. Lovely company. I stress this because nobody – nobody! – gets my Dad's company at length like that. That trip was priceless and I'm feelin' very lucky.

I find it hard to leave home for any length of time, never seem to feel "ready", always waiting for some future when I'll feel up to date with all of the things I need to get done. But I told him that if my work was accepted into yonder award exhibition, I'd do the road trip with him.

So we went to Broken Hill, and I'm in love with it. It's the red soil, so soft to walk on. Love love *love*. No wonder My Dad keeps wanting to go back. He's done two solo trips up through Central Australia since retiring. He's social with his family but very much a loner, so going it alone seemed normal for him. But he said two beautiful things while we were there. One was on the way back from Silverton, where we walked a decent distance along a dry riverbed together. Since retiring he's becomes a walker like me, so we were in our element. (The *quiet!*) He said '*Of all the walks I've ever done, this has been one of the nicest*'.

He then told me he wished he'd asked me to join him on his Central trips, which took me completely by surprise. I wish I'd thought through my response before opening my mouth to speak. Instead of saying *that would've been really nice*, I said '*I thought you wanted to go alone – you should have asked Aunty One or Aunty Two to go with you!*'.

I meant that he's so close to his sisters and they're also retired enough (without teenage kids to look after) to have gone with him.

231

I hope he didn't think I meant I wouldn't have wanted to travel with him. I want more than anything to be the kind of person who could do that sort of thing.

Now, of course, I'm worried about his self-imposed loneliness. Which he may not even feel. It kills me to think that he's the lonely victim of his own personality. We're similar enough for me to think he might be.

I hope to, and I mean well, but will I ever do that trip with him? Not as a tourist, but as a doer of things? Something more useful than looking and feeling all wishy washy. Something that involves rolling around in that beautiful red soil.

_____

I'm also in love with a camel we met on the roadside. History walking around us on four legs[es]. It was a great kisser, and now I want a camel for Xmas. Please.

Also on the roadside we met a rustic-yet-feminine woman who thought we were in trouble because we'd pulled over, and wasn't that nice of her. (That's why she had to become part of an elaborate sexual fantasy that sustained me for the rest of the trip. And there I was thinking I was into men lately. My mistake.) I'd asked Dad to pull over so I could walk on the red soil and listen to the absolute silence. A silence full of birdsong and little else. I can't find silence at home, even when I'm hiking. Always a hum of cars. So this moved me, left me hungry for more. And with a resolve to find my way back to it somehow. Take my kids with me.

_____

Went to see the exhibition, and the novelty of seeing my own work on a gallery wall still hasn't worn off. All of those polished floorboards and nice people and their artwork. Aren't humans clever.

So much to say, so few energies to say it with. A helluva lot to process for my little head. Had fun is all.

_____

Goats on the roadsides. So many of them. Do we call them feral, or leftovers? Like the camels.

And monumental quantities of litter. Before we even arrived at Broken Hill, that long road strewn with empty water bottles and food packaging. How do humans fail to care about the impact their careless actions have on the world around them?

———

Back in the real world: full(ish) moon over Eastlink tonight. How do I love thee, Eastlink, let me count the ways. I love everything at the moment. What a many splendid thing.

———

Wednesday, 23ʳᵈ July, 2008.

There's No Savin' Ya

Today I wore the necklace that First-Born gave me for my birthday. The one they swore they didn't steal, a very sweet declaration. They loved me when they gave it to me, proof that they sometimes do.

I'm not really a "pretty" necklace type, but I've been reworking a manuscript that made me think about them being young n' vulnerable, so wearing it was a sentimental thing. Like wearing the macaroni necklaces they make for you in kinder. And just about as stylish.

This made the timing of the phone call from the mediator funny. If you turn your sense of humour on its head and pinch it into a weird shape. He was really nice, actually, and probably told me more than he should have. Very gently. *There's no hope for you,* kind of thing. I should be devastated by this, but I'm so far gone I'm larfin'. That crazy kid o' mine.

He saw First-Born on their own and saw through their act. I like him because he's perceptive and frank about it. Told me how they like to blame me for things, then described them very well, for a stranger. Said he can't help because First-Born won't take responsibility for their role in the situation (well duh). Said he can see them controlling our lives and that it's not healthy. Said I'm going to need more specialised help with this one, and then wished me luck. You could hear the pity dripping from his voice.

I wonder how often he has to tell people they're so well and truly up shit creek there's no rescue party able to get them back? It would

233

have been useful to have referred me on to this fantasy specialist who offers help to the un-helpable. Or at least told me how to find them. Told me who or what they are.

Wow. Anyway I'm not too fussed. First-Born's been okay, so I'll cruise along and wait for those small opportunities that sometimes present themselves, where they let me be friendly and we have a laugh. Humour is their thing, so I can work with that.

They now have their learner's permit, and I have to start teaching them to drive. That might be fun? What happens when they realise that to teach them I have to [repeatedly] tell them what to do?

Yep, the future's looking bright. Maybe they'll get sick of all of this and just start being nice eventually. I miss them. A lot. I miss family life the way it used to be. Repeat repeat.

———

Thursday, 24th July, 2008.

Deification

I'm converting to Jamie-Oliver-ism. What he did on tv last night! Chickens the world over are erecting monuments to him as we speak.*

My friends'll rue the day they laughed at me when I suggested you CAN make changes to the world, even when it's as big, bad and ugly as it is today. All you have to do is find the right way to educate people. Encourage them to be less selfish. It'd help if you were as famous as Jamie Oliver, but STILL.

Anyway, it's a wonderful step in human progress, and everybody should be filled with hope. Especially if they're a chicken.

* *Jamie's Fowl Dinners;* a program drawing attention to the cruelty of factory farming.

———

Then I read a Reddit post about free range chicken products selling out in the UK after the show aired. One comment refers us to *The Omnivore's Dilemma*, by Michael Pollan, which describes how a [misleading] free-range label can be abused to trick consumers into believing they're choosing a more ethically produced food. A reminder that even human kindness can be exploited under capitalism. *Fuck.*

Saturday, 26th July, 2008.

Garson

I am, as we speak, in hiding. I'll have to start wearing a balaclava and develop a shifty look in my eye. Any minute now the newspapers are going to label me "The Hot Chocolate Bandit", because this afternoon I walked out of my favourite café without paying.

It's not my fault I can't keep up with the world. I go there, as per usual, only to find that instead of paying when I make my order, I'm supposed to take a seat and be served. They've changed the way they do things (i.e. they're now doing things WRONG). Don't they know some of us don't like change? The waitress told me they're also about to install automated ordering, whatever that means.

Anyways, I had the Saturday paper and was reading about books, the hot chocolate was top notch, and the cafe was as nice to be in as ever, once I got used to it. I stayed for a long time. Then when I'd had my fill of both newspaper and beverage, I got up and left, because that's what I always do. Except, this time without paying. And now I'm a common criminal – I didn't realise until hours later that I'd even done it.

If I go back and turn myself in, are they gonna take me out to the kitchen and make me do dishes? *Oh the shame.* After I've made my confession and paid them next time I'm there, they're probably going to keep my mug shot on the wall behind the counter and start counting the cutlery every time I try to leave.

The moral is, good service sucks. Also that if you want to steal a hot drink, the best place to hide it is in your belly.

It's All Good

I'm supposed to be going to sleep early, but I have so many euphorias bouncing around in my head I can hardly contain them. Some are euphorias that result from hard work. Some are from *Dark Knight* (the new Batman movie), which is so good I can't help feeling amazed by the cleverness of people. (Is it cool to be excited by a Batman movie? Possibly not. Forget I mentioned it.)

Then there's the euphoria of receiving nudie shots from Friend Girl A, who's kind enough to trust me with her body, and I didn't realise until then just how nice a gesture that is. I've had a painting in my head that requires her body, only I have such good manners I hadn't asked her yet. So she's said yes, and she's said *duh,* because she's apparently hinted before that she wants me to paint her naked, but I'm so thick (more of a sledge hammer girl) I didn't pick it up. Not to worry, I now have a future of imminent boobage and naked skin, and that's gotta be a good thing.

Also, this evening I went with my sisters and My Lovely Mother to see *Mamma Mia,* and it's such a *happy* movie. You don't know what fun is until you've seen that movie. Can you imagine the world without ABBA? ABBA and Meryl Streep. What a wonderful era this is to live in.

Thursday, 31ˢᵗ July, 2008.

F*%k Off, Euphorias

I hate poetry. It makes you love it and sweeps you away and it's such a rush, but then you start writing the stuff and... I'm never going to write poetry again. I SWEAR. (Like this: *Fuck.*)

These things have been kicking around in my head for weeks. I've been reading and reading and I keep finding more good poets, but then even the good ones write bad stuff and the bad stuff makes me chuck. I keep writing because it's all just in there and spilling out, and I start to wonder if I'm turning into *one of them.*

"Them" can't tell the difference between good and bad. So I've decided that my work-in-progress is bad and have screamed at it, and deliberately not sent it off when I was meant to. Even though it was ready.

For the record, I also this week hate teaching. And old people. I was asked to give a one-off Introduction to Writing class to an elderly social group, and VERY CAREFULLY chose a piece for them to read (no sex, no violence). Buggered if one old DEAR didn't keep interrupting as they were reading aloud – one of the most beautiful, sensitive stories you can imagine – with *'This is revolting, oh – oh no,*

I'm going to have to leave the room'. She didn't leave the room at all, which is a pity because I really wanted to say *good riddance*.

Poetry has put me in a very, very bad mood.

She then turned her nose up while the rest of us tried to reassure her of its value. I was dumbfounded. Everybody else loved it, but she made me think *what a waste of time*. I would much rather have been at home that day, reading a [not-poetry] book.

This not-sending of things off is bad of me. I've done it about five times this year now, and it ain't gonna get me anywhere. But it's good to hate things. Hating things lets you eliminate them from your list, so say goodbye to hanging out with cerebral people because my time from now on = going back to painting, drawing and a fugly big project upon which I'm supposed to be well and truly focused and yet, am not.

I'm spending far too much time alone. I have to, is the problem, or I won't get important things done. And that's why poetry sucks.

———

August 2008

Demonesque

I don't know why somebody would go to the trouble of re-writing a perfectly good past, especially when that past involves me being a wonderful mother. As in, "maternal", not mofo. But every now and then First-Born comes out with some high-calibre revisionism.

Tonight it started with the oranges. Until recently I forgot how much juice you can get out of an orange, but having rediscovered it I've been squeezing jugs full of fresh orange juice (or delegating the task to Son), and the joy it provides pretty much makes up for my terrible cooking. Tonight First-Born made a bitter comment about how they've been asking me where the squeezy thingy is for years, and suggested that I'm a cruel/bad/evil mother because I've kept said information from them.

I think if I wanted to be mean to a child I could come up with something more impressive than hiding the squeezy thing. Which incidentally is in the cupboard above the bench, next to the glasses, where anybody with eyes can see it.

Then that stupid ad for some stupid indoor cubby house for kids without any imagination at all came on the tele, and it reminded me of my kids being young and I asked '*Do you remember we used to build enormous tents in the loungeroom with sheets and blankets and cushions n' such?*'. First-Born answered [bitterly] with '*Yeah – until you told us we couldn't do it anymore*'.

I said no such thing. I loved those tents. They took over the whole house and I let the kids sleep in them for nights on end. So I pointed out to them that they were changing the past to make me look evil, and they should be careful about all of the good memories they're throwing away.

They backpedalled on the comment, until the real memories started poking through. Sad, huh.

Oh well. They're at their ex [?] partner's house, probably doing alcohol and teenage sex, but with any luck they'll dream about innocent things like tents and remember a time when there was peace on earth and their lovely mother didn't have horns, tail and pitchfork.

I'm going to erect a tent in the loungeroom this weekend. I'll wait until they bring GrandKitten home with them, though. GrandKitten'll go nuts – it'll be like having young kids again.

I wonder if when First-Born grows up they'll re-re-write the past back to its original state. Or if it's gone forever. Sigh and double sigh. Double, triple, quadruple.

Monday, 4th August, 2008.

Starvin' Marvin

I'm not sure about this idea of art galleries being just about the art. I went to St Kilda Road today to worship at the temple, and have to say ye gods have let us down. Aren't renovations supposed to make things bigger and better? Well, my friends and I waited for ages for the NGV bistro renovations to be over, so that we could get our grubby paws on their roast vegetable ciabattas. We had to go through withdrawal after the place had closed, but were sustained by the knowledge that it would one day re-open and ciabatta supplies would resume.

So I looked at some art, then headed to the new and improved bistro, only to find a little coffee/cake scenario in its place. NO MORE ROAST VEGETABLE CIABATTAS. What were they thinking? How could they do this to me? Don't they know that some of us have so little to look forward to? It doesn't make sense. The downstairs job they've got going is too noisy and cramped. This is the end of a fine institution. Whole civilisations crumble over something like a good ciabatta.

First I lose an arrow at the archery range on Saturday, then I lose an hour and a half of my life because Son made me watch *Tremors* (pitiful movie), and now I've lost my gastronomical joy. Next time I'm bringing a cut lunch.

Tuesday, 5th August, 2008.

Forward Thinking

Plan One: sit down between gesso coats to make a plan. In which case, the real Plan One is to dig my way out of here with a spoon. In which case, I must be feeling trapped.

The problem is that despite being wonderful [!!], I can't stand my own company. I really do have nothing to look forward to. I discover this every weekend. My weekends are full of people, yet also not. Then the new week starts and I have my work, but no reward at the end of it. Sense of satisfaction? Get fucked. Getting shit-loads done each week? Well of course, I've moved mountains lately, but who cares. It's all just a lot of nothing in the end.

This is one of those transitional phases you have to go through when you change your life around. Circumstances change and you can't keep your people with you the way you'd like to, so you need new people, and you'll keep needing new people until you have a new tribe to belong to.

The good thing is that on Sunday morning, in the middle of struggling unhappily through the weekend, I unrolled a small bit of canvas and started playing with an idea. The euphoria snapped right back into my head. Not happiness, just that absorbing contentment you get when you're working. I have to make sure I don't let too much time lapse between projects. Hence the gesso; prepping a larger canvas so I can get this one going. If I never stop, I'll never feel lonely.

Anyway there's this woman I think I might ask to sit for a portrait soon-ish. Or later-ish. Apart from having an interesting face, she's a loner of sorts and I'm fascinated. Loner because the kind of work she does needs to be done in isolation (she says). I want her to sit for me so that I can ask her *'What's it like to be you?'*. I really, really wanna know. I spend my life fending off the isolation. I hate it. I love being alone to work, but when I look up I want there to be people there. I want to know how she embraces it like that.

In the meantime I have to embrace it myself. I have an enormous amount of work to neglect while I do my real stuff. In which case my plan isn't really a plan, it's just a reminder to keep going, because it's as close as I'll get to happy. And if I don't have work behind me I won't find new people, because I'll be empty and not worth spit.

———

I know that flopping down in front of the tv on a freezing night like this is supposed to be fun, but one more minute of Brigit Jones and I'll have to scream.

———

Wednesday, 6th August, 2008.

No Worries

I discovered cat scratches on one of my paintings a few weeks ago – just light ones, but visible to me. That made me get off my arse [eventually] and hang my newer paintings on the walls, because it's the only safe place. One of those paintings is Son's portrait, my second large oil ever.

It's one thing to show your paintings to people and have them appreciated, or to lean them up against a bookcase in your workroom where you can still see them, but it's another thing entirely to hang them on your wall. Once it's on the wall it's not just a painting anymore – it's a presence in the room, so for half a week these large eyes have followed me whenever I pass by. I stop and look, and realise again and again how much the painting works.

It's making me emotional, actually. Partly because of the subject and the expression on his face, those eyes half-glaring in a stop-painting-me way. But also because of the technique. It's steeling my resolve to do what I damn well want (i.e. paint). Because I can. This is as close as I'll get to confident, and it's a good way to feel.

When you're painting it's all about the act of seeing and constructing in a way, so for a long time afterwards that's what I see when I look at the work. This time, though, I'm on the other side of the process, and it's strange to be the audience of your own work. Without cringing.

I cringe when I look at my old work, which I've been steadily painting over. I only have a couple more large old canvases to go. I'm not even calling them paintings, I hate them so much. I can't wait to have them gone, but the kids have said they don't want me to paint over them, so now I'm stuck. My practicality versus their sentiment, which is nice when you think about it, but still. Also that photographer who came out to the house at the beginning of the year to document some other pieces for me and said *'Don't!'*, said *'What a shame'*.

What would he know? It's not like he's hanging them on his walls.

I have photos of them (that's bad enough), and I save hundreds of dollars and a good few hours if they get recycled. Plus I've run out of walls to hang things on, and it's very easy to kill something that's going to otherwise spend its life shoved in a corner gathering dust.

Anyway, not a problem yet. I have fresh canvas to work on for now, and no guilt to keep me from it. It'll work out well in the end.

Thursday, 7th August, 2008.

Cars are for Private

Where's a phone booth when you need one? I wish my car (Ex-H's car) had more heavily tinted windows. Sometimes, for some strange reason, I start to feel really restricted by my clothes. It used to happen a lot, not so much recently. I'd feel so nauseous and convinced I'd die I had to rip my bra off ASAP, bugger the consequences.

Today I was inexplicably tired and as soon as I got into the car, there was that feeling. So I ripped off my coat and tied my hair up into a pony tail, undid my bra, so my neck was bare and my arms were sleeveless, and apart from straps falling gradually down towards my elbows I was well and truly free to breathe.

No big deal, really, because I was sure that when I pulled into the car park at work it'd be so dark nobody would see me in my naturally slovenly state. I thought I'd be able to pull myself together discreetly, sort of like Superman in his phone booth. *Exactly* like Superman in his phone booth. But thanks to Eastlink I got there too early, and student-who-knows-my-car pulled up beside me. There I was with boobs akimbo; I had to perform the fastest bra do-upping ever.

Poor Superman. Doing up a bra is one thing, but those tights must have been a complete bastard to pull on and off.

I don't think my student caught me. He didn't raise his eyebrows or look at me like I was some half-naked freak. Which is lucky; I wasn't in the mood for people, and definitely not in the mood to have to explain myself, especially without a better reason for being alone and less-than dressed. Although, he did stare at me a lot during class, when he thought I wasn't looking. I know this because I see all. Anyway, he didn't need to stare so much, seeing as I may have saved him the trouble of undressing me with his eyes.

I guess that's lesson three-million-and-one against wanton stripping. At least my windows weren't fogged up – that would've been really sus.

———

About the News

I don't know what's more boring – the Olympics, or Nicole Kidman's baby. Although, I heard it being referred to as her "first-born" as I listened to the report, and was shocked that news people could be so insensitive. She has adopted children, so using the term "first-born" suggests that only the act of birth matters. I haven't heard them say it since, and gawd knows they've gone on and on about it, so I guess somebody corrected them somewhere along the line? The news story thus reverted to its original boringness.

Apart from too long, how long do the Olympics go for?

———

Friday, 8th August, 2008.

Damn Right I'll Judge Him

This is a quote from an article about the *Family Fortunes* documentary on John Olsen (*Home is Where the Art Is*, Ruth Ritchie, Sydney Morning Herald, 2nd August, 2008):

> *Nobody in their right mind would pass judgment on a living legend and obviously charismatic genius such as John Olsen but he'd be a mixed blessing as a father.*

Is she kidding? Anybody could be forgiven for saying the man's [allegedly] an outright cunt. I don't know a single person who was able to watch the part where he described abandoning his kids and leaving for Europe without being appalled. The look on his face, the tone of his voice, the way he callously described saying '*Bye bye*' without the any hint of retrospective remorse. And then the footage of his eldest daughter with tears in her eyes.

And this journalist gets all adulation-y about him? Seems to me it's more than reasonable to call out bad behaviour, especially in a potential role model, because that's a great deal of sub-standard manhood wrapped up in one egocentric parcel. He used the word "justifiable", as though his "art" is so brilliant it excuses his lack of responsibility. These are human beings, *Genius*. Grow *up*.

Sunday, 10th August, 2008.

Hell Freezing Over

This morning Son looked out through the windows and asked '*Uh, Mum – what's wrong with the rain?*'. When I followed his pointing finger I could see SNOW!! It's never snowed here before, because it just doesn't. It was so exciting I had to sit down and watch it like it was television. It was pretty, and for a whole half-hour or so life was a picture postcard. I forgot that snow is silent. *Nice*.

Monday, 11th August, 2008.

interruptus

I'm having a fantasy where I get up at 5 am, do some work, and then make my kids a family breakfast of eggs and freshly squeezed orange juice. That's my sole purpose in life right now.

Small purposes are good and manageable. Not so much big purposes. I keep being interrupted from the depth of painting by stupid phone calls.

I didn't mind having to pick Son up from school because he was unwell, but I did mind Old School Friend calling out of the blue because she needed a hug. Well and truly out of the blue; I haven't seen her for about two years, possibly on purpose. She took me by surprise, it was too late to pretend I wasn't home.

Anyway, who am I to begrudge somebody a hug? I don't hate her or anything, she just bores me shitless. So I warned her that I'm painting (and will stop for nobody), and she turned up. I stripped as many painting clothes off as I had to, hugged her long and sincerely, put said clothes back on, and continued painting. I'm so proud of myself, on accounta I didn't know I had the capacity to be so rude. She had her small son with her and I didn't even bother entertaining him. (I ignored a child!! So cool.)

I don't mind people watching me paint, but she shook my equilibrium a little. Possibly because I couldn't get the sordid details of her gossip in one quick sitting, so I was left with half a story and now need to get involved slightly to hear the rest. Possibly also because I can't stand her breath. It's not bad or halitosisish, there's just something about her insides that's thick and suffocating and smells like plastic. I almost can't stand being physically close to her.

Picky picky picky. I'm a good friend to have, yes? Anyways, when she left she took my calm with her, and I had to play *You Fill Up My Senses* (*Annie's Song,* but who calls it that?) five times in a row, trying to get it back. It didn't work. Even though I sang louder each time. My neighbours must want to shoot me by now.

Doesn't matter, I got a lot done. I'm about to enter the essential I-hate-my-painting phase, where it looks like shit and I have to fight desperately to bring it back from the brink of disaster. I go forth with courage.

A Little Too Lady-Like

Obviously I'm not talking about myself. Needing a good read tonight, I picked up Sonya Hartnett's *The Ghost's Child,* and I'm trying so hard to like it. Am reading with my best manners on. But. But but. I don't know what's gotten into her. I flinched at the first page because it's condescending. Then there's the nature of the story, which is fairytale-ish, but in the worst possible way. Apart from anything else, there's the concept of naive love without sex – a bit of fluttering in the stomach doesn't cover it. Wild man on beach plus unconventional female on beach plus no supervision plus both over eighteen years of age equals there'd be fucking.

Before even that (you see how I skipped everything else to get to the fucking, even though there is none?), there's such a big problem with the storyline of main-protagonist Rich Girl going on round-world trip with Rich Father (as you do) and recounting the experience like she's pushing a traveller's shopping trolley. A few beautiful descriptions (atta girl, that's what we want from Sonya), but so little contextual depth.

I'm trying hard not to be mean. The writing's good, in that it's well crafted. But the story has me so puzzled. She's my age, but she's telling a fanciful story that reads like it belongs to two century's ago (era context notwithstanding, it still doesn't fit contemporary readership). I think it might work for very sheltered private school girls who're of old-fashioned mentality. Maybe. *Anne of Green Gables*-esque.

So now I'm worried about Sonya Hartnett's imagination, because it's sporned this flight of fancy. It's so repressed or old fashioned (I think my mum would love it) that she's either very young and fanciful in her head, or she's trying to subdue the reaction to her lusty nom de plume novel, which I haven't read. Yet.

Hopefully I can finish reading this without drifting off.

I'm writing this whilst enduring a telephone conversation with Old School Friend, and the process of typing silently is preventing me from dying from boredom. Going going... gone, *oh thank fuck for that.*

Tuesday, 12th August, 2008.

Speaking Of...

It's clear that I'm not going to succeed in not-being mean tonight. Really, I do care about Old School Friend. I'd just prefer to care in small doses. And not late at night. And from a great distance.

When she called I thought *great, here's the rest of the gossip*, but then I realised I don't find the story interesting after all. Especially the stuff about the hippies. Does she not remember who she's speaking to? Obviously not, because she was telling me about going to a witch wedding. And Confest. And she said '*You should come with me next time!*'.

All of my other Confest-y type friends know not to say that to me. They just *know*. They also know that if they've had an experience sleeping under a full moon with crystals lined up on the roof of their car, I'm not the person to tell about it. Unless they want to be LAUGHED AT. And they know that comments like '*I felt so much moon energy pulsing through me*' are gonna be met with derision. Nay, blatant unkindness.

This is what I'm up against. How can I not be mean when there's so much to be mean to? I used to be such a nice person. Thank goodness I grew out of *that*.

Wednesday, 13th August, 2008.

Blurgh

I finished reading *that book,* and I'm holding... back... meanness. No, I can't, it was *TERRIBLE*. It's like an adult concept in a baby story and doesn't sit well with me AT ALL. Today's imagination is so much more sophisticated, and some back-in-times just shouldn't happen.

How did she *write it?* And how did it get *published?* How even-more did it get shortlisted for the CBC Young Adult Fiction award? Fuck and fucken fuck. It's the most luke-warm, shallow rendering of complex thought I've ever read. AND NOW SHE'S MADE ME COMMENT IN ABSOLUTES.

It's just that it's so abstracted it's stripped of character growth, lacks emotional depth, has no extremes to latch onto, and in fact has to be read like a blah list of blah things that happened. The imaginative nature of it is, I'm sad to say, boring, and gets stupider as it goes on because she gives us less and less real world context.

If thinking about lives that could-have-been is her way of going through a mid-life crisis, I hope it passes so that she can write a real book again. I'm sorry. *So* sorry. But I can't even pretend to be generous with it. Am I that hard-nosed? I don't know, but now I'm desperate to read something with real meat to it. Whimsy may be invented with good intentions, but it makes me wanna puke.

p.s. Newsflash: if my sources are correct, she's actually won the damn award, and it'll be announced this Friday. Why in the YA category I have no idea. *Fark*. Is it possible I'm wr-wr-wr-wrong?

———

Thursday, 14th August, 2008.

Karma

If I was a nicer person I wouldn't be having a shit day. If I didn't care about my childhood friend's plasticky breath and hippy tendencies, or if I was more kind about the work of usually-brilliant authors who accidentally write the occasional crap novel (sorry).

If I was nicer I wouldn't have decided suddenly this week that I hate teaching after all, and have nothing left to give my students. I'd have nice things to look forward to. Nice is good, I like nice. I don't need spectacular, nice would do. It's not like I'm asking for much.

I don't want to have to fix problems anymore. I'm tired. Today I can't even paint, so I've been forcing myself to do housework in the belief that it'll make me feel better. Because vacuuming makes the endorphins kick in. If I do it vigorously enough.

Ah fuck it, I wish I was a man. Not just any man, but a complete motherfucking arsehole. Emotions, more than anything, get in the way of my work. I understand that women can be complete motherfucking arseholes, too, but if I was a man-arsehole I'd be unstoppable. I'd have some desperately under-loved bitch to do the vacuuming for me. I'd pay her with sex. Bad sex – I'd take my orgasm and run.

So forget about being nicer, it's the arseholes who have better lives. This way towards happiness, get out of my fucken way.

———

Monday, 25th August, 2008.

Two Minds

It's bad enough not being able to find music to like, but not being able to find music you like when the weather's dismal is the pits. So that was a bitch of a week. Every time I picked up a paint brush I felt so guilty, and I'm tired of feeling guilty, especially when it's raining and I can't even force myself to like music.

So I hate my life, which has no soundtrack at present. Even silent movies have soundtracks. Hence, this is the stupidest life I've ever had.

On the other hand, it's not raining anymore and who needs music anyway? I've rediscovered *Catch 22*, one of my favourite novels to listen to on audio. I used to listen to a version read by Alan Arkin (from the movie – so much character in his voice), but it was a disintegrating library tape and abridged, so now I listen to a full version and get way more mileage out of it. Also, despite how many times I've heard the story, I can never remember how it ends. There are advantages to being this stupid, the best being that I'll get a big surprise. Again. (Goldfish, meet Rock; Rock, meet Goldfish.)

I tried listening to it while I walked this morning, and it was hard. I know I've said this before; that when you're painting you can give your work full attention AND give full attention to the book you're listening to. It's like being two [brilliant] people. Living two [brilliant] lifetimes at once. But when I walk I can't listen to non-musical audio, because my thoughts wander. I concentrate really hard, but one small tangent and I'm off. When I walk I have only *one* mind, and it's not even nearly brilliant.

So I had to force myself to listen properly, and eventually somehow managed. Then I walked smiling. I laughed out loud. And was so happy.

I love Joseph Heller. I still have about seven hours of story left to go, so today's work'll be pure pleasure. And if I can learn to dance to his book I won't ever need music again.

———

Tuesday, 26th August, 2008.

Circus Rudd

Blaming the parents for truancy as a blanket rule is just plain wrong, and the punitive measure of cutting welfare for thirteen LONG weeks is just crazy. Welcome to our police state.

We've suspected for a while now that KRudd PM is just John Howard in a monkey suit, and yesterday pretty much confirmed it. (Actually he confirmed it when he didn't stand up to Japan about the whaling, but now he's double-confirmed it.) The truancy punishment proposal is an enormous can of worms and way too monumental to even begin approaching. In the trial locations it makes "some" sense, because there are huge social problems generally and it's difficult to initiate effective prompts for social change on a large scale. Education is a very realistic answer, and needs to be encouraged. But even in those places there are parents who struggle to get their kids to go to school because the kids refuse, and punishing those parents is not the answer. Punishing them will lead to homelessness, because tenant-parents will be evicted. Some children who do go to school will starve to death and be effectively punished because their siblings wag.

And duh – poor people are called *poor* because they have *no money*. Take away their income and they'll have even less money. The social problems will be exacerbated until they're out of control. (Welfare groups must be terrified of the impossibility of helping people survive if this goes through.)

Parents – those saintly creatures who stress long and hard about their children's future, because truancy is one of the most stressful things ever – will end up slashing their wrists because instead of a measure that deals with the teenage problem, the government will be introducing a system of blame that suggests the parents *allow* their children to skip school. Do they think all penniless parents don't give a fuck about their children? Do they think that children in welfare families get fed McDconalds and the rest of the money goes on parental booze while the kids run wild in the streets?

Some parents do neglect schooling, granted. But there are a lot of children out there who have pretty serious problems. The blanket approach is way too presumptuous in regards to circumstance. And as one parliamentarian suggested, how do you punish the parents of children who *don't* receive welfare? To make it fair?

My suggestion: PUNISH THE FUCKING CHILDREN. Those who are *not* in locations of widespread social disadvantage are just regular kids who enjoy a lack of recourse or the luxury of not having to answer for their behaviour. Bring the police in and make it formal. Run regular reform-school-ish day-long classes for truants that they have to attend, and give them serious consequences to face if they don't. A kick up the teenage arse would do this country a world of good.

p.s. Save the whales [!!!].

———

Thursday, 28th August, 2008.

The Week That Was

Last weekend I managed to do some spectacular people avoidery. I'd get off the phone after deflecting potential visitors, smile to myself, and say arrogant things like *you've still got it.* And yet, I still got landed with a few visitors that wouldn't leave.

Annoying Friend is the one I felt most guilty about, because she got an outright lie from me. The worst thing was that by the end of the weekend I started to believe my own lies; I felt like I really *had* been away for the weekend and darn it, wasn't it just exhausting to have both stayed at home working my guts out *and* gone away for a holiday? I oughtsta not knock myself out like that.

It was worth lying, though, because a lot of work went into that piece. I've finished it now (finished? finished enough), and am ready to get stuck into the next one, so that I can finish that too and get back to what I'm really supposed to be doing. Except, now that it's finished I hate it, have rolled it up and packed it away, so that I don't have to look at it.

Problematically, now that it's gone I keep turning around to look at it, and it isn't there anymore. I feel a sense of loss, because it was a big presence in the house for so long. It's like I've spurned a lover. A lover so ugly the only person who's gonna love it is its maker, and that's me and I hate it, so I guess that's the end of it.

I'm so tired. I haven't slept more than an hour or so for two nights in a row. I'm not manic, just wound up. So in love with what I'm doing while I'm doing it. It doesn't matter if I'm making crap because I'm getting better at it, therefore it's betterly made crap than it used to be. It looks good rolled up and packed away. In case you were wondering.

251

The good news is I got good news this week. I've been feeling guilty lately because everything I do is such a gamble, the fruits of labour not appearing until years after said labour has been performed, if at all. It's making me wonder if I should be doing something more useful. Remembering that I don't have the capacity for usefulness (I've tried!). BUT THEN, I got feedback on my manuscript and suddenly uselessness seems like a great idea again. I feel alive, because the words I loved throwing together have been loved by somebody else, somebody articulate and intelligent who said such nice things I'm teary about it.

Again it comes down to this: I am *allowed* to do these things. I have *permission*. My writing touched somebody and their writing in turn touched me. A verbal intimacy. Goodness knows I don't get out much these days, so that's as good as life gets.

———

Sunday, 31st August, 2008.

Breathe In, Breathe Out, *Don't* Listen

You can avoid the hippies all you like, but they'll get you in the end. I thought I was safe doing a yoga class at the gym, because it's not pure yoga. It's yoga without the hippy element. If you put a Bullshit Rating on the classes, they're supposed to come up with Zero.

Until today, so far so good. It's a nice way to enjoy being in your body. In fact, with Other Instructor it got very transcendental; by the time she got us through the meditation part at the end of the classes I couldn't stop smiling because I felt so good.

But today I had to go to a different class because we had my nephew's 21st party on Friday night (bogan theme – we all wore wife-beater blue singlets and I like the look, so maybe I can be a cross-dresser after all). I invited two of my nieces back to stay with me overnight. They're among the most serious offenders in the visitors-who-won't-leave category, so I went today instead.

It was okay until we got to the meditation part. She nearly pulled it off, but then said these fateful words: '*This is your heartfelt expression*'.

I suppressed a very serious bout of giggling. A few sentences later she said '*The final element to focus on is the space between your eyes, where you'll find your inner eye, your third eye*', and by that point I was having trouble suppressing an outright guffaw. She crossed the fine line between inner peace and inner delusion. It's impossible to find inner peace if somebody's both offending your inner rationality and tickling your inner hilarity. Don't even mention my inner bad manners, which were threatening to burst.

Now I'm scared to go to the class Reformed Hippy teaches, even though I promised. She lived in Byron so her Bullshit Rating's probably off the scale. If I hear her saying that shit I won't be able to contain myself and she'll have to send me to the principal's office for disrupting the class. Maybe I should warn her. Or she should warn me. In any case, proceed with caution.

Still Sunday.

Where Are My Trusty Scapegoats?

This should be easy now that I've found my third eye (oh HA HA), but today's work is looming like big, looming things do. In fact, the loomishness is getting overwhelming, and if you consider that today's work was supposed to be yesterday's work, you'll understand just how looming it is.

Granted, yesterday's work was delayed by visitors-who-never-leave (duzn't matter, I love those girls). Also, after they did leave, instead of starting to do this work I went swimming. And then instead of finishing swimming after twenty laps I just kept going until well after thirty. My arms were like dead wood, and who can hold a paintbrush up to a large canvas if their arms are dead wood?

Am I avoiding it, or do I just not know how to resume? The problem is that I did a study. I have a friend (who shall remain nameless) who laughs at me when I tell him that if I do a study, I get too bored by the subject matter to do the actual work I was preparing for. He seems to think that this boredom reflects my small cranial capacity. It's not small boredom, mind, but huge boredom, as in *I-never-want-to-look-*

at-it-again boredom. And seeing as the study just happened to have gotten out of control (it being the work I just finished, which is huge and involved), going to this one straight from that one would be like finding love on the rebound, and we all know that's bad news.

My big drawing's still packed away, but I photographed it and every ~~two minutes~~ now and then I open the file to look at it, drawn to the colour and the texture. Whether it's good or bad doesn't matter because that texture makes me want to eat it alive, and there's no-way no-how I can go back to the oil painting and paint the almost-same thing smoothly. So I don't know what to do.

I could take a flying leap, but I don't even know if I can do that with oil paint yet. If I get it wrong, I won't have time to let it dry to make it un-wrong.

The best thing is to avoid touching it for a while longer. The house is full of teenage boys and therefore smells like teenage boys. Who can concentrate with them here? (Well, me, usually.) I could read art books. Or even do work I'm supposed to be doing. (Pffft, like *that's* gonna happen.)

Dammit – every week I'm hit with distraction after distraction, and now when I want one there's no distraction to be found. I wish somebody would bother me today. Then I can blame *them* for my wasted time.

———

September 2008

Comfortably Numb

Doing this painting is like trying to push a baby out. Remind me never to do a study first again, because as predicted, even though it's different, doing the same image twice is as boring as all fuck. Or it could just be the subject matter. Or that I haven't given myself time to play with it. Or maybe I should just start my life all over again, and begin with finger painting on butcher paper.

Unfortunately, that's the most logical step forward, and the most tempting. I'm just not ready for the real world.

Anyway, who cares. Everything's been travelling along okay for a while, so when I picked First-Born up from school to take them to the doctor I got shocked all over again by their perfect shittiness. Then I remembered they've been doing this all along, I've just been ignoring it. Can't ignore it when you're trapped in a car and it's yelling at you, though. Telling you how you repulse them just by existing.

I'm finding it harder to even care. For the last few months my reaction's been automatic = I just go numb. Try not to think, absolutely try not to feel, and absolutely don't cry. Much. Just a little wet around the eyes.

Moving my poor old body physically becomes difficult, but I drag my sorry arse into the doctor's surgery, open a book to read and there, I've shut the situation out. So it shits me no end that by the time we're back in the car First-Born starts conversing with me. Like a normal human being.

Just like Ex-Wife, actually. When she visited last weekend she was all *I love you I love you*, which is really nice because she gives good love, but she thinks I've somehow forgotten the revolting things she said to me recently.

So I accept her love, but also I kinda gape at her, dumbfounded. My tolerance astounds me, and not in a good way.

What I hate is that everything good is mostly in the future. I'm sick of the future, it's so damned far away. The future can go fuck itself. Goodness should be evenly proportioned throughout life. It's hard to keep looking ahead and saying *it won't always be like this.* Because what if it *IS* always like this? And between now and the future there's so, so much time that's going to be spent on not living properly.

Head down, work hard. Yah, I get it. Keep on going and hope for the best.

Thursday, 4th September, 2008.

The Lost Book

I didn't even know if I liked it or not, at first, though I leaned more towards not. I've been reading *The Lost Dog*, by Michelle de Kretser, and it's spellbinding. Still, it didn't do much at the start. Lots of beautiful observation, but long passages that were nothing *but* observation. And all of those things that happen without being explained – ya go back to re-read whole passages to see if you can work it out, and decide you're stupid because it doesn't make sense to you. Nobody likes to discover they're that stupid.

The sense of *inadequacy* it provokes. I guess that's what we call a laborious read. She has clarity problems, I'm saying. Surely it's not me having comprehension problems (*her fault!!*). Which makes it something you have to be quite educated to enjoy, which makes it too elite, for example, to give to your mother for her birthday.

Despite this, it started to grow on me. And then I was addicted. I discovered how addicted I was when I lost the book. I realised I must have left it somewhere at work, and knew I wouldn't be able to get it for a whole day and a half, which meant a whole day and a half without reading it, and that prospect was mortifying.

Now I have it back but don't have time to read, so I have to consume it in small mouthfuls, which offends my well-cultivated habit of book gluttony. But what a nice thing to be immersed in. And what a beautiful brain. (Hers, not mine.) (Though mine does scrub up ok on occasion.) Gosh, the things a book can do to you. It's just like love.

———

Monday, 8th September, 2008.

Let It Go

Easier said than done. I went back to my evil painting, attacked it, saw that attacking it was good, and managed to salvage some of it. I worked it up from the bottom, rough as guts, and that's how I want to paint. It's how I *will* paint – it was like reading my future in tea leaves. A *revelation*. All well and good, except that by the time I got to the top I was back to working the paint in smoothly, and I hated it again. Which might be a good thing, because if I hate enough I can attack it again. But what an angsty way to work.

I'm trying to walk away from it but I can't stop thinking about it. I lie awake at night. I get up, I work on it some more, *hate hate hate*. If I was brave I'd put my foot through it. So I'm making a deal with myself. If I haven't roughed up the middle by this afternoon, I'm not allowed to touch it until it's time to paint something else entirely over the top of it. Which I'll end up doing anyway, so why am I bothering? Why do I do any of the stupid things I do? I'd like to know the answer to that one. Anybody?

———

Tuesday, 9th September, 2008.

Logistics are a bitch. So is sobriety. So, for that matter, am I. Just by accident, though, because it's hard to make time for somebody who you know isn't going to be a proper friend at any stage, because you have nothing in common, not really, once you subtract the sex thing. The problem with young people – I mean apart from them being young in the first place – is that they have time to be friends with anybody. Just add another person to your phone book and voilà, instant friendship.

I wish I could be like that, but if I add more people to my phonebook they end up just being more people to feel guilty about neglecting. Starting with now, because Young Guy with Beady Eyes keeps asking for a second date (was the first time a date?) and I keep delaying it. I really want to see him (body saying *please please please!*), even though I don't want to (mind saying *don't invest time in something that's going nowhere by default*). (I hope body wins this one.)

I hate dilemmas. The pros are that he makes me laugh and I make him laugh and hell yes I need another night out. We've already been drunk and naked so we don't have to bother with all of the getting-to-know-you stuff. The cons are that he keeps asking for more getting-to-know-you stuff, and that takes time. What does he want that for anyway? I'm old enough to be his – well, not quite old enough to be his mother, but definitely old enough to be his mother's younger sister.

He's so young I can't take him seriously. (I promised myself the next one would be older than me.) Also he lives too far away to be convenient. Surely if you're gonna use 'em up and spit 'em out they're supposed to be convenient? I suppose it'd be easy to invite him here, but I don't think the REDRUM on my bedroom wall is going to give us much of an atmosphere.

I dunno. It was uncharacteristically easy to hook up with him when I'd only known him for half an hour, but now that it's been a couple of weeks it's just plain difficult. This is why I was never good at being twenty-one.

Wednesday, 10th September, 2008.

Kids 1 & Kids 2

The good news is that it's okay for kids to spend half their life on computers and X-Boxes. Last night Son showed me a basic stick-figure animation he's been working on for a school project, and not only is it outrageously funny (paroxysms of laughter, I had tears streaming down my face), but it's outrageously clever because of the gestures and movement of the figures. He knows the visual language of bodies because he's learnt the subtleties of pretend-human movement from games. So all of that computer and X-Box time has been useful, like applied research, which means that technically he's spent half his childhood working.

This is nice. This is real living. Just like bringing his pastings home from kinder to show me. And he was so relieved that not only did I get his jokes, but that they had me crippled. He was funny with his script the way he's funny with his stories, and his class is going to laugh so hard during the presentation they'll need tissues and incontinence pads.

———

I'm feeling sorry for First-Born because I was mean to them. I'm not sure how intentional it was, but I suspect I've been childish. They slept-in today and I didn't wake them for school. I did the same thing last week. Ever since they got vile about me being involved in their schooling at all, because it's *none of my business,* and I told them *okay then, I won't bother.* And then I didn't bother.

When they finally got up they said that they'd wanted to make it to school every day this week, and I realised that me not-waking them stopped them from being a better student. *Damn.*

———

Friday, 12th September, 2008.

Yes, We Have No

Now that's what I call a day. How many lifetimes? I've lost count. But the fact that I finally had breakfast at 9:15 pm is demonstrative. Well, we were out of bananas, and I don't start any day without a banana. It took me ALL DAY to get to a shop.

I gave up working on projects to go to the city to pick up one of my paintings this morning, and I survived Kitchen Nazi's road rage. In fact, it was funny. She waved her fists at people (literally) who were blissfully unaware as they rode along in their capsules, and I sat in our warm capsule enjoying a feeling of complete and utter calm. There was sunshine, and it was so warm. There's a freedom in giving the day over to somebody else's control. Today was like a holiday.

Possibly because I also gave up [wagged] work to go to Son's presentation, and I'm so glad I did. It was the most human thing I've done in years. Irresponsibility is my new middle name. Except it's not irresponsible at all to be inside your child's life. I got to hang out with

259

the mums, it was still sunny, and I brought a few extra kids home with me, performing my third giving-up of something for the day.

That being, I gave up a hot date with Young Guy so that I could take Son and his friends to see *The Mummy III*. And although there may have been a point as the credits rolled where I asked myself '*You gave up more very reasonable sex for that?*' (it was so corny, and Rachel Weisz wasn't cast so everything seemed "wrong", although Michelle Yeoh is the most beautiful woman in the world and made it worth sitting through), I'm still glad I did it. I feel so *normal*. Like a real person living in a real world with her real kids. Today, by doing a hundred things wrong, I did everything just right.

Oh well, body still cares but mind would happily unload the burden. My kids first, and everything else one thing at a time.

———

Wednesday, 17th September, 2008.

On Doing Things Properly

Being good isn't all it's cracked up to be. I'm not used to being sensible and organised, so I forgot I'd written a piece weeks and weeks in advance for a competition. Yey me, you'd think. Except that having forgotten, I started writing something new, was too unsure about it, didn't send it, then discovered the earlier piece days too late, and found it to be better-written than I'd thought it was, ergot I should have sent it off. The lesson I learn from this is, being too organised doesn't work.

It's not the only thing I haven't sent off. I've met every deadline I set myself over the past few weeks but haven't submitted anything. Because I was being sensible. I have to say that of all the things I end up regretting, being sensible is the thing I end up regretting the most.

Now I'm wondering what other work I've done over the past few months and forgotten about. Fugly Novel Project? It'd be really good to discover I'd already done *that* revision work. If only.

———

Doesn't matter. Don't particularly care. Have been a nice kind of busy, very focussed, and able to hang washing on the line when it's sunny. When people drop in I haven't had to say *piss off*. Plus because it's the last week of term some of my students have been sneaking wine and horse doovers into the classroom. That adds up to happy living.

———

Thursday, 18th September, 2008.

Speaking of Which

I practically *am* doing Fugly Novel Project in my sleep, because I have a virus of the forearm, which also has the rest of my body feeling like it's been kicked in the ribs/legs/shoulders. That's possibly not its formal name, but you know, whatever.

All because last week I said out loud '*I never get sick – never*'. Ye gods get pissed off when they hear humans say that, and punish you by sending the plague. To your forearms. To make them throb.

Ye gods be appeased; being unwell can be very peaceful, so I see this as an opportunity to slow down and rest. While I'm working. Propped up against about a million pillows on my bed with my laptop, happy as a pig/mud combo.

Happy is an exaggeration, but we can get away with calling it contentment. We'll call it happiness-proper if I'm better by the weekend, because I've been promised a girl's night out by Neglected Friends, one of whom has requested (nay, she has *demanded*) that I be there. Which has made Other Friend fear for the woman's heterosexuality, because she's purportedly obsessed enough with me to make people think it's a crush.

I think it's cute because she's fantastic to get smashed with. If she's obsessed with me then I get to hang with her all night. Fuck the world and its viruses, I'll go out anyway. It's been a difficult few months and my forearms and I have been working hard. We deserve to get well and truly drunk.

———

Saturday, 20th September, 2008.

To Succeed or Not Succeed, That is the Question

What I love about Fugly Project is that even though I've been working away at it, I'm going to fail to finish it on time, and the failure's going to be spectacular. Uneventful, but spectacular. With that failure will come the most amazing release. I know it, and I'm waiting for it. Oh so patiently.

Also I'm happy about it. With release will come freedom from every bit of pressure I've ever put on myself to be something I don't want to be. What will be left are the bare bones of it, which is where I've placed all of the value (i.e. the work itself).

It's not until you start doing something that you realise how little it matters to you. Also how little you matter to the world, therefore the things that seem so monumentally important to you are really just nothing to anybody. It's liberating.

Anyways, not long left. I'll keep working. I won't go dancing, that can wait. And when the deadline passes I'll have done well whether I've finished or not. I can drop the bits of it I don't like, polish off the ones I do, and walk off into real life.

Wednesday, 24th September, 2008.

Gesundheit

I caved. For the last month or two while I've been working away at Fugly Project, new novel has been pushing its way into my head. It's been bizarre having two fiction things actually happening at once, as opposed to just fighting for supremacy at the front and back of my mind. And frankly, a little bit annoying, seeing as I gave it strict instructions to stay put. But yesterday I started making more solid notes than usual, and notes became a passage, and that's it, I'm in.

Rule Number One: do *not* enter project before you're ready for it.

Now there's a whole little world forming and I can't stop it. I don't want to stop it. It's like saying no to a sneeze you know is about to happen. All of that nice anticipation. Who says no to a sneeze? Sneezing is so pleasurable.

Apart from being concerned about the novel taking over before I'm ready for it, I'm flummoxed by the lack of humour in this one. I don't think I've written a long work without humour it in before. You can tackle any issue by using humour, and yet here I am with an issue to tackle, and my work doesn't feel the least bit funny on the inside. In

262

fact, I don't think there's any personality there at all – just a series of responses to situations. I'm hoping it's just because the narrator hasn't evolved yet. I don't even know if he/she is a he or a she. All I know is that he/she is dead serious, and that's scary.

It shouldn't scare me – I read serious novels all the time, and I love them. No reason why I shouldn't write that way. I do it in short pieces. I think. I might have to check on that, but I'm sure I do. So now I have to work out if this seriousness is a result of my having been less consistently happy than usual (it's been a hard year), or if it's just the nature of the work.

Have I become a very serious person with a grave countenance and gloomy outlook on life? Not that I'm thinking about it, with Fugly Project demanding so much attention. If the antibiotics have kicked in (*please* have kicked in), I'll get more than three hours of being alert today. That's at least three hours I shouldn't be wasting here. Oops.

Sunday, 28th September, 2008.

Disconnection

I dunno 'bout this. I summoned a lot of discipline and instead of approaching it bit by bit as I have been – like a small, afeared creature – I worked solidly on finishing a small section of Fugly Project, thinking that a bit of finishing would at least bring the whole thing into the home stretch (spring carnival metaphor, because the world smells like flowers). But it seems so blah. When I read the original writing I discover it to be quite strong, which makes me realise that while I make the necessary structural changes, I'm working like an automaton. I'm writing without any punch whatsoever; I have the personality of a mannequin.

No offence to mannequins. I have no idea what I'm doing, what I should do, or what I want to do. I have no drive left of my own so I've just been going with the flow. I plan to work, I do work, but when Son or First-Born ask for my time, I drop what I'm doing and enjoy being with them. (I lost track of how many times First-Born hugged me when I saw them the other day.)

Yesterday, when My Lovely Mother asked me to join her for a walk, I dropped everything to be with her. Which was also nice, because when she was in Sydney last week I missed her. (I missed my mother! I felt like I was four years old.) So, sun shining, work be damned. We walked through the reservoir park and sat on a high bench with our legs swinging for over an hour and a half, just talking, with her telling me things she's never told me about before. I thought of the work waiting for me at home and realised it's just not important.

That work, for years, has kept me away from things like this. It colours everything you do, so that you're never free from it. Ever. I don't want to be that person anymore – I want to be the daughter that sits in the sun with her mother and is free to stay there for as long as they both want.

Getting well and truly personal, I haven't done any art work for about two weeks, but every now and then I need something from my work room and as I walk through I look at the portrait of my father, and automatically whisper '*I'm sorry, Dad*' under my breath. I'm not apologising for the portrait – he's dead proud of it, in fact the whole family are and have been e-mailing it around (my niece told me), even though nobody's seen it in the flesh.

I think that's why I'm apologising to him; because I make work and it sits in my studio and I don't show it to anybody anymore. I'm apologising for being useless. For not knowing how to do anything other than write or paint or draw things that have no place in the world. I don't know what's worse about this – that I keep slipping in and out of this profound, guilty sadness, or that I talk out loud to a painting.

Last night: a friend's 40th birthday. I almost didn't go. I had work to do, having spent the afternoon walking around in the sun. (Fucking fuck – when am I going to learn?) Plus I knew the party would be full of people from another planet. So I went for another walk, it got late, I was about to start work, then realised how stupid that is. My friend has so much love, and I was about to let her down.

So I went to the party, and everybody was free and happy and welcoming. My friend took me aside, told me she'd made the spare room up especially and exclusively for me, in case I wanted to drink and crash overnight. That's how lovely people are.

Right this minute, these things matter. Also, there were chocolate-dipped strawberries, which made the night perfect.

But I didn't stay. I was stone cold sober and being hit-on by Single Guy, who was okay at first, with his intimate voice close to my ear, and his friendly invasion of my personal space, and some cute conversation about the see-through fish. But in the end I couldn't stand him or the situation, because he was so bitter about his ex and we had nothing in common.

Why would you want sex without some sort of foundation? I can't stand being this disconnected and yes, I found it offensive, even though I shouldn't because he hadn't done anything wrong. No more sex with strangers, I don't like it. What a stupid everything.

Monday, 29th September, 2008.

Fables Are So Yesterday

I tried very hard not to dislike *The Boy in the Striped Pajamas*, by John Boyne. So hard. I was dying to read it because I'd come across a few rave comments about it, and thought it must be flawless. Maybe I'm just too old for this sort of thing, but I can't help seeing the condescension behind the writing.

I could insult a few people by saying this, but I think the raving people were too kind on the book because of its subject matter (Holocaust). I was harder on it *because* of the subject matter, which is dealt with so badly. For example, heavy use of English expressions that I suspect don't translate well into German, frequent play on words likewise. Historical details that shit me up the wall with their clunkiness. Storyline – not nearly enough people have criticised the storyline. Try as I may, I couldn't suspend my disbelief.

Mostly, though, you can tell when an adult has forgotten what it is to be a child by the way they speak [down] to them. There's no way that child could have been so ignorant. Nine year olds are innocent, but they're not morons. And the evasiveness (actually all of it, this adult-author misconception of children's dumb wonderment) reminded me of Sonya Hartnett's latest (sorry sorry). She corners the market on euphemism, but he comes in close by avoiding the subject altogether. What kind of writer writes something like:

> *Lieutenant Kotler grew very angry with Pavel and no one.... stepped in to stop him doing what he did next...*

...and then doesn't tell us what happens next? 'Scuse me, but if you're going to write a novel addressing particular horrors, then don't shy away from those horrors. Grow some authorial nads. Children see worse than that on television, and in less noble contexts.

Coulda been a lot more sophisticated than that, is all I'm saying. Oh, and pet-hate: this happens twice in the book, but I'll give one example, Page 70:

> *On this particular morning neither Mother nor Father was at home.*

WERE WERE WERE. Why are people so unkind to plurals these days? I know this is a complicated plural, but there's an editor somewhere that needs to be slapped over the knuckles.

Tuesday, 30th September, 2008.

Readin', Ritin', Rithm'etc

I was worried when I picked up Kate Grenville's *The Lieutenant* because the print's so big. It's been aligned thematically with *The Secret River* because of its historical content, so I was expecting it to look intelligent, and that's when I realised that big print looks unintelligent, like it's been written in crayon, or like a school assignment that's been printed with a huge font to disguise the lack of wordage.

Big print also makes me think of people who shout at blind people as though they're deaf, even though they're who big print is for. (No! I do not make sense!)

Gosh, I had no idea I was so shallow.

It's not a happy read, I can say that much. Do I admire it? Not as much as I admired *Secret River*. I think with this one I wasn't as convinced by the story – I need to know more about which bits are based on fact and which aren't. Specifically. With *Secret River* I trusted her characterisation and let myself get lost in her intense reconstruction of our history. It was stunning.

What I especially admired in *SR* was the way she presented us with a moral dilemma as readers. She tore my empathy in two and what I felt about the characters and their situation was in direct conflict with how I feel about our history. I was barracking for the good guys who were also the bad guys, and also barracking for the bad guys who I knew to be the really good guys, knowing that the good guys (who were really bad guys) would win, and the result would ultimately be bad.

Hindsight is a bitch. Kate Grenville, more than any other author I've read, was able to demonstrate the complicated nature of pioneer morality/ethics when it comes to race relations. It's an amazing approximation of experience, I wish every Australian would read it.

But not *The Lieutenant*. Or yes, it *is* worth reading. It just doesn't do the same thing, or have as much power. I only found the punitive expedition powerful. The sacks did it for me – my only real emotional reaction. With the rest I got the feeling she'd stuck to a few facts and skimmed over a lot of the periphery, as though she'd already exhausted her material with *SR*...? Which is fair enough, I couldn't imagine writing the same thing twice, even if it's different. So I guess her strength is the horror of moral dilemma, and the extent of human depravity legitimised by "civilistation". A good and useful way of torturing your readers.

———

October 2008

Mi Amore

I started reading Steve Toltz's *A Fraction of the Whole* last night, and I'm *in love*. The voice! I haven't read a voice-driven piece since... since the last time I read one, and that's a long, long time. I'm delirious with excitement, and have to sing all praises now because I'm only a hundred-and-a-half pages in. There are five-and-a-half-hundred pages still to go, so if the Sheer Brilliance isn't sustained I could fall out of love, and not have recorded this sun-shining/birds-singing feeling.

Promise to myself: although books are wonderful, next time I fall in love, it has to be with a person.

Friday, 10th October, 2008.

What You Learn When You Don't Quite Make It

It's still mi amore, but we're *having a little break*. Being un-famous means you have to prune your writing back until it's just a stubby trunk. None of that flowery rubbish allowed – you've gotta be sparse. At first you resist because the ramble allows you to spew so much wonderful thought, but then you realise the value of economy. Not economy of style, but economy of message, which makes the writing not just palatable, but easily digestible. And it allows the profound to stand out.

Fraction of the Whole, in the end, was too encyclopaedic. (This makes the title ironic, no?) Not in a useful way; I got the sense that Steve Toltz was saying Everything He Ever Wanted to Say. Instead of saving some of it for later. And although it stays brilliant – BRILLIANCE NOT IN QUESTION – it draaaaaags so much at the end I found finishing it excruciating. Maybe I wasn't supposed to read it all in one hit?

I think he thoroughly deserved to be given his Lucky Break (publication), but I can see that they didn't make him work hard enough to earn it after the fact (pre-publication hacking). The stuff you learn when the Lucky Break happens slowly.

It's like *Dark Knight*, when you get to the point you think of as the climactic conclusion, but then the movie keeps going. Except, it gets away with keeping on going, because it uses excellent action to advance the plot. Maybe Steve Toltz needed to add a car chase?

———

Saturday, 11th October, 2008.

So Close and Yet So Far

After writing a lot, I'm ready to start painting and drawing again. It's been a month. This is okay, because it's just like chocolate, in that when you're young you think you have to eat ALL of the chocolate NOW, as though it's going to run out, but as you get older you realise that if you only eat a little bit now, the rest of the chocolate will still be there later, so you can just take what you need *as* you need it. (Need, not want.)

Finally, after years of struggle, I've learnt to apply The Chocolate Principle to art and writing. No more tug of war. I now know that I work project by project, so if I'm working on one I needn't feel pulled toward the other because it'll still be there when I'm done. Then it'll assume top priority, and harmony will prevail. In other words, I can do both, and I can do them without an anxious struggle.

Enter Fugly Project [AGAIN], stage left. Motherfucking thing. Deadline slipped by quite painfully. I worked, knowing the futility of the whole thing, and then let it go. A week later I got an e-mail telling me, *okay we'll give you to the end of the month.* Did I ask for an extension? No! I was about to paint!! I just finished the first proper short story I've written since forever, and the process of writing was so calm and considered it was like an unnatural form of bliss. After a lot of thinking there were three full days of research and focus, and in the end a finished product.

It took me so so long to shuck the unwanted expectations enough to slip back into the right headspace to write. Then Fugly Project

269

returned to continue haunting me. Why won't the world just let it go? I'll give it five days – if I can't see the finish line by then, forget it. Damn the pseudo-kindness of those extension-giving people. It's like they're giving beef steak to a starving vegetarian.

––––

Sunday, 19th October, 2008.

Thought Dumping

I stopped hating Fugly Project some time early during the week, and haven't looked up from the computer screen since. Except to go to work about a million times (two jobs = eats up so much time).

But: I miss painting like crazy. Went for a picnic/portrait drawing session with Reformed Hippy and friends last week; apart from that, no time for art.

After seven hours of straight writing today, finally sick of Fugly Project again. Not for bad reasons, just head so full of dissected ideas and loose threads in the process of being unpicked and re-threaded = going into a mindscream. Went for lovely long swim, went for lovely long walk, now desperate for lovely long sleep, but have to get up at zero o'clock and work for as many hours as I can before going to real-world work, then will be too tired to do more 'til zero o'clock the following morning, when it starts all over again.

(PLEASE MAKE IT STOP!!!)

Unfortunately: suspected Fugly Project wouldn't end up being inside the word limit and now know it won't be inside the word limit, which makes it a suicide mission. Maybe that's why I'm enjoying it now. The revised objective is to make it half-way decent as a story and nothing else, *go fuck yerself evil world.*

Wonderful thing: my lovely First-Born xx

Also wonderful thing: my lovely Son xx

Discipline: when it's finished and at its natural length, will give it one more brutal slaying and hope like heck it's still not within the word limit, so that I don't have to revise the other part.

A relevant aside: Reformed Hippy read my short story and sent me text at 1 am last weekend saying '*Sorry if I woke you but had to tell you you're brilliant'*. Normally the penalty for sending wakeful texts in the middle of the night is Death, but people who send I-love-yous and flattery get an instant pardon. Subtract the bias of friendship, and *brilliant* gets reduced to *not crappy*, which means my story worked [!!]. (Just so happens I'd been to a party and was still up anyway, so went to bed relieved and happy.)

Not so relevant aside: took train to Bendigo during week to see Robert Jacks Drawing Prize exhibition. Love the train, love shunting yards, love Bendigo station, love the churches, loved that it was sunny, loved the guy playing piano accordion at an outdoor café table across road from gallery, loved that it sounded like Gay Paris (even though I've never been to Paris), loved the exhibition, loved that I did so much writing on train on the way, loved that I did so much writing on the way back, hated that I then had to transcribe hand-written work into computer.

Real life: Mine Uncle is starting to love his captors = is becoming institutionalised = when we take him out he longs to go back to the nursing home but = good that he visits the day room now and has friends and loves one of the staff members and isn't he beautiful, yes.

Also real life: when we went to Bush-Dwelling Brother's property a few weekends ago, First-Born and her friend insisted on being in the car with me and they didn't hate me even once [!!] = eight hours of driving = did I mention my lovely First-Born?

Exhausting: too tired to work but too pumped to sleep = long night ahead *oh lawdy*.

———

Sunday, 26th October, 2008.

Aftermath

Okay they can go now. I'm over them. I was over them at 1 am. I was over them again at 4 am, after having spent three hours fighting back the urge to mop my upstairs floor, which is literally BLACK with teenager dirt. I can't wait to mop it. It's like when there are crumbling small rubbishes to vacuum up and they make that ace rattling sound as they go up the hose, and you can see the difference as you go. (Exciting!)

271

As far as parties go that was the biggest First-Born's ever had. We got a photo of everybody sitting up the driveway, which is uphill, and in the photo it looks like stadium seating.

I was going to spend the night locked away in my room reading, but instead I invited a friend over to satisfy my week-long craving to watch Hollywood pap, specifically *The Devil Wears Prada* (I know, but I couldn't help it, and technically you're only pathetic if you watch it alone). We huddled over my laptop on my bed, and what with the wine and the conversations about how absolutely real Hollywood is [!], the movie took four hours to finish. Go figure. And then the floor; thank goodness I didn't let any of them downstairs (sanctuary). Then I had to be responsible and supervise, and it was like rounding up cattle. I had to *nip at heels*.

The things ya gotta do to be a good mum. Apparently I'm the *acest mum on the planet* (First-Born's Friends' opinions), and yeah yeah, sure sure, it was a great party, but really, fuck off already. I DID NOT SLEEP and I am WRECKED.

Since I got up from my pitiful few hours of not-sleeping, they've all been saying *'Hi First-Born's Mum!'*, as though I can continue being ace to teenagers for more than a few hours at a time. I've been replying with *'Fuck off, Scumbags, I hate youse and want you all outa here'*, but they're not taking the hint. (The hint is: LEAVE MY HOUSE NOW.)

The longing to mop that floor is insane. And to disinfect the door handles. And to hose the inside of my house down. Today's possibilities are endless.

Stamina

I wonder if going to bed before 8 o'clock will make me a granny. I love today. I love also that today is about to end, and then it'll be tomorrow. I mopped three times (five bucketfuls of black water!! teenagers are filthy!!), and even though it wasn't fun after the first time, I didn't mind. I'm glad First-Born's going to have such good teenage memories.

But also, *ouch*. Yoga, swimming and mopping = my muscles are wasted. So I had the nicest shower of my life, found some pyjamas and put them on. They're no good for sleeping in but excellent for making a statement along the lines of *I'm-not-going-anywhere-today*. I wish I could wear pyjamas every day.

I was too tired to read, but I enjoyed holding a book up to my face and watching the words get blurry. Sat in my clean house and enjoyed having all of the windows thrown open with a nice breeze blowing through. Watched *Sharkwater* again with First-Born's Best Friend, after everybody else had gone and First-Born had crashed for the afternoon.

I don't feel lonely today because last night was the first time I've invited a friend over in ages, and that's all you need. She was the first person to see my paintings, which undoes the art loneliness. Not sharing work is unhealthy, and also impractical. When I finished the last painting I didn't submit it as planned, because I had no idea if it was any good.

Who cares, not even me, really. Thats the beauty of it. With clean floors comes great peace.

———

November 2008

Monday, 3rd November, 2008.

Enough Already

I did *Obernewtyn* and survived. All in a row. I didn't mean to get so sucked in. Not that it's a bad thing. Oh hang on, *yes it is*. Just because of Book Four, though – an overdose of information. I think by the time Isobelle Carmody (who I LOVE) got to Book Four she'd discovered the Fat Book thing. It's all in there. And then some. And then some more. And then SOME MORE. Long after I've already had enough and then maybe TOO MUCH. Book Four has the whole kitchen sink, and it's full of dishes, and even if it wasn't you'd find those grey bits of lettuce clogging up the drain hole.

IT'S MAKING ME EXTEND MY METAPHORS.

After reading Book Four again I hate information. I'd love to edit the fuck out of it. Although I did develop a new skill, a process of identifying which paragraphs are useful, and which are reiterations. Which give me good information, and which are going to shit me up the wall. Using this recognition, I managed to skip whole pages. Poetry I skimmed like a stone on a pond. Even then I felt the need to jump ahead about fifty pages at the halfway point, because I couldn't stand it anymore. EVEN THOUGH I LOVE IT. I started to long for the real world. I started to hate writers and their imaginations.

But anyway it's fine; Book Five makes up for it. It helps that I haven't read it before, and I didn't start skipping paragraphs until towards the long-winded end. And as much as I wish Isobelle would stop being so generous with the information-giving, I can't wait for Book Six. I hope it doesn't come out for a long time, though. Or maybe soon. Let me go back there – *please*. Ohmigawd, how long is she going to make us wait this time????

———

Thursday, 13th November, 2008.

I Heart Art Exhibitions

Because I have no life beyond art and books, I took my disconnected self up to Sydney again, to see the Dobell and Portia Geach Portrait exhibitions.

Fun staying with Prodigal Niece as always, but no kissing of young lovers this time, no romance. I was lonelier than lonely but it's my own stupid fault because I wanted to be alone and therefore didn't invite anybody to come with me. In fact, I wanted to be alone so that I could ponder how lonely I am at the moment, and what that means. You can imagine what a barrel of laughs I am to have around.

And yet there's art rapture, always. Wandering around Sydney anonymously with my blistered feet in a state of 50% bliss, 50% social inadequacy. And though in art speak I'm not supposed to use the word *love* to describe my reaction to art work, I loved both exhibitions. Also the Yinka Shonibare exhibition at MCA. But that moment has passed so enough about that.

The Portia Geach = I haven't seen before and was so worth the trip. These happinesses. The Dobell was as good as last year, but also a bit of sameness there. I wasn't quite as blown away. What was missing? I'm not sure. Perhaps the balance was tipped further towards abstract? Who knows? Who cares? Was good enough.

———

I Also Heart the Household Guide

I wish I could write a gushing fan letter to Debra Adelaide, because after the painful interruptions caused by work shifts and the feeding of children and the visiting of sick uncles and an exasperating need to sleep, I finally finished reading *The Household Guide to Dying*.

There I was in Sydney, bare feet on floor boards by a solid window covered in years' worth of cracked paint, looking over the harbourbridge-operahouse-artgallery, feeling mellow from reading and finishing, as though it was a sad and beautiful glass of wine. It made me cry. Thank goodness Prodigal Niece was at work and I had time to pull myself together before she and Her Better Half got home.

So emotional, all the way through. And something else; as the death approached my breathing changed, grew laboured, as though my breath was running out with hers. A book that'll kill you – great.

When I started I was worried because she uses two structural/ narrative elements that I've used in Very Important Manuscript. Nothing scarier than seeing that somebody has beat you to the punch, and done it so gracefully that you can't even say *damn!,* or wish they hadn't. Makes you feel redundant and quietly humble, as though somebody else is better at being you than you are. But actually my manuscript is different enough. She's far more refined and writes with such gentle manners. She must be beautiful on the inside.

I love finding somebody new to admire. And being so moved on a personal level that I can't even tell anybody about it. A little more disconnection, but this bit's welcome.

Speaking of Manuscript

I'm trying to do a rushed brain dump to clear my mind so that I can shut myself in and not look up until the revision's complete. Bit of synaptic polishing and a tidying up of the neurones. Memory could do with a bit of a scrub.

A snot-load of work, and eventually the joyful process of parting with another few hundred dollars for the manuscript assessment. The last one declared me to be on the brink of finishing, and was so full of outrageously good and emotional responses that I have to use it to scratch together some confidence. (The dreaded C word!)

Enough. Work to do means getting rid of interruptions. Minor problem = that I love my friends again. Damn them to hell. Friend Alice In Wonderland rang this morning and told me what I've been missing at Small Art School, and gosh I've missed her. I've missed everybody and everything. So I needed to remind myself that I had reasons for leaving, and that doing so allowed me invaluable time for painting and writing and the finding of self [ha ha] after a gruelling year. I've plumbed great depths whilst pissing the latter half of the year away. But isn't it funny how you manage to get so much work done without even realising it?

Doesn't matter – I have an interview for Big Art School soon, so possibly I'll belong somewhere again. This period of being alone to work is a necessary transition between one life and another.

In the meantime, I'll catch up with art friends and by the time I get home I'll be ready to plunge into writing. I'm both excited and afraid. With all of the good writing things that've happened (*so many* good things), I can't seem to reach a point of accumulation, where the hard work pays off for real. That only happens in la-la land, I suspect, and never to me. Okay sometimes to me, but not in The Big Way.

This manuscript means a lot to me personally, but despite the response being so positive each step of the way, the thought of maybe-publishing is a tease – a real possibility that may not actually eventuate. The last appraiser said she/he wanted to see it reach a broad readership. I wept, honest to goodness, as I read his/her report. After all of that lonely work, suddenly a human being with a mind who understands what you were getting at.

But still, ya gotta do better. Hence, hard work ahead.

———

Tuesday, 18th November, 2008.

He Means Well...?

It's been two weeks and Ex-Husband and I aren't madly in hate yet. Something to do with those walking-on-eggshell skills I mentioned. I had no idea I was so good at being docile.

The sad thing is that all year I've been comparing people to him, and they fall short. He's still my yardstick for partnership, not even Ex-G-Not-G changed that. And when he's interstate, as I hope he will be again by the end of the week, we're great friends. Sort of. At least the memory of our old friendship keeps us going. So I meet people and think '*I doubt I could be as comfortable with you as I was with him*'. But then he gets here and I'm not comfortable at all.

Something to do with him being a cold motherfucker (joking) [?]. Plus he's too resistant to my controlling ways (joking) [?].

And even though I tread carefully and we're getting along fine, I have privacy issues, because he hovers around. *Everywhere.*

Looking over my shoulder. Therefore I'm not working on anything. Just waiting. I can't even finish this thought off properly. I hope time passes quickly, because I'm dying to paint again, and can't start until he's gone. Something to do with the comments he made about it not being a suitable thing for somebody to do. I guess that's it; he's so condemning that I'm not willing to put myself in a position where I find anything important to me being condemned. It'll threaten my sense of being Practically Perfect.

Sigh. I remember when he wasn't like that.

Nor am I touching my manuscript when he's around, because I know he'll interrupt my thoughts and work patterns. He used to be so supportive, but now when he's not being lovely he's being holier-than-thou, and I'm the biggest *thou* in his life.

Mostly it's the coldness that gets me. Keeps my barrier up. Then he'll look at me and not understand why I don't respond when he's being warm. I feel sorry for him because he's shut everything good out. He's the kind of person who thinks it's an achievement to not-eat for days on end, and you just can't save somebody like that. He hates the food-eating chaos of us. He needs to fall in love with some half-anal woman who can put some warmth into his life.

In the meantime our friendship is very shallow and I wish he'd lighten up because it doesn't need to be like that. I hope he leaves soon – not to get rid of him, but because I want my life back. *Please.*

———

Author Overdose

If I wasn't a glutton I'd have stopped after one. Savoured it for a while, rolled it about on my tongue. And I could have done that, because *Shiver's* beautifully written. The only other novel of Nikki Gemmel's (aka Anonymous) I'd read was *Bride Stripped Bare*, and seeing as I also enjoyed that I thought I couldn't go wrong with *Cleave*.

BUT. *Cleave* is awful. No offence, NG. Really. But the bits of *Shiver* that I took in cautiously (i.e. some aspects of the sexuality) I absolutely hated in this book. When she writes sex in *Shiver* it can be very intense and poetic. Vivid, I guess. In *Cleave* I found the poetry missing. Maybe she was trying for another frontier, trying to do a *Shiver* equivalent.

The way she writes her characters = makes me think I can see her sitting over a computer, pouring herself in. Too transparent? I can't put my finger on it. Could be the nature of the emphasis. The place sexuality has in the narrative. Seems performed rather than felt?

Also I don't give a flying fuck about the characters in *Cleave*. They're boring. The attempt at "mysterious woman" seemed so contrived I lost patience. I stopped reading less than half-way.

Most of all, though, I hated it as a writer. I've confessed before to hyphenating often, so this might [still] make me a hypocrite, but here's the thing about hyphenated word combinations: they should only be used when there's a natural need for them. Make them up by all means, go nuts, but don't make them happen because you think your paragraph needs some cleverness. Every time she did it I felt this excruciating sense of the voice being forced..

Examples: '*hurt-cold milkshakes*'; '*desert-dry*'; '*snail-cold*'. Not bad on their own, but when this kind of combination appears every few paragraphs it starts to grate on my nerves. Especially because some are so weird and contrived they sit unnaturally within the text. NIKKI GEMMEL, I SCREAMED AT YOU.

Maybe I hated *Cleave* because it seemed like an exercise in writing character rather than something to care about. *Shiver* had interesting concepts to explore. Read *Shiver* and then stop, is my advice. Then if you ever meet Nikki Gemmel you can smile and be pleased without any secret feeling of distaste. I'm going to do my best to forget all [half] of *Cleave*. I'll probably hang on to a residual memory, though – just enough to ensure I never pick it up again.

Friday, 21st November, 2008.

Very Important Mission

I thought I could study to prepare for my interview at Big Art School, but realised as I compiled my thoughts that studying to be yourself is stupid. So I did yoga instead. Then undid all relaxation by hiring a truck and carting huge canvases and millions of smaller artworks in to the city. (Friend Boy A's advice: bring the actual work, not just photos.)

In the waiting room the eighteen year-olds were shitting themselves, while I sat there calm and rather pathetic, seeing as I'm the age of their parents. I know this because they had their parents with them, which was good because it meant I had people to talk to while we waited. In fact, it was starting to feel like a party. I've been so alone lately that being with people who love art was thrilling. I'd been looking forward to this interview because of the art-loving people prospect. I wanted to pinch them to make sure they were real.

So, the interview. When I was in Grade Three and making my holy moly communion with the other effing xtian children, my teacher (Mr Clifford) ceremonially placed the chain around my neck (decorative, not yoke) and said '*Trust you to have a big veil, Miss Fontana*'. That's what I was like going in to my interview with my many and oversized works; the one who does things a little awkwardly and makes other people shake their heads in exasperation. (Friend Boy A, *your* fault.)

But I didn't care. Don't know how to describe the interview – good, I think? I was told by a friend that the man who interviewed me is a bit of a pants man so I'd have gotten in on my cleavage alone. Pants Man himself told me later that I scored high, but ya never know. I really liked Pants Man, by the way, and would love to have him as a teacher. The female interviewer kept asking me what they could offer me, and suggested I might be too advanced skill-wise for the course. I kept explaining that there's so much more I need to learn, and it's about context and confidence, and working with people as opposed to in a vacuum, that I have no grounding or starting point, but her questions were alarming. I've only been oil-painting for a year and that makes me a beginner no matter how much or how little skill I have. Also, skill doesn't make you interesting. Interestingness comes out of your development as an artist, and I have a lot of developing to do.

I'm too lonely not to go to art school. They took me in again later to ask if I'd be interested in studying at a higher level, but I can't afford it. I want this one – I'm humble enough to know I don't have what other people have. I'm a lost little puppy, albeit an old one. I do worry about not getting much studio time, though. She was right about that. We'll see. I'll just have to be very, very organised if I get in, and go into it with a solid and workable plan for each twelve-week semester.

Chris Fontana

So. The lovely Ex-Husband gave me a whole day of his time and effort, to help me with the truck and the carrying. Very lovely. He ties the canvases in so carefully it's like he's handling dynamite. (*'Where's the kaboom?!'*) He's a nice man. All of the meanness is just habitual, because he's alone so much in the field. Just needs re-training, is all.

———

Still Friday.

Anti-Friendliness

I'm repossessing his halo. I feel guilty thinking this, because he can be so kind and generous (to myself, and my offspring), and obviously I'm so grateful for his help yesterday. But he later got mean about it. I wish he wouldn't do that. I feel like I'm watching him go through a transformation, something akin to Humble Man morphing into Troll.

I'm scared of him. It's more than needing to be very careful not to rock the boat; when I'm on that boat I don't even breathe. The man seems to hate me. Perhaps he hates me and doesn't realise it? Maybe his brain has manners that won't acknowledge something like hatred out loud? Technically he's allowed to hate me because I'm his ex-wife, but realistically it doesn't make sense.

So what to do. Nothing – I just have to sit it out and wait for him to leave for Perth again. I would have liked to have enjoyed his company, but no matter what I do he finds something to criticise. And if the kids do something wrong, he criticises me, as though giving birth to them makes me indirectly guilty. There's an edge to his condemnation that wasn't there before.

No, he's turning into a nasty little man and is unpleasant to be around. I'm trying to point out when he's being mean, so he can re-learn how to interact with humans without hating them for their alleged imperfections. I'm the right kind of person to teach him about human imperfections, I have so many of them, but it's not working.

I don't like being scolded like a child. He needs to acknowledge that our values have become less aligned, and that doesn't make either of us bad people. Just different people, who deserve to go about their business in peace, trying not to get in each other's way.

281

Now his miserable mood is dragging me under. As he intends it to; a reflection of the displeasure I cause him. At the moment I just bounce around throwing every bright side possible in his direction in the hope that he'll catch one and find a reason to be happy. Needless to say he finds that irritating.

I really am scared, but I don't know why. Just intuitive. The volatility and unpredictability of a person's moods, brought on by my annoying presence. Surely I'm not *that* bad?

––––

Saturday, 22nd November, 2008.

Closet Ice Sucking

It's getting harder to hide my little lemon Calypo dependency "problem". The only way to really melt a Calypo to a perfect state of squelch is to sit it in the sun on the window sill for a few minutes. Not too liquidy, not hard-as-rock frozen.

Also the car dashboard, for when you leave the shop and don't have enough patience to wait to get home to the sunny windowsills. I usually sit two on the dashboard (they need to be eaten in pairs). It makes me drive super carefully, so that they don't slide every time I turn a corner. Until I forget and take a sharp corner and they go flying. I try to catch them and suddenly I'm not driving very carefully at all.

Really, the window sill's the only way to be inconspicuous. Therefore, you can imagine how upset I am with this prolonged rainy weather. No sunny window sills! I've had to be inventive when it comes to Calypo melting. The heater duct makes them too liquid. The oven works okay until I get sprung and the kids start laughing at me for melting icy stuff in a cooking appliance. Ditto for the George-Foreman-gorilla; when the kids found my melting Calypos oozing out into the drip tray they squealed with disbelief and then laughed at me all day.

It'd be easier to be an alcoholic than a Calypo addict; an alcoholic can hide their booze anywhere, and not have to wait for it to half-melt. I can't handle this sub-standard melting. It's giving me no joy.

––––

282

Monday, 24th November, 2008.

Brain Cell Blaster

I almost forgot about this. A few weeks ago, First-Born and I stopped at a radio station van, because they were giving away free things and we just happened to be passing. Among the free stuff (mostly rubbish) they gave us a *Women's Weekly* magazine.

This might be the first time I've looked at a *Women's Weekly* at somewhere other than a doctor's waiting room. Is it possible that the content becomes even crappier when you're flicking through it at your kitchen table?

I came across an advertisement for [Unnamed Weight Loss Product], and the personal endorsements in the ad are SO BAD I have to quote one of them here:

> *The great thing about [Unnamed Weight Loss Product] is that I feel completely energized and it makes exercising easier – I just love the look of amazement on my family's faces when I go jogging. And it's not just exercise but I now have more energy to work and wash and iron and cook and clean – not to mention running around after husband, kids and dog.*

Here's to womanhood! But somebody please tell me again, what century are we in?????

Monday, 24th November, 2008.

Sands Through the Hour Glass

Ex-Husband's still here, and is so slow in packing up his things it looks like it'll be forever before he leaves. For the last couple of days he's been quite friendly, due to my caution. But now I need to stop walking on eggshells. I have work to do, work I need to be buried in. I need to work uninterrupted and without threat of criticism.

By the end of the week First-Born will be on holidays. They dominate the house, the mood of each day determined by where they are and what they're doing. Which means I'll only have Wednesday and Thursday of this week to be by myself, and that's going to be stolen from me by Ex-H, who also dominates the house. Makes me realise how many directions I get battered from. No wonder I spend so much time alone; people are a pain in the arse.

My plan of action so-far has involved preparing the house for being peaceful. Today: fresh bed sheets, cleared my desk ready for writing, will tidy up the main studio for painting, will plan my next painting. But I'm itching to start the actual work, and I've run out of preparatory things to do. No, he needs to go now. Before he gets mean again.

Other plan of action: so that I can enjoy the kids being home AND get my work done, I need to start getting up at about 4:00 am every day, to do some work before they wake. I used to do this every day, back in the glory days. I want that life back.

————

December 2008

Hideous Smiley Face From Outer Space

The two eyes have moved far enough across the night sky to now be on the underside of the moon, which means if you were able to twist the planetary alignment into a face of any sort it'd be a miserable one.

They ruined it for me. I don't know who they are exactly – was it Friend with Rich Parents, who texted me while I was walking at night to say '*Look at the sky; Venus and Jupiter are aligned with the moon to make a smiley face!*', or was it any number of news crews who announced the smiley alignment in the first place?

I have no idea why this bothers me so much. All I know is that both Ex-H and Son told me about the alignment and I looked up and there was this wonderful bright thing in the sky. While I walked the whole world was clear. Being on the foothills I could see the city off in the distance, and all of the pretty lights (which are only pretty if you don't think about the ugly urban sprawl that makes them), and still this bright alignment stood out so much I couldn't take my eyes off it.

When Friend sent that text I suddenly saw it as a face and couldn't stop seeing it as a face. That made me think of humans, and I'm so sick of humans anthropomorphistically hijacking nature that I hated that face with abandon. They *ruined the planets*.

Well anyway, I have fondness for Ex-H again because he finally left today. Notice *he* didn't ruin the stars (made no mention of smiley faces). And even though I was wishing he'd go, we do actually get along [sometimes]. I'd gotten used to him being here and now everything's different even though it's technically gone back to being the same.

I know I'm repeating myself, but I feel sad for him, being on his own. I had to corner him in his room on Saturday to tell him how evil he was becoming again, and try to get him to accept that he needs to learn how to interact with people, because I don't want to hate him, because he's my friend.

He was lovely again after that. And now he's gone I can overlook the small but escalating meannesses, and will have forgotten them within a week. I don't want him to feel unwanted. Perhaps I feel guilty about not being able to see the nice man I married in him anymore. I see glimpses, but his intolerance wipes it all away. How does he find joy in his life?

But look! House to [almost] myself! I can write here again! The happiest guilty feeling I've ever had.

Thursday, 4th December, 2008.

The Anti-Lust

No offence to Ex-H, but he's a libido crusher. It's not manners to talk about it, but I'm quietly fascinated. Just having him in the house for a month killed my sex drive, so much so that I was only vaguely aware of my self-imposed drought, and wouldn't dare let myself think anything that was going to make me go blind. Now that he's been gone a day it's all come back, and I can see just how much I'd let die inside.

I also didn't paint or draw while he was here, and to write I had to summon great powers of concentration to block his presence out (I couldn't hold on any longer).

What is it about some people that kill you inside? That's an insult to him, but really it's just a result of his Marvin the Robot ways. Persistent negativity. If I'd tried to paint, one bastard comment from him would have poisoned the whole thing. Sometimes repression is a matter of self-preservation.

Doesn't matter, all over now. Am walking with a spring in my step.

Speaking of Which

I was walking tonight and finally got to see Dog Woman in action. Dog Woman's house is in the middle of our street, has an ad hoc railing boarded up over the front porch, and about a million small dogs frequently breaking out and running up and down the road.

Dog Woman herself never makes eye contact, so I thought she must be one of those eccentric people who everybody knows but nobody ever speaks to, because she can only relate to animals. The occasional squawking noise she makes when they get stuck up on top of the carport doesn't help.

So I'm disappointed to discover that she's nothing but a strange bogan. She was saying goodbye to the only human I ever see visiting her, walking him out to his car, when three of the small dogs came running up the road towards me. For one mortifying moment I was worried they'd try to hump my leg, but they only nipped (with teeth!!) and jumped. That was nothing – it was more mortifying that she was suddenly animated, half talking to me and half talking to her friend as she called after the dogs with the lyrical strains of '*Come 'ere dickhead... here dickead, come'orn dick'ead...*'.

I mean, is Dickhead actually the dog's name? I have a sneaking suspicion that it is. I was trying not to be a snob, but she's leaving me with no choice. I've started thinking such snobby things as *the value of the properties on either side of her must have plummeted after she moved in*. Not to mention their quality of life. We've inadvertently bonded as locals, but I hope like heck she goes back to lowering her head every time I walk past.

———

Friday, 5ᵗʰ December, 2008.

Battle Tactics

It's time to declare domestic war. Again. My kids are so lazy. I love them, but really, we can't live like this. Warfare's the only solution.

Back to my old solution of locking the plates away. And the cups. And the cutlery. One set of everything out for each of us. Visitors can be instructed to bring their own plates and utensils.

I'm a better strategist than I was before. This time when they get desperate and start looking for alternative things to use as plates, they won't be able to find picnic sets or mixing bowls. If they get desperate and are still too lazy to wash their own things, they'll just have to use their fingers and drink out of shoes or something. I *will* win this time. I *will* succeed.

———

The Anti-Climax

For me and GrandKitten both. GrandKitten because she's on heat. I tried to consult the oracle for advice on what to do, and the only practical suggestion anybody made was to gratify the cat with a cotton-tip.

Um... no. Isn't that bestiality? I'll just stick to giving her a cuddle and a tummy rub. And get her spayed next week. First-Born's supposed to do it, part of the promise they exchanged for being allowed to keep Kitten in the first place. Alas, too late – her suffering is killing me.

My own anti-climax stems from looking forward to the local Xmas fireworks tonight (real ones), only to hear them go off half an hour early. AGAIN. That's two years in a row I've missed them. And if I missed them, then Son has missed them, too. What a household of disappointed creatures we are.

———

Still Saturday.

The Burden of Things

I was hoping to get some writing done tonight, but I'm finding it hard to work because of the hideous bits of blue couch that are spread between the garage and First-Born's bedroom.

I was backing down the driveway after a long, hard afternoon's work when I noticed this fucking big thing blocking my way in the garage. Only days after getting rid of a lot of Ex-Husband's excess things, First-Born decides to buy a shitty old couch at a fete.

I HATE COUCH-SELLING FETES.

They paid thirty dollars for it, and this is the kind of couch you wouldn't even take for free from a nature strip. In fact, you wouldn't be able to *pay* somebody to take it.

It's a modular thing and they can only fit the corner piece in their bedroom. Which means the rest of it is *my* problem. My mum, who I called immediately to scream '*Help!*' down the phone to, thinks it's hilarious. Who can write under this kind of pressure?

I'm too tired to deal with couches. Maybe if I try to donate it to charity. Would that be cruel? Or when their Biological visits on Tuesday I could ask him to be fatherly and deal with it.

'*Today they're your child*,' I could tell him; '*Congratulations on your new couch!*'. And get him to take it to the tip.

After all of poor First-Born's home-renovationish effort, I'm a dream-crusher. But on Tuesday I'll be a dream-crusher with a manageable house.

Sunday, 7th December, 2008.

Wall Flower

She's too *young* to be a spinster. And the way she yowls and crouches down to offer her raised hind is just so sweet. Now I'm worried – what if by not letting her out to find a mate and get it over with, seeing as she'll be spayed soon anyway, we're making her feel unloved? Is protecting her from life-threatening feline venereal diseases really that important?

Every time I look at her she makes eye contact and assumes the position, making her little trilling noise, as though I can help her with it. The guilt is going to eat me alive by the end of the day.

But today is for writing; I have to somehow shut her out of my head so that I can concentrate on my manuscript. Determined to post it tomorrow. Which means I also have to block out the houseful of teenagers. This cat music is making it very hard to think.

Monday, 8th December, 2008.

Done

I'm officially sick of my own voice. Happens every time. But I've posted off my manuscript and am quietly pleased to have cropped around 16,000 words, reducing the length by 60 odd pages, which is the equivalent of chopping off about one leg.

Two days ago it was still my baby, but now I hate it, and I hate the letter that accompanied it, and will spend the next few weeks cringing at the idea of it being read, if I happen to think about it at all, which I hope I don't.

Onto higher things, I now have to crop about a hundred percent of dirt from the kitchen floor. That's the problem with finishing. Suddenly the real world. Once tended to, I'll return to the not-real world by starting a painting, if for no better reason than to give myself an excuse to ignore the housework again for another three weeks.

Also in the real world I'm still dealing with that little cat-in-heat problem. It's cruel keeping her inside. I've never seen a cat in heat before, and it looks like agony. I wish there was another way, perhaps something to do with nurture versus nature. For instance, instead of dressing her in a sexy red collar with a love-heart clasp, First-Born could have dressed her in circumspect, church-going lilac?

Thursday, 11th December, 2008.

What It's Like

Yesterday I finally started to feel excited about being accepted into Big [Elite] Art School. (By the way, I got accepted into Big [Elite] Art School.) When I first heard I took the news calmly, even though it's so hard to get in. I wrote '*Whoo!*' into a text to my friend, but I didn't feel *Whoo!*, even though I'm pleased. Everything's neutral these days; everything just "is". It's like I don't expect anything good anymore.

But yesterday – excited. Started planning how smooth it would be if I could be outrageously and uncharacteristically organised. I went for a lovely long swim, and as I swam I planned the writing I could start work on, the art works, and the cooking I could do each week to make sure family life would be stable despite the extra commitments.

Then I came home and made soup. The soup was training for the many soups I could make next year. I even enjoyed cooking [!!], because of this stable life ahead.

But then it was later and First-Born happened. Yelling, vying for world dominance. Any hopes for a stable future are pipe dreams.

I still sleep under the REDRUM wall. I haven't had time to paint over the graffiti, and anyhow I can't just paint over red oil paint.

Whenever I think of it I wonder if painting over it is the wrong thing to do, as though I'd be removing an essential part of First-Born's personality and emotional makeup. Sometimes I wonder if it's wrong to cover up the reality of our life. Mostly I ignore it, but when I do look at it I realise the sanctuary of my bedroom is contaminated by anger.

So despite the inclination towards being happy, these days I find happiness difficult. It's not just that there's no happiness – it's the prospect that there'll never be any happiness. And I'll be alone forever because I can't bring anybody into our lives. I hardly even invite friends into the house anymore.

I've failed my children. I love them and worry about them, but First-Born's always so angry at me. The other day they seemed to be in a good mood, but then said *'The main thing I've learnt from you is what not to do as a parent, and that's the only compliment you'll ever get from me'*.

They're usually more devastatingly clever with their insults – so clever I can't quote them here. It's wrong of me to admire their way with words when they're directed at me, but I do. So quoting this one makles me squeamish because it was such a childish thing to say, and conversely there are so many times when they've told me I'm wonderful and said they couldn't imagine life without me.

When I dropped them at their ex-partner's last night, they said *'Thanks for the lift, I really appreciate it'*, but I couldn't even answer them. I feel sorry for them because they think these little bits of niceness undo the damage. But I can't trust niceness anymore. I don't believe in it as a sustainable thing.

I don't think I'll ever have the family life I love so much. I can't even bring myself to put up a Xmas tree, because I can't feel festive. There's just no point in pretending there's anything to enjoy. And yet, I should be performing normality for Son. For his sake.

What a stupid way to live. It separates me from people. Not good.

I Have a Theory
Maybe it's like Samson and Delilah. Not Delilah – she's irrelevant. Samson though, yes. It's the hair.

In my happy memories, First-Born has light, strawberry-blonde coloured hair. A much lighter hint of red than mine. I have a photo of them swinging one-handed from a flying fox at a park, with their other arm in plaster (broken wrist), wearing purple overalls. It's one of my favourite images of them; happy, laughing, active, enjoying the world.

Part-way into Year Seven at school, they coloured their hair. At first they went brunette, and it suited them but already I couldn't recognise my child anymore. Then they went uniform teenage black. Emo. Stunning to look at, but impossible to see.

It's like somebody snuck in and replaced one of the puppies in my litter. Only on the odd occasion do I glimpse the real them. I've been wanting to paint their portrait, but can't because I can't generate a composition in my head, because all I can see is black hair and anger.

Warning: BLACK HAIR DYE MAKES YOU ANGRY. Samson knew it: don't mess with the hair. So if I can sneak in and un-dye First-Born's hair when they're not looking, they'll transform back to their real self, and I'll know them again...?

———

Sunday, 14th December, 2008.

In Transition

Feeding an elderly woman at work today, *Moonlight Shadow* started playing on the radio. Some days go so slowly, until one song speeds things up, turning life into something tolerable for a whole three minutes. Those three minutes are therefore worth writing home about.

A woman at work who studied printmaking and who talked art with me over tea break. I was so excited until I later walked into the staff room and found her reading *Women's Weekly*, not even at gunpoint, thus realising I could never really be her friend.

Two thoughts, no one to tell them to. The friends you tell these inane things to are the ones who're in your life daily, and I'm waiting to see who my next daily people are.

I'm nervous about being at Big Art School with a male friend who stopped being my daily person this year, when he stopped needing me. Until mid-year he kept saying '*I wish you were here*' (at Big Art

School), and then suddenly nothing. A man thing? Love on a needs-only basis?

———

On Your Marks, Get Ready...

Two blisters (thumbs), two stretched canvases (enormous), four coats of gesso (each), and seven replays of my Cat Stevens playlist whilst the deed was being done. Plus one listen to Nick Cave's *Murder Ballads*, because all of that peace crap inevitably leaves you hankering for a good butchering.

Now I'm ready to prep for painting. A portrait diptych. These will be risky ones, although aren't they all. They're in my head, and therefore must be expelled.

Am wondering how to start the next novel, too, given the painting schedule I have ahead of me. Without losing this generally peaceful approach to everything and everything's et ceteras.

How do I squeeze it all in when the soup has run out? How was I to know that one pot of soup wouldn't last the whole summer? What, you mean I have to cook another one? Why must children be fed every day? Couldn't they be more like plants, and need watering only once a week?

———

Normal

Contrary to popular opinion (i.e. my own), I'm not a complete failure as a mother [!!!]. One night last week I was about to go for a walk and asked Son to go on cat patrol, which involves preventing four cats from following me up the street. (All very cute, and it makes me feel mother-nature-like when I return and they run out from underneath parked cars to greet me in the dark and follow me home, but I'm sure one day it'll lead to gruesome death.)

Instead of cat patrol, he chased them home and came with me. An offspring on my night walk!! He talked, and talked, like we were a normal mother and son thing, and I realised that despite the anger of one teenager dominating our lives, I've still managed to provide a semblance of "home". Son isn't suffering some weird withdrawing-personality disorder; all is well with the world.

On that note, he has such a beautiful personality. As does Firsrt-Born, when they're Jekyll and not Hyde (or is Jekyll the bad one? I never remember). He also doesn't mind me getting excited about Xmas lights. I'm so relieved. Parenting's not so hard after all – I don't know what I was worried about.

———

Over-Exposed

Sometimes I have so many women throwing their naked bodies at me I just don't know how to cope. I've booked one in for a sitting because that's the painting I'm working on (therefore essential), but have told the other to postpone their social visit even though I haven't seen her for so long and miss her quite a lot.

At my most lonely, why am I wanting to be so alone?

The drawing's done, the painting's started, I'll interrupt progress for Xmas and then go back in, planning to resurface in about three or four weeks.

Funny thing about nudity, though. I don't have a vision for it (except for the current painting, and that's not about nudity as such), so when somebody offers to model I'm stumped because I have no starting point, no visual desire. It's like being offered money but refusing it because you don't know what to spend it on. It will come to me, though. I just have to give it time.

———

Thursday, 25th December, 2008.

I Giveth, I Taketh Away

Love is… seeing two little apples bobbing on their branch in your rear vision mirror as you're driving along on Xmas eve. Love isn't… falling in love with an apple tree you bought as a gift for your big sister and then keeping it for yourself.

Is that bad? It's just, how can you not love a fruit tree? And have you ever smelt an apple tree in your car? *Have* you? You understand.

It was a spur of the moment thing. I'd planned to give her a massage voucher, but then I thought about her amazing life as I was pondering my love of fruit trees, and realised that her amazing life has no apple trees in it [!!]. I went to the nursery, bought feijoa trees and an apple tree, and after the disaster of falling in love with the apple tree before I was even home, Mum told me over the phone that I couldn't swap the trees over because Ye Olde Sister doesn't eat feijoas [!!].

I'm now fast becoming close to realising my dream of having an orchard to watch over. This fits in with the plan for my Great New Life, where I get up early every morning, go for a walk, and tend my orchard/garden before breakfast.

And my sister? I got her that massage voucher. Maybe I'll give her an apple when they ripen. (Well she *is* a teacher, so that'll be perfect.)

Propagation of Species

When I was buying the fruit trees I looked up Fuji and Gala apples because I noticed there were a lot of them at the nurseries, and found the descriptions usually said '*with a sweet pleasant albeit not outstanding flavour*'.

These apples are designed for transportation and longevity, not for flavour, and that's why we're perpetually disappointed with our lunchboxes. New generations of children growing up with unsatisfied palates, turning to McDonalds when hungry because apples no longer give us a flavour hit.

I have a plan. I'm going to get rich and buy a lot of properties, and I'm going to plant as many original apple trees as I can, so that they just keep on propagating. I'll tattoo Caring for Apple Tree instructions onto the fences, rent them out to fruit tree lovers.

I'll do the same thing with plums, apricots, feijoas, nectarines and peaches. And give fruit tree saplings to everybody, to plant in their back yards.

In 1970s suburbia we grew up surrounded by backyard fruit trees. How can anybody expect to get up onto their sheds to fight their plum wars without climbing their peach tree? How can they even have plum wars without an abundant supply of fresh plums?

All of which have flavour. Supermarket fruits are increasingly insipid. We should all be very disturbed by this. Is everybody just too busy to notice?

———

Tuesday, 30th December, 2008.

Soup Kitchen

In keeping with my plans for Our Perfect Life, I made another pot of soup. Not just any soup, but an internet recipe soup, which always involves some degree of risk. It's just that cauliflower soup took over my mind and I couldn't find it in a book, and couldn't let it go.

Lovely Friend came over last night after I'd finished work, witnessed my efforts, and called me a Paragon of Domesticity, giving me a real kick. Then we went off to see a movie, found ourselves at a bar with a bottle of red instead, and I remembered being human. (Mental note: do *not* neglect good friendships.)

Back to the soup, where all roads inevitably lead. The recipe starts like a curry, with the frying of onion and garlic and cumin and coriander. I can smell the words as I write them. I have to remember this – the loving of paying attention to the immediate things in life. Things being slow enough to taste and savour. And the warding off of teenage anger with a soup talisman. My rock and foundation.

I have permission to get back to the painting now, and a perfect life you betcha. If we overlook the sad fact that I manage these domestic pargaonisms so seldomly they become noteworthy as a Major Event.

———

Wednesday, 31st December, 2008.

Ye Gods

All gods are human, that's what I'm most afraid of today. Because of the Abba interview, which is really just a Bjorn interview but anyway, Abba is Abba.

I know I'm going to watch it. How can I not? But I'm worried about the potential spin, and the falling of gods into mortality. I need them to remain deified. Instead of listening to *Brave New World* as

296

planned while I painted today, I listened to Abba, in case the magic is stripped from my life by 8 pm tonight.

It's New Year's Eve but yes I'm staying home for this. My feet will be sore because I'll have just gotten home from work. It'll be me, Abba, and nice bowl of soup. Then painting until it's time to walk to the top of the hill to watch the fireworks that go off in every direction at midnight. This time, no visitors. Just me and my paint. As it should be.

———

Still Wednesday, Still 2008.

YEY GODS!

There was no spin! He was lovely! He's making me use exclamation marks! !!! !!!

I should never have doubted. It's just, I guess every religious fanatic has their faith tested, and this was my test.

What a wonderful way to see in the new year.

And now I have to decide: go to party in Warrandyte, or not go. Really, who goes to Warrandyte? It's full of hippies. I think if it wasn't New Year's Eve I'd go. Perhaps if they throw another New Year's Eve party, only at some other time of the year? I'll suggest it in my invitation-declining text.

———

Acknowledgements

Most of the preparation for these volumes has taken place quietly in the shadows – somewhere between Purgatory and Solitary Confinement – where I skulk around as I work. I couldn't survive this lonely business without the feedback of good friends, so thank you to everyone who listened when I leaned out of my turret to scream into the abyss.

Thank you to my mother, for anchoring me in the real world daily, with warm companionship, support,... and an endless supply of chocolate.

A special thank-you to Chris Gabriel for being such an enthusiastic sounding board when I needed to ~~rant~~ think-out-loud, and for your support when I came across inevitable technical problems. Your bystander company was a balm during ad-hoc troubleshooting attempts.

Thanks also to Sarah Rudledge for being on the technology cheer squad, for generous layout/design advice, and for your practical and moral support. Most of all, though, for teaching me that sharing is the thing that makes "Art" worth it.

Thank you to Diane "Grabby" Glenane, for the sound of your reassuring voice as it echoes across the valley when you call from your own turret. Screaming into the abyss isn't so bad when you know somebody is working away on their own projects at the other end.

Last but not least, thank you to Dr [Empress!] Josephine Browne, for your thoughtful feedback, invaluable conversations, and for *knowing*. Because through all of these endeavours, we are kin xx

www.ingramcontent.com/pod-product-compliance
Lightning Source LLC
Chambersburg PA
CBHW050547190726
48283CB00007B/2038